Digital Fictions:
Storytelling in a Material World

New Directions in Computers & Composition Studies
Gail E. Hawisher and Cynthia L. Selfe, Series Editors

Digital Fictions:
Storytelling in a Material World

by
Sarah Sloane
University of Puget Sound

 Ablex Publishing Corporation
Stamford, Connecticut

Printed in the United States of America

Library of Congress Cataloguing-in-Publication Data

Sloane, Sarah.
   Digital fictions / by Sarah Sloane.
   p. cm.— (New directions in computers & composition studies)
   A revision of the author's thesis —Ohio State University.
   Includes bibliographical references and index.
   ISBN 1-56750-482-5 (cloth) — ISBN 1-56750-483-3 (pbk.)
   1. Fiction—Authorship—Data processing. 2. Experimental fiction—History and criticism—Theory, etc. 3. Authors and readers—Data processing. 4. Fiction —Technique—Data processing. 5. Creative writing—Data processing. 6. Storytelling—Data processing. 7. Literature and technology. 8. Hypertext systems. I. Title. II. Series: New directions in computers & composition studies.
PN3377.C57S59   2000
808.3'0285—dc21   99–39596
                                           CIP

Ablex Publishing Corporation
100 Prospect Street
P.O. Box 811
Stamford, Connecticut 06904-0811

For Judy

The reader who opts for the old way of reading, for the one-way street, the reader who is determined to slide toward death by the shortest route, without putting up a fight—in other words, to read across rather than down—will be surprised...

—Milorad Pavic (1991)

BOOKISH: Given to books; acquainted only with books. It is generally used contemptuously.
—E.L. McAdam and George Milne (1963)

Contents

Acknowledgments

In 1990, I was a nervous graduate student about halfway through the first draft of my dissertation, the bare bones of this book. As I wrote, I began to hear radio reports that the remains of Amelia Earhart's plane had been found: researchers had dug up a wooden chest buried on a small island in the South Pacific, a chest marked in such a way that they figured it had to have come from Earhart's ill-fated flight. I wrote furiously as I listened to announcers describe the plan to scan the reef for the wreckage of her plane. (They never found it.) The researchers speculated that Earhart's aircraft might have landed on this shoal, just off the island, and eventually slid into the rising tide, her radio broadcasts gone unanswered. In the intersections of the account of the story carried by National Public Radio, my faint memory of childhood books about Earhart's final journey, and my own lackluster, fearful writing about women, men, and new technologies, I had an inkling of the sometimes bizarre contexts within which we compose. I posted a quotation from writer Scott McLean above my desk: "...we all move in many circles out and away from the small-self of one meter." Today, almost 10 years later, as I put the finishing touches on this manuscript, I consider the important circles of people around me.

We all move in widening ripples, in and between many communities of colleagues, peers, and friends. I began writing these acknowledgments several years ago, when I was visiting my partner, Judy Doenges, at a writer's residency at the Headlands Center for the Arts in Marin County, California. The artists there, and their eccentric assemblages of materials, challenged me to make a book as rich, milky, and febrile as their own studio installations of compasses caked in ice, radical definitions of the River Styx, a medical hemostat nipping the binding of a book, and the long, silent profiles of cornstalks drawn in dried milk on the floor. One artist looked around her sunny studio and said to me, "[t]he windows are in real-time but the walls are historical." My visit to the Marin Headlands Center was valuable to me, and ultimately to my dissertation and this book, because I saw first-hand some results of rigorous rearrangements of the parts of our world, as well as a faith in the whim, the oblique, the noncanonical and uncatalogued, the rip, the quick cut, and the resulting *bricolage*. I saw afresh that art is a rhetoric of human inquiry, perhaps spoken in a different register or drawn from a different palette, but essentially the same activity of symbolic action as is composing with language. I recognized anew that my interest in computers and fiction was tied to a long aesthetic tradition, one that views both visual and verbal arts as kin, as versions of a mimetic act that helps us understand the relations between self and others, between self and world.

Ongoing conversations with a number of important friends, family, teachers, editors, students, colleagues, and my partner have all shaped this book. This series' editors, Cindy Selfe and Gail Hawisher, have proved to be the patient and encouraging presence that any fledgling writer would be very lucky to have. Let me just mention the long gestation of this book: eight years. If only I believed more in organic and expressivist metaphors for the writing process, I could acknowledge them as the most sure-handed and capable midwives in the profession. Their faith and support have been the greatest help to me. Thanks, too, to the anonymous reviewers who looked at the first and last drafts of this manuscript and made valuable suggestions. Friends and teachers at the University of Massachusetts (Amherst) and Ohio State University have also provided invaluable support: At UMass, Anne Herrington, Charlie Moran, Marcia Curtis, and Sara Stelzner sparked my interest in the teaching of writing and inspired me to continue my graduate work in rhetoric and composition. At Ohio State, Andrea Lunsford, James Phelan, and Lewis Ulman were the members of my original dissertation committee who oversaw my writing of the first draft of this book; they helped me germinate a great many of the ideas presented here. It was a great pleasure and privilege to work with each of them. Graduate students Cindy Cox, Faye Purol, Jim Buckley, Ruth Ann Hendricks, and the late and much missed Eric Walborn provided crucial support, nurturing, sustenance, shots of ouzo, and humor, at precisely those moments when they were most needed. My Ohio State study group—Mindy Wright, Kelly Bellanger, Heather Graves, Donna LeCourt, and Carrie Leverenz—also helped me form the first ideas of this book (as well as gave me the will to stay in graduate school).

I also owe a warm thanks to Joe Bates, who was kind enough to befriend a disconsolate English graduate student at Carnegie Mellon University and to invite me to his computer science gatherings, to teach me some of the main ideas of the new discipline of artificial intelligence, and include me in many fascinating classes and discussions about AI, its successes and discontents. I appreciate the generosity of digital fiction writers who have spoken to me over the last eight years about their work, including Michael Joyce, Carolyn Guyer, Stuart Moulthrop, Joe Bates, Phoebe Sengers, Peter Weyhrauch, Scott Reilly, Abbe Don, David Graves, and Brenda Laurel. Thanks especially to Stuart Moulthrop, who made our serving together on the Modern Language Association's Computers and Emerging Technologies Committee a pleasure.

More recently, my students and colleagues at the University of Puget Sound have been a real support during the revisions of this book, support ranging from generous funding to words of encouragement. I am grateful to the University of Puget Sound Enrichment Committee for granting me a summer research award and a junior sabbatical that gave me time to work on this book. Members of the

Women Studies Advisory Committee, especially Nancy Bristow and Connie Hale (not to mention our faithful work study students, particularly Julie (O'Donnell) Moore and Kristy Maddux), have helped me keep a sense of humor and faith in the aims of higher education, not to mention aid in preserving whatever shreds of sanity I might have left. Stuart Smithers, my friend, colleague, and comrade-in-arms at Puget Sound, has helped me through every step of the bumpy path we call a career in academia. And my friends teaching across town at Pacific Lutheran University, Susan Brown Carlton and Erin McKenna, have also helped me tremendously by modeling how to be creative and powerful teachers, and how to be writers that try to say something real.

In addition, all my students, past and present, have taught me a great deal. As my dissertation director, Andrea Lunsford, once confided to a group of her own students, "People are infinitely interesting." In my students I have found a wonderful community of people committed to learning about language, rhetoric, and the world; I express my gratitude to all of them for their energy, intelligence, and senses of humor. In particular, I want to thank Andy Volk for his knowledge of computers and Teresa Giffen for our thoughtful conversations and her exquisite writing. Also, I'd like to thank the founding members of the Italian Cooking Club—former students Emily Hove, Ben Steele, and Lindsay Herman—who have taught me the meaning of good food, good wine, and good living, not to mention the pleasures of doing dishes in purple-checked aprons.

My brother, Tom; my sister-in-law, Jane; and their children, Carrie and Matt, have never failed to entertain me and to keep me interested in the evolving narratives of their rich and complicated lives. Will Carrie be an artist? Will Matt become a civil engineer? What is the correct response when their guinea pig eats a clue during a scavenger hunt? My mother, Virginia, and my father, Tom, have also always provided models of art and critical inquiry that are of the highest standard. To these family members I offer my warmest appreciation.

I would also like to thank a few of my favorite cultural icons—Ellen DeGeneris, Linda Hamilton, Hillary Clinton, Agent Scully, and Blondie—for the models of courage, humor, intelligence, and talent they offer us mortals.

But most of all, my love and thanks to the woman to whom this book is dedicated. Judy Doenges—partner, friend, long-time companion, confidante, writer, artist, pal—has been a great blessing in my life for the last 15 years. I cannot imagine having written this book without her steady love, understanding, and friendship, not to mention the well-placed quip that reminded me of the world outside of this book—and the books outside of these cyberworlds. I never forget that Judy writes the real thing, short stories and novels on the page, while I dabble in the digital, mindful of the gap between theory and practice, sneaking in my poems where I can. To Judy I dedicate the following chapters.

Invocation: To the sailboat warehouse moon upon the occasion of writing my first book*

You float outside the door tonight
and see me enter this packed house.
Sailboats half-dressed gather here
to gain their bones and ream their sides.
They talk of water all night long.

In luffing sleep I landed here—
this incubator of half-born parts—
surgeon's tools untended lie
near box-saws, uncut vessels, knives.
You see the crowd in this dark house.

New hulls anchored on sawhorses, sticky shells,
assorted ropes, metal flanges, gloomy sterns,
stacks of centerboards, rudders raised
in disorderly piles pack the place.
The cool dust of new boats is everywhere.

Broad shelves of equipment glisten
under you. In your dim, speckled light
sails spill over the blurts of hulls,
meet the abrupt edge of booms, pivotless, still.
Unfurled jibs murmur in their ghostly pools.

My eyes are useless here—
their double, skittish flirts
at hanging things. The visual knots
of molded board and folded cloth
float past me in your lit house.

The floorboards creak, the steambox mumbles,
the seacharts shift inside their drawer.
Your aching light furls towards the dawn—
the violet tooth of this night sky.

* This poem originally was published in 1986 as "Sailboat Warehouse" in *Sun Dog,* 7(2), p. 37.

1

An Introduction to Computing Fictions

WORDS

What is it to them to fly, to stop
To flutter away
from the tall woman?
The starlings in the snow.

In a line they bend wing
and peck the grass and mud between
old snow piles.

They move
like sentence fragments.

They fly from the woman
who walks thoughtfully
around their meaning.

Their tracks come and go
signs in the snow.

FOREWORD

A Foreword to a reader is a hindword to an author. The author knows what has been written, the reader has yet to find out. The author, when [s]he does not use her foreword to acknowledge help received in [her] completed labours, sometimes stands at the threshold which the foreword is, biting [her] nails and wondering whether a brief warning, an apology for inadequacy or excess, an avowal of mediocrity where [s]he had intended brilliance, might not be a courteous gesture to the person who has had the kindness at least to pick up [her] book.
—Anthony Burgess (1986)

The replacement of the old narration by information, of information by sensation, reflects the increasing atrophy of experience. In turn, there is a contrast between all these forms and the story, which is one of the oldest forms of communication. It is not the object of the story to convey a happening per se, which is the purpose of information; rather, it embeds it in the life of the story-teller in order to pass it on as experience to those listening. It thus bears the marks of the story-teller much as the earthen vessel bears the marks of the potter's hand.
—Walter Benjamin (1955/1988)

The true literature machine will be one that itself feels the need to produce disorder, as a reaction against its preceding production of order...
—Italo Calvino (1986)

Digitality is with us. It is that which haunts all the messages, all the signs of our societies.
—Jean Baudrillard (1983)

Most histories of the 20th century note October 4, 1957, the day when the Russians launched a satellite called *Sputnik*, as the signal event of our century. Few historical surveys offer even cursory acknowledgment of a far more important date in our century's sweep, a date ultimately more profound in cultural implication, technological progress, and global influence. That date is the one that marks the U.S. government's commitment of funds to start an agency that would invent the backbone of the Internet. On January 7, 1958, President Dwight D. Eisenhower requested startup funds from Congress to establish the Advanced Research Projects Agency (ARPA), a government agency that would go on to invent DARPAnet, then ARPAnet, and finally, the vast computer network that connects tens of millions of people around the world today, the Internet. Just a few days after Eisenhower made his request, Congress approved the funding as part of an Air Force Appropriations bill, and "ARPA went into business" (Hafner & Lyon, 1996, p. 20). By 1969, the first node of ARPAnet was installed at UCLA, and within four years, 37 nodes were in place to allow the traffic of information between its users (Denning, qtd. in De Landa, 1992, pp. 117–118). Today, of course, the worldwide computer network includes tens of millions of nodes, and is growing daily. However, theorists like Paul Baran of the RAND Corporation (De Landa, 1992) designed ARPAnet with a simple goal in mind: to ensure that U.S. communications networks would survive a first-strike nuclear attack by the Soviet Union.

By designing a communication system that was decentralized, distributed, and redundant (so that the loss of any one node would not summarily shut down the system), ARPAnet would ensure the durability of wartime communications. In short, owing to cold-war fears triggered by a tiny Soviet satellite, President Eisenhower created a government agency that invented the Internet: a computer network that would become the basis for a linked global communications system whose capabilities and permutations we are just beginning to comprehend, whose implications for textual form, circulation, and agency we are just starting to understand. In particular, if it were not for the Internet in its various incarnations, past and future, we would have no World Wide Web, no computer games, no MUDs, MOOs, or MUSHes, no Web-based soap operas or HTML fictions, and no shared virtual spaces devoted to narrative at all.

I enjoy the fact that I was born the year that the Space Age dawned—not to mention during the half-century that has seen the evolution of the Internet—in part because of the perspective such an historical position offers me. At the end of the 20th century, I find myself as an associate professor of English living in the Pacific Northwest and putting the finishing touches on a book-length manuscript; I am sensitive to the ironies of writing a paper-based *fin de siècle* book about computers, and remain hopeful that my stance of ambivalent humanism is the right one to take as we consider storytelling in/on computers. My life so far has taken me from rotary telephones to touch-tone telephones and videoscreens; from black-and-white televisions to color ones to the ones connected to today's digital cable services; from drive-in movies to *Riven* to Spiderworld (Sloane, 1999b); from pencil to typewriter (first mechanical, then electric) to computer keyboard; from writing by hand to writing with hands to encountering virtual worlds via helmet and glove; to the local Seattle Cinerama to watch the first *Star Wars* prequel.

As I write about these digital stories in these changing cultural contexts, I wonder what accidental traces of a pulp- and print-based literacy, what thumbprint on this clay pot, to paraphrase Walter Benjamin (1955/1988), I am leaving behind as I write. I wonder in what telling ways I am blind to the influence of some of my own contexts, even as I make a conscientious effort to acknowledge my own historical position. Every word here is haunted by what has already happened in my life, and what I know of what has happened in the world. However, while stories, oral histories, narratives, and other reworked memories often present some essential truth untellable in any other way, they are also notoriously unreliable. And it is this unreliablity, the ways in which my contexts inflect and infuse my own ideas and ways of talking, my own story, as it were, that I wish to acknowledge from the outset. And it is the power of the story that I wish to emphasize throughout this narrative.

In the interests of establishing some shared vocabulary as we begin talking about digital fictions, I offer below my working definitions of the following terms: materiality, storytelling, and the problem of naturalization.

The Material World

One of the contexts within which we both compose, you as a reader and I as a writer, is the one alluded to in the title of this book and in Madonna's 1984 hit song: the material world. I mean a number of things by this adjective, *material*, which I discuss at greater length in the next chapter. But let me pause here to pursue some of the larger meanings of composing in a material world, meanings different from what Chris Haas means by the term in *Writing Technology: Studies on the Materiality of Literacy* (1996), itself a very interesting attempt to identify a field of inquiry she calls technology studies, and which attends to material as "[the] mass or matter," the physical spaces and implements of writing (p. 4). Like Haas, I see writing as an activity that is individual, material, and cultural, but, unlike her, I see cultural concerns blurring with the material, and the individual infusing the cultural and material, both in conception and in practice. Overall, my book is far more preoccupied with the ways in which cultural context inflects stories told on computers.

On the other hand, I do not take on the much wider scopes of material feminism or philosophical materialism in the book, nor do I undertake a full Marxist critique of the patterns of consumption and material production that haunt post-capitalist societies like our own, interesting though such perspectives might be. (See Berlin, 1996; Jameson, 1991; and Lyotard, 1984, for valuable examples of such perspectives.) Instead, by referring to "material world" in the course of this book, I take *material* to be related most closely to Baudrillard's (1983) *simulacrum*, in that it is the stuff by which texts deliver meaning—and that while it is derived from matter and concrete reality, perspective, and period, it is not itself matter. It is that stuff that represents matter, just as a film gives us a cut of the real world and digital stories represent some of the concrete realities embedded (both explicitly and implicitly) in their codes and programs. I also mean *material* in architect Michael Benedikt's (1987) sense of "material carriers" (p. 4): words, celluloid images, or buildings, for example, that in themselves carry material and cultural traces. According to Benedikt, these "material carriers" transparently convey the ideas and codes of the web of culture that surrounds both the thing itself and its myriad representations and iterations.

The Compact Edition of the Oxford English Dictionary (1971) indicates a primary definition of *material* as "[o]f or pertaining to matter or body; formed or consisting of matter; corporeal." This concise definition leads me to specify even more carefully that I mean something slightly different from such conventional definitions of material. I refer, of course, to the *secondary corporeality* that I see as a dominant element of digital fictions, as well, in fact, of all digital texts that might be "peopled," "inhabited," or "populated" by agents, 'bots, or characters. This secondary corporeality echoes Walter Ong's (1982) notion of *secondary orality*, a term used to describe the ways in which features of oral cultures are reenacted in new media or technology. Sherry Turkle's (1984) notion of "a second self" is also an early iteration of the idea, just as Norbert Wiener's *God and Golem, Inc.* (1964) Richard Powers's *Galatea 2.2*

(1995), and Marge Piercy's *He, She, and It* (1991) comprise implicit critiques of secondary corporeality.

My notion of secondary corporeality might be yet another "making visible" of a contemporary theoretical idea, in this case Kirby's (1991, 1997) claim that the debate between essentialism and anti-essentialism encourages "somatophobia" (cited in Adam, 1998, p. 134), a fear of the body that is traced by some feminists to a sense of our body's betrayals, a misplaced disappointment that leads to distancing self from flesh. Some feminists would claim that digital fiction's emphasis on secondary corporeality (and the disguises and deceptions that interactive computer texts permit) is prompted by our lives in a culture that overvalues youth, health, whiteness, wealth, and being very thin. The somatophobia implicit in the joys of secondary corporeality might also be understood as social constructionism's implicit denial of the physical body (Sloane, 1999c). Secondary corporeality, or the image of bodies scripted and inscribed in digital fictions, is one element of these texts' implicit questioning of the categories of identity, body, and the singular self.

In my understanding of *material*, then, I do not mean raw materials, nor essence, bulk, terra, or physical domain. I mean something constructed. By *material*, I mean the matter from which structures are made, including structures such as allegory, narrator, or plot, as well as all the material traces of such discourse, everything from page to scripted behaviors. Ultimately, I suppose, I am understanding material as *fabric*, and the uses to which material is put by programmers, as *fabrications*. The mimetic enterprise of digital programmers, writers, and readers, finally, is different in nature and influence from the mimesis of more traditional fictions.

Michael Benedikt (1987), who envisions architecture that resurrects the category of the "real" within a postmodern discourse of design and buildings, understands *material* in a way similar to mine. Benedikt posits a new architecture that would offer a "direct aesthetic experience of the real" and reject a world (and buildings) whose being is solely "symbolical" (p. 4). Within such direct aesthetic experiences, *material* is ultimately discarded, and only *matter* remains. In such cases, Benedikt explains,

> Objects and colors do not point to other realms, signs say what they have to and fall silent. Conventional associations fall away: a flag against the sky does not conjure a stream of patriotic images—soldiers, funerals, moonwalks—like some TV documentary, but contains in its luminosity and sharp flapping a distilled significance unique to the actual sight and sound of it. We are not conscious ("Ah, this means that...") of reference, allusion or instruction. These processes become transparent as their material carriers either disappear, like words, or like bells and old trees, collapse upon themselves to become crisp and real... (p. 4)

In my opening invocation of the material world, then, I am invoking the critic's sense that Benedikt rejects, the very sense that "Ah, this means that...," which Benedikt hopes contemporary architecture might be able to overcome.

Benedikt's distinction between the material and the real (or raw) world, between the thing and its allusions (and illusions), is echoed obliquely by critic Sven Birkerts's (1994, 1999a, 1999b) concerns about the pace, depth, and content of our "media-saturated" lives and his sense that we are living more and more in a simulated world (points discussed in more depth in Chapter 4 in this volume). Let me quote him briefly here, though, to extend our working definition of *material* and to acknowledge the ways in which Benedikt's dichotomy between thing and allusion (a dichotomy that also allows the notion of secondary corporeality) is expanded by Birkerts into a critique of the entire concept and project of this "second world," which is the subject of our study. Birkerts writes,

> Our technologies, and our technology driven employments, have created a secondary world that we inhabit in lieu of the first world that our immediate ancestors, and all of their ancestors before them, inhabited. This original world was determined in many essential ways by the brute realities of nature—by weather, by terrain, by the time required for various processes, and the intervals of long-distance communication…. For the real we are substituting the virtual. (1999b, pp. 27–28.)

While later in this book I disagree with the premises of Birkerts's valuation of hypertext fictions, I borrow his words now to underscore the meaning of material I intend to extend in the chapters that follow.

The material world, whether it belongs to Benedikt, Birkerts, Madonna, or myself, is different from the real world. And the material worlds created by programmers and navigated by readers in the digital fictions under study here constitute a peculiarly fitting reminder of a grave weakness of postmodernist ideas: that the raw or real exist no matter how we disguise or avoid it, no matter how many ways we might shuffle the deck and build the houses of cards that represent it. And it is the responsibility of literary critics like ourselves to understand the dynamics between sign and thing, whether we call that sign a second self (Turkle, 1984), a secondary world (Birkerts, 1999), a simulacrum (Baudrillard, 1983), a material carrier (Benedikt, 1987), or the delicate weave of cultural codes and ideas I call secondary corporeality.

Storytelling

[O]n some occasions, in connection with aesthetic activities, we humans might like to exercise our prowess with symbol systems, just because that's the kind of animal we are. I would view the poetic motive in that light.

—Kenneth Burke (1966)

Storytelling, or the art of narrating fiction, is arguably the oldest form of conversation and certainly remains one of the most interesting. When stories are told through the agency of software, hardware, and programming code, in the form of secondary characters, words, and worlds, these material creatures (and carriers) shape and inspire their readers in ways not very different from the rhetorical resources of all stories. The ancient art of storytelling is not lost but reformed by digital fictions. And it is that reformation of the ancient art of narrating fictions that is under study in the following chapters.

Within the larger context of a discussion of how and why memory is story-based, Roger Schank (1990) talks about the importance of "indexing" stories in our minds so that they are easily retrieved when we have similar experiences. Schank explains,

> The more information we are provided with about a situation, the more places we can attach it to in memory and the more ways it can be compared to other cases in memory. Thus, a story is useful because it comes with many indices. These indices may be locations, attitudes, quandaries, decisions, conclusions, or whatever. (p. 11)

Schank's project quickly becomes one of identifying particular story scripts and skeletons, and their indices, goals, and lessons, in his attempt to identify the way memory works. But the larger thesis of his book appears to be that not only is memory story-based, but so is much of all cultural knowledge, and by extension, so is culture itself. While I sometimes disagree with the cognitivist premises of Schank's work, I think here he is absolutely right: stories are the basis of how we understand our world and how we explain it to others. A literary critic of a different bent, Kenneth Burke (1966), defines the quality of telling stories as a central quality of our being human. When we acknowledge, as I do, that storytelling is both a central activity of human beings and a primary means of organizing information and experience in our lives, we are ready to explore the implication of an artificial voice narrating the stories of a virtual world.

In the following chapters, I attempt to take advantage of my precise historical, literal, and transitional locations and to describe the works and ideas of a community of scholars and practitioners who read and write digital fictions, including interactive fictions, hypertext fictions, MUDs, and other computer-mediated games and narratives. I examine the relations between stories and their participants by assuming a critical stance that is equal parts semiotic, feminist, and postmodern, a critical stance that is as much of a *bricolage* as are our machines and their writings. I also take a critical posture that allows me to see stories as embedded in the lives of their creators and writers.

Following the critical work of Mark Johnson and Robin Lakoff (Johnson, 1987; Johnson & Lakoff, 1999), I explore how the body is revealed in the stories we tell, how our limbs, skin, ligaments, eyes, and ears leave traces in the metaphors and overarching rhetorical designs of the language we use to tell stories within the situation of the computer. I am looking for traces of primary corporeality in the secondary corpora of digital fictions. Finally, in the course of this book, I record my own reactions to digital fictions, observing how my feelings range from frustration to wonder as I leave the traces of my readings, my thumbprint, as it were, on the stories readers and writers create and study on these millennial machines.

The Problem of "Naturalization"

Seeing is sometimes not believing. In Shoshona Zuboff's *In the Age of the Smart Machine: The Future of Work and Power* (1988), an excellent, prescient work on the transformational qualities of information technology in the lives of workers at pulp and paper mills, she highlights the problem of researchers who "naturalize" an environment they claim to be investigating by not seeing those features that have become "transparent." Researchers lose sight of some important aspects of a setting when those aspects become too familiar, expected, and predictable—or, in Zuboff's terms, too *natural*. Zuboff says,

> The most treacherous enemy of [such] research is what philosophers call "the natural attitude," our capacity to live daily life in a way that takes for granted the objects and activities that surround us. Even when we encounter new objects in our environment, our tendency is to experience them in terms of categories and qualities with which we are already familiar. The natural attitude allows us to assume and predict a great many things about each other's behavior without first establishing premises at the outset of every interaction.... *Awareness requires a rupture with the world we take for granted;* then old categories of experience are called into question and revised. (emphasis added, p. 13)

By seeing afresh storytelling practices, both through our own careful observation and the perspective new storytelling technologies afford us, we can better understand and follow the intricacies of literary exchange between readers and writers of narrative.

Computers, these boxes of plastic and metal cabled and plugged into the walls of our workplaces, libraries, homes, Internet cafés, and workplaces, provide a rupture in the way we see stories and offer an opportunity to analyze them afresh. Computers, the latest writing instrument in the 20th century's parade of technological innovation, interrupt that smooth parade by a technical leap so grand that suddenly eye and ear are riveted by what the hands can find. Much of what we took for granted in reading and writing stories, much that we no longer saw, is today thrown into sharp relief by computers. The challenge (among many) that computers implicitly pose to those of us who study narrative, is to avoid analyzing these new stories solely in terms of "categories and qualities with which we are already familiar" (Zuboff, 1988, p. 13). Today's networked computers give us a new window into what happens when we read and write fiction, and that window affords us a perspective that complicates the models of reading and writing based solely on encounters with paper-based fictions, and interrupts models—for example, the rhetorical triangle—based on both speaking and writing. Today, when we read and write stories at computers, the interactive, immersive works of fiction with which we interact and dance force us to reconsider our models and theories of storytelling, and to revise those models once we see how neither social constructionism nor cognitive psychology adequately encompasses them.

Current articles about the processes of writing digital fictions tend to be either discussions by programmers about their own adventure game programming languages (Betz, 1987; Lebling, 1980) or how-to essays addressing freelance writers who wish to compose in this new genre (Banks, 1985; Crawford, 1984). And while a growing body of literature (such as articles and books by Aarseth, 1993, 1997; Bolter, 1991b; Heim, 1987, 1993; Joyce, 1995; Landow, 1992a, 1992b, 1994; Lanham, 1993; and Murray, 1997) addresses the implications of computers for composition in general, none of it describes, in detail, the collaborative process by which programmers, authors, and readers compose digital fictions. (Jay David Bolter's (1991b) description of the new "writing space" of computer fictions comes closest to detailing the layered collaborations that characterize the composing process of this new genre, but he distorts his discussion of interactive fiction with a description of *Afternoon*, a work of hyperfiction, and he does not discuss MUDs or MOOs.)

This particular historical moment, one in which the art of telling stories is denaturalized, provides an opportunity that we must seize. Our "old categories of experience," while certainly relevant, demand revision and refinement. Digital fictions force us to reconsider the rhetorical triangle, narrative theories (especially reader-response theories and semiotic models of reading and writing), and composition theories (especially those that construe reading and writing as independent cognitive processes) and pedagogies (especially those in creative writing classes). Digital fictions demand we revise or extend the important work of theorists like Wolfgang Iser, Andrea Lunsford and Lisa Ede, Linda Flower and John Hayes, Wendy Bishop, Wayne Booth, and Cynthia and Richard Selfe, among others, so that we can better model the hybrid processes of reading and writing on computers. The ways in which computers today allow us to innovate multilinear narratives, engross us in engaging graphics, move us with synthesized music, and compose words and worlds with real (and shifting) rhetorical power, forces us to look anew at what a story is and does—how it *acts* on its readers and participants. Text-based interactive fictions, hypertext stories, MUDs, and computer games like *Myst* and *Riven* force us to reestablish the premises by which we understand story, both as genre *and* as rhetorical action.

On the other hand, the computer's very novelty today has distracted important theorists like Landow, Bolter, Murray, Haas, and Aarseth from accounting for the ways in which computers change reading and writing in particular genres. Intelligent, thoughtful analyses of computers and their historical contexts offered by these writers do not sufficiently differentiate among the genres computers support, nor the diverse reading and writing practices different kinds of people bring to this tool. (I should note, however, that Haas [1996] approaches an answer to these important questions in her expert-novice studies.) These critics rightly observe that today's computer is an innovation, a dynamic, interactive delivery system whose coded gestures, layered interfaces, and audio-visual elements are often meaningful (depending on the reader) and always linguistic (when we understand language in that sense that Kenneth Burke did, as a kind of symbolic action). However, by concentrating on the ramifications of this box, by sweeping together genres, reading habits, different hardware and software packages, composing processes, and rhetorical conventions within too general discussions of how the computer has affected writing and reading, many of the critics of computer-mediated communication miss the rhetorical invention, the emergent genres, and the interactive drama of computer-based documents. Furthermore, by collapsing categories as diverse as computer-assisted instruction, computer-mediated communication, and synchronous electronic communication, some contemporary researchers are missing difference and nuance within more narrowly focused studies and groups. This general focus on computer as information delivery system is the only real mistake I see in the otherwise useful and interesting work of Chris Haas, Jay David Bolter, Victor Vitanza, Myron Tuman, and some of the most recent writers for the groundbreaking journal *Computers and Composition*. (See, for example, the interesting essay "The Mysterious Disappearance of Word Processing," by Bernard Susser [1998], in which he notes that word processing has almost disappeared from accounts of writing with computers. He suggests that nonetheless the need for word-processing instruction remains pressing, and urges instructors to continue teaching how to use word-processing packages in general.)

Because the computer "ruptures" the world we take for granted, because it affords us this new window into composing processes, suddenly its presence seems overwhelmingly important to some researchers in rhetoric and composition. While the attention to word processing *per se* may have waned as it has become more familiar, even almost ubiquitous, the general capabilities of various computer systems still receive undue attention from researchers into reading and writing practices. An analogy might be helpful. Imagine how we would smile and roll our eyes at a colleague foolish enough to attempt an understanding of first-year writing, for example, by concentrating on the qualities of the *pencils* they use.

Can you imagine a Conference on College Composition and Communication (CCCC) panel addressing pencil pedagogy, pencil rhetorics, and penciling across the curriculum? We would discuss the ramifications of a sharp point and the material constraints of graphite. We might ask: Is it a Supreme or a Ticonderoga? Does a writer sharpen it between drafts? Is a 2 or 2B lead better? How does the pencil affect revision, in general? What is the pencil–audience relationship? How does the mechanical pencil's precise, perpetually loading strokes model the economic system under which it was constructed? What does Freud say about the pencil? How does the presence of the eraser contribute to a "delete strategy" of revision; to a writer's self-confidence; to the writer's sense of the durability of her words? What happens when a writer closes her eyes and writes with the pencil? What about the economic conditions of loggers or the cultural influences of fairy tales about woodcutters? What are the material processes that underlie pencil production? And so on.

Certainly, such questions might lead to interesting insights into the composing process, but such questions would also miss much of what is most interesting in the manipulation of symbols that is the metacognitive activity underlying what people do when they write stories, arguments, or memoranda and other documents. The novelty of a particular delivery system, the computer, has obscured the far more interesting phenomenon of how different sets of words act on their readers in this new environment or *scene*, how computer-based genres evolve, and how readers and writers are taking on new roles that earlier models and language do not adequately describe. In this book, I endeavor to concentrate not only on pencil potential (or, in this case, computer capacity or digital daring), but instead to focus on a particular set of rhetorical acts that is complicated and facilitated by computers. Yes, within the writing space (Bolter, 1991b) of the computer, spoken words are made visible again; yes, the temporal is made spatial (Ong, 1982); and yes, computer texts show some signs of a secondary orality (Havelock, 1986; Ong, 1982), but in terms of this book, what is most important is how a single genre changes, and our models and ideas of literacy change, owing to the computer. Our primary enterprise is to examine a few individual stories, and the narrative and rhetorical theories we use to describe them, as we consider their presence in and on computers.

Computer systems come and go, operating systems are rejuvenated in new versions every month, chip-speak is an argot in constant flux, and every day we hear announcements of new kinds and capacities and speeds of processors, power supplies, bandwidth, and interfaces. Focusing on a particular genre of computer-based texts and a specific set of rhetorical acts, in all their infinite permutations, rewards our attention. Instead of sweeping all computer-generated texts under one rubric, then, this book, therefore, concentrates on a single genre: fiction. And instead of understanding digital fictions as the simple realization of post-structuralist theories, I opt to look at the ways they are both modern and postmodern in their encyclopedic, digressive, and complex forms.

Finally, I make every effort I can think of in this book to heed Zuboff's (1988) warning about the blinders attached to assuming "a natural attitude," and to see clearly how this particular rhetorical act or genre, the fictional narrative, is realized online and onscreen by contemporary computer technology.

What Matter Who's Speaking?

> *New questions will be heard:*
>   *"What are the modes of existence of this discourse?"*
>   *"Where does it come from; how is it circulated; who controls it?"*
>   *"What placements are determined for possible subjects?"*
>   *"Who can fulfill these diverse functions of the subject?"*
> *Behind all these questions we would hear little more than the murmur of indifference:*
>   *"What matter who's speaking?"*
>
> —Michel Foucault (1977)

> *"I yam what I am."*
>
> —Ralph Ellison (1972)

When Michel Foucault participates in the French post-structuralist critique of the ascendancy of authors (as they are construed by their readers and interpreters), he offers us the set of questions listed above; this set is intended to supersede preoccu-

pation with the biographies of poets and novelists and to get to the heart of the matter, to the question of *how* something was said rather than *who* said it. Foucault's last
question (quoted above) seeks to shift our attention away from an author's status and
life and toward a consideration of the author's *function* in the texts critics examine. I
read Foucault's (1977) essay as an important departure from the thinking of both
New Critics and New Historians; Foucault directs our attention to the limits of concentrating on just the text itself (as some New Critics do) and to the fallacies of reading literature as semiautobiographical writing (as some New Historicists attempt).
Instead, by asking us to pay attention to *authorial function*, Foucault's essay asks readers to explore the ways in which the name inscribed on a title page and made visible in the various paratexts surrounding that inscription (book jacket photos,
reviews, interviews, critical reception) invent a category that should be included in
our literary analyses. One consequence of this Foucauldian emphasis on function,
however, is the figurative murder of the author herself, as also discussed by Roland
Barthes (1977) and Italo Calvino (1986). As the latter says in his provocative essay
"Cybernetics and Ghosts," the ascendancy of the "eye of the reader" will guaran-
tee the disappearance of the author:

> What will vanish is the figure of the author, that personage to whom we persist in
> attributing functions that do not belong to him, the author as an exhibitor of his own
> soul in the permanent Exhibition of Souls, the author as the exploiter of sensory and
> interpretive organs more receptive than average... (p. 16)

Calvino continues here by calling the Author "that anachronistic personage, the
bearer of messages, the director of consciences, the giver of lectures to cultural bodies" (p. 16). I confess to growing progressively less happy with Calvino's claim here,
and overall with the Foucauldian notion of authorial function, the closer I get to
completing this book. That is, the closer I get to achieving *narrative telos*, the more I
want to assert my active authorial presence, to throw off this papery shroud and
shout out my own raw presence, right here and now. Ultimately, even though narratives may never really end, stories may unfold in many directions, and authorial
intent may always be suspect, when push comes to shove, it matters a great deal, to
this writer, anyway, who is speaking.

Within any writing, but especially within any so-called creative writing, the
need to pay attention to *who* is speaking (as well as within what compass, within
what scene of reading or writing she speaks) is more important than Foucault
might see. We have to listen to the full chorus of participants whispering under
the page. (Searle [1983] made a similar point when he asked Derrida to consider
the acknowledgments he makes within the space of his published essays.) By
acknowledging myself, my own preoccupations and predilections, my habits and
blinders and experience, I find myself stepping into a critical perspective that is
one kind of feminism: I subscribe to the idea that the personal is not only political, but it is *critical* as we build our models of reading and writing. In her valuable

essay "Towards a Black Feminist Criticism" (1996), Barbara Smith, countering Foucault's claims quoted above, instructs us that "[f]or books to be understood they must be examined in such a way that the basic intentions of the writers are at least considered" (p. 122).

Bodies usually live on the other side of the page, and these living, breathing entities are still connected to words even when those words are published on paper. You read strings of symbols set on a page, but every one of those symbols has a history of authors, editors, etymologists, publishers, friends, and colleagues haggling over a rogue meaning, deleting lines with cross looks and red pencils gripped by callused fingers, or smudging the screen with a fingerprint as they lean into a particularly tenacious tangle of words. A company of quarreling people underlies every line you read, but in our race for certain objective truths, we forget how opinionated, how saturated in its rhetorical situation, how responsive to its immediate and distant contexts, all criticism and theory must be. In keeping with Barbara Smith's claim, in the course of this book I'll make an effort to talk more than is perhaps customary in an academic book about the voice, perspective, place, and person behind the story to which you are listening.

I write at present within a critical community characterized as post-structuralist, and I am predisposed to see text and world as heterogeneous and fragmentary, open to multiple interpretations, and subject to rupture and aleatory influence. I understand writing as an act contextualized by personal belief, history, and culture, as well as by the demands of the immediate rhetorical situation; I understand reading as an activity of responding to texts and their symbols on the basis of personal perspective, educational training, and past reading experiences. I think my own theoretical position is best expressed in the plural, not the singular, and that my perspective is both expressivist and social constructionist. In other words, my own understanding of how the reading–writing relationship coheres and inheres is itself disjunctive, incomplete, contradictory, and evolving.

I write also in a "first world" country as a member of a privileged class—white, educated, and female—and I write as a teacher at a small liberal arts college. My readings and writings are informed by the rhetorics, slogans, and publishing apparatus of a "late print culture" (Bolter, 1991b) that is rapidly becoming a multimodal culture. As I write this on the Power Macintosh 9600/200 my university has bought for my use, I see in my surrounding cultures vigorous aural, visual, and graphic rhetorics rapidly converging in computer games, on television, in plays and concerts, and in a form of multimedial presentation that is increasingly interactive and insistent, almost intrusive. Because I am a woman trained in rhetorical and literary analysis, because I am a carbon-based human being who is living through the transition from late print culture to early silicon culture, digital fiction seems a promising site for research into contemporary rhetoric and literature.

As I write today, I tell myself that I am writing a piece of nonfiction prose that represents in its inconsistencies, its allusions, its irregularities and irruptions, its false starts and blind leaps, a *cusp*. I am writing on the cusp between genres, media, voices, and forms. (According to my dictionary, a "cusp" is a term used by mathematicians, architects, and astrologers to describe the point at which two arcs or curves intersect; it is also a transitional point or time.) The text you hold in your hand is a text woven at a particular moment in history out of the intersections of several threads, a veritable knit and purl of textures and yarns: codex book and computer screen; memoir and memory; practice and theory; anecdote and data; first-person address and limited omniscient address; the literary essay and rhetorical theory. At each of these cusps, in each of these encounters, I intend to examine the boundaries, to name them and to explore their lineaments as they evolved in the course of writing this book. I write to demonstrate and simultaneously explain the problems and possibilities of computer fictions, especially when those narratives are realized by and in the technologies, voices, and preoccupations of those who compose at the end of the millennium.

PLAN OF THE BOOK

From my close readings of dozens of digital fictions, three categories of rhetorical analysis emerge clearly: *materials, processes,* and *locations.* As I explain in more detail in the following four chapters, when we describe and theorize about how these three critical categories might account for the complexity of digital fictions, they become bases for a better understanding of the rhetoric and dialectic of stories in general. Furthermore, by developing these three critical terms to replace the three points of the rhetorical triangle, I am working toward a rhetorical theory that encompasses the dynamics of all contemporary storytelling. Moreover, by including the firsthand accounts of writers and readers of computer fictions, I hope to provide a historical record of what contemporary computer composers think, feel, and say about these fictions. I hope this work will help researchers, teachers, students, and other scholars to appreciate better the joys and frustrations that contemporary digital fictions inevitably bring. I write to move beyond the pencil and arrive somewhere else, where you can hear me and I can imagine you, at least for a little while.

This book's perspective resists some current research in computers and composition, specifically that which finds in these computer fictions a liberal democratization of the reader–writer compact and new possibilities for women readers to identify with their characters or avatars (most of whom are male and some of whom have more freedom than we do); I also try to avoid the epideictic rhetoric that claims that these computer-mediated stories are helping readers cross into a new frontier: one where readers can more fully come into their own as readers who vote on where they are going. Instead, this study sees the greatest value of digital stories as lying simply in how they encourage us to consider new categories of stories and prompt new terms of analysis. A close study of the enthusiastic rhetoric of the people who write computer fictions deserves to be done in an effort to illuminate its roots in the peculiarly American lexicon of independence, capitalist dreams, and autonomy; we might fruitfully trace its echoes back to the rhetoric of our country's primary documents (for example, the Constitution) that enshrine our rights to freedom, property, and happiness. But this book does not offer such close study. Instead, this book uses digital fictions as a new site from which to ask old questions about textuality, narrative, authoring, and reading. It takes advantage of the window into reading and writing processes that computers, in general, afford, and examines how a particular technology, the software and hardware of computers, affects the voice, content, preoccupations, processes, and responses of readers and writers of fiction, as well as the textual form of these new stories.

Many narrative theorists today offer us a critical apparatus that cannot wholly account for digital fictions; the dialogic character of digital fictions needs to be complemented with a better understanding of their dialectic. In my following treatment of digital fictions, I extend some existing rhetorical theories of how stories act on their readers. I pair and extend the important work of several theorists of rhetoric and composition and literary critics. Reading the useful metaphor of Jay David Bolter's (1991b) "writing space" against the "readable space" (*espace lisible*) of Roger Chartier (1994) and Michel de Certeau (1984), for example, reminds us to attend to the many contexts within which readers and writers compose multilinear narratives. Linda Flower and John Hayes's (1981a) work on the cognitive processes of writing, paired with Wolfgang Iser's (1978) notion of the implied reader or Kenneth Burke's (1957) inquiries into the philosophy and rhetoric of literary forms, read in tandem with Andrea Lunsford and Lisa Ede's (1990) questions about the social character of writing, helps us create a reader-response criticism that better accounts for digital fictions. By comparing and extending theories of rhetoric and narrative, we can develop a three-dimensional portrait of readers and writers communicating imperfectly over the plane of a story they have jointly composed. We can better realize the slipperiness of meanings as we interpret the symbolic worlds of digital stories; and we can better understand the range of collaborations when we remember literacy is always steeped in history, and that literacy acts (Street, 1995), too, are always imbricated in culture.

Also in this book, I address some of the recent criticisms of digital fictions. Sven Birkerts's (1995) Luddite notions of how computers are crippling commerce between readers and writers, or between readers and writers and their own souls, deserve a serious response, which I attempt here. Jay David Bolter's *Writing Space* (1991b), Richard Lanham's *The Electronic Word* (1993), and Geoffrey Nunberg's 1997 edited collection, *The Future of the Book*, are important exercises in placing our current experiences with computers in a historical context, and the quibbles these critics raise are often important. Too often, though, the critics of digital fictions fail to look behind the screen to see *who* is actually speaking, and *what is being enacted rhetorically*, when all is said and done. Today, we are in a far better position to analyze the content, voices, and forms of a particular genre of *cybertexts* (Aarseth, 1997) than some contemporary Luddites allow.

In Chapter 2, I outline some of the central themes and rhetorical concepts important to developing a rhetorical theory of digital fiction. We examine some of the historical literary precedents of digital fictions, including Oulipian textual games, French and American experimental fictions, and the Dada and Surrealist movements' play with randomness. We explore how contemporary theories of the reading–writing contract incompletely characterize or contextualize that relationship, especially when the relationship is built in part by programmers encoding their worldviews in digital stories. The postmodern farrago becomes a decentralized, distributed communication network that diffuses and constrains the stories it carries. We look also at some of the very first "story generation systems," including those developed by Lebowitz (1984, 1992), Meehan (1976), and Sharples (1985, 1999).

In Chapter 3, I more closely examine the *material* experience of reading computer-based interactive fictions. I examine the experiences of readers and writers as they intervene—-through the agency of a keyboard, and as a programmer-writer or character-participant—-and direct the narratives, including their sequence and quality of narration, to greater or lesser degrees. I examine the rhetorical resources of one kind of digital fiction, the text adventure or interactive fiction, paying particular attention to three of the narrative techniques typical of interactive fiction: multiple perspective, nonlinear progression, and second-person address. My examination of these texts is informed by Wolfgang Iser's (1978) concept of an implied reader interacting with the gaps in an indeterminant text. I also describe Carnegie Mellon University's Oz Project, the site of ongoing research into making interactive fictions that exist in both text- and graphics-based forms. Finally, I speculate that current interactive fiction composing processes are harnessed to an outdated realist epistemology, one that posits a univocal, objectified reality and ignores the force of social context in meaning-making activities such as reading and writing.

Chapter 4 of this book examines the *processes* of composing hypertext fictions. In this chapter, I explore whether differences in reading digital fictions are the result of differences in how computer fictions are composed. I explore how hyperfictions, primarily those published by Eastgate Systems, are written by interviewing three current writers of hyperfictions. The central problem of hypertext fictions, as this chapter explains, is that the expectations of its readers do not match the intentions of its authors. We listen to the voices of Michael Joyce, Carolyn Guyer, and Stuart Moulthrop, and look at their respective hypertext fictions, *Afternoon* (1987), *Quibbling* (1993), and *Victory Garden* (1991). We consider Sven Birkerts's (1995) critique of the genre and find its origins in his nostalgia and entrenchment, and its realization in a complaint that is itself heavily coded and cultured.

In Chapter 5, I explore the practices of reading and writing required by contemporary MUDs, MOOs, and MUSHes, explaining the problem of reading digital fictions that is related to the dissonance between the reader's actual locations and her textual representations (secondary corporeality), as realized in the online world. By looking at the differences and distances between physical locations and contexts of the reader and his or her projected location (following Turkle, 1997), I explore how MUDs make explicit and visible the tension between textual constraint and plural identity (not to mention between modernists and postmodernists). The meta-geographies of MUDs and many other computer games require the invention of navigational tools and commands such as the use of cardinal directions, maps, compasses, virtual bookmarks, and magic spells and vehicles for traversing cyberspace. Furthermore, the spatial metaphors that underlie MUDs prompt readers to rely on these navigational aids so that these readers' attempts to engage digital fictions become little more than scavenger hunts or a series of battles. I suggest a generative theory of digital fiction that relies on a rhetorical awareness and analysis as an alternative to the objective, monologic epistemology codified in many current commercial digital fictions. I propose that researchers assume a modified and responsible social-constructionist epistemology that will acknowledge the influences of location—cultural, historical, ideological, and gendered—on the actions of programmers and writers as they fill in the gaps or indeterminacies of these digital fictions. Furthermore, I challenge structuralist conceptions of story that implicitly posit a single ideal reader. I develop a claim that the natural and necessary complement to a view of readings as contextually determined would be a composing *process* that explicitly acknowledges the variety of readers there might be in an expanding global community. Finally, I question whether the notion of artificial intelligence and the very *material* of its composings—the computer and its binary machine language underlying the scripts and algorithms of higher-level programming languages—might not be constraining the capacity of a reader to participate in a fictional world.

I am all too well aware of the brief lives of books that address questions about computers. They have a shelf life about as long as a gallon of milk. So, I hasten to make clear, the value of this book lies not in the accuracy of its soothsayer's predictions, but in its focus on a particular rhetorical act, the story, and in its inquiry into a set of categories (materials, processes, and locations) that may be useful to both theorists and practitioners who wish to understand stories in general. I do not know how digital fictions will evolve, nor am I able to predict the shifting lineaments of their reception by critics and other readers. I hope, though, that this book will help us answer the question of how stories change when they are read and written on computer. What is gained and what is lost by the presence of story within this new literary space? How do our working definitions of authorship, textuality, and reading shift to encompass the practices of people engaged in using the computer to write characters, plots, settings, and motives? What parts of narration are enhanced, what rhetorical strategies misshapen or erased, by digital fictions? Responsible critics and rhetoricians must take note of the activities and actions of scribal culture as they are extended by computers, and we must make a record of these changes.

In the end, if there is such an end, I hope you will read my chapters as tentative and provisional, as the first draft of a set of categories, and ultimately a theory, that may account for the narrative structures and rhetorical capabilities of digital fictions. Read these millennial notes as an earnest effort to understand the processes of reading and writing as they are realized via a new set of scribal tools, etched in silicon, electrons, and air, enlivening the flickering interface of a new medium, and enacted in a new contract between readers, writers, and stories.

In sum, digital fictions are a new site for understanding a familiar transaction: storytelling. Part of the challenge of understanding the rhetoric and dialectic of digital fictions is our natural desire to compare it to something familiar. In our search for the right analogy for digital fiction, whether we choose books, cinema, or oral storytellings, and whether we demonstrate it implicitly in our metaphors of desktops, pages, bookmarks, palmtops, story guides, or pick-a-path plot trees, we are sometimes blind to the real possibilities of digital fictions. We haven't yet taken advantage of the perspective computer fictions give us on traditional questions of how authoring works, how stories are delivered to readers, and how readers make sense of these dynamic artifacts. If we reject the Ongian hypothesis that different writing technologies change consciousness, as I do, and if we reject the notion of digital determinism, which says a particular computer platform supports only certain story ideas and dynamics, then we need to explore better what these digital tales tell us about what it means to be human at the beginning of a new century.

In a movement parallel to the way digital fiction conflates reading and writing processes, bridges social-constructionist and realist epistemologies, and breaks down the boundaries between reader and writer, these new narratives push us toward a new understanding of story that is rich with tentativeness, parallel possibility, and unboundedness. The rhetorical resources of digital fictions engage readers and writers in a fundamentally new way, not yet sufficiently explored.

2

Theorizing Digital Fiction

A MILE OF NARRATIVE RELIEFS

Apparently a mile of narrative reliefs
leads the way to the Buddha
a giant stone head
worn down to its marrow
in the photo in the book
I am holding in these dreams.

An orange fungus ripens the face
the neck the robed torso
the abandoned softening stone
a pit of an ancient idea
whose fruit long ago withered away.

There are stories lost
along this river path
their stone panels broken
in the heart of the world

—some tales defaced or falling away, others,
well, their outlines grow more definite
in the sorrowing rain.

The worn edges of relief
make some of the stories look like poems.

Every voice in the thundering sky
finds an echo in these old old stones
their engravings shadowed by clockless light
their dull characters frozen in opaque laughter.

The rivergrown statue's giant eye
watches half-seen narratives progressing recklessly,
the unending clouds mending their broken frames—
mile after mile of stories
waiting to be told.

TERMS OF STUDY

If men learn this, it will implant forgetfulness in their souls; they will cease to exercise memory because they rely on that which is written, calling things to remembrance no longer from within themselves, but by means of external marks; what you have discovered is a recipe not for memory, but for reminder.
> —Socrates in Plato's *Phaedrus* (Hackforth, 1952)

The typewriter had a rhythm, made a music of its own I don't mean the script I mean the type-writer. In those complicated sentences I rarely left anything out. And I got up a tremendous speed.
> —Alice B. Toklas, about composing on a worn-out Blickensdorfer typewriter (Souhami, 1992)

The computer on his desk has only recently supplanted his old typewriter, which sits in its case on the floor. "I was afraid that it would be like writing on a television screen," [Cheuse] says.
> —Alan Cheuse (1998)

[N]ot everybody likes to read in order. And some do not like to write in order either.
> —Milorad Pavic (1991)

If at one time literature was regarded as a mirror held up to the world, or as the direct expression of feelings, now we can no longer neglect the fact that books are made of words, of signs, of methods of construction.
> —Italo Calvino (1986)

During the last two decades of the 20th century, English departments in the United States have been animated by intensely felt debates about disciplinary boundaries, canon formation, the relations between literature and composition, and what the curricula and goals of such departments should be. The very nature of the acts of reading, writing, and speaking have been complicated, problema-tized, questioned, and probed by theorists schooled as structuralists, post-struc-turalists, phenomenologists, psychoanalysts, feminists, Marxists, New Critics, New Historians, and cultural critics. Critical theories, often borrowed from the French post-structuralists (such as Jacques Derrida, Monique Wittig, Roland Barthes, Michel Foucault, Luce Irigaray, Hélène Cixous, for example) and handily reworked by British and American critics (including Wallace Martin, Jane Tompkins, James Berlin, Terry Eagleton, Stanley Fish, and Sandra M. Gilbert and Susan Gubar) have contributed to our discipline's conversations about how reading and writing might be best understood and taught. Several other contem-porary theorists have argued that the computer's recent entrance as an instrument of our late-century discourse enacts, enables, or emulates the best and worst of some post-structuralist ideas (see, for example, Aarseth, 1997; Haas, 1996; Landow, 1992a, 1992b, 1994; Murray, 1997). However, I want to argue here that computers not only mirror a number of intriguing post-structuralist theories, but more importantly, they anticipate other theories and realize new structures that correct and extend many post-structuralist notions.

When Jay David Bolter, for example, claims that "postmodern pronouncements seem to fit the computer" (qtd. in Tuman, 1992b, p. 24) in ways uncannily apt, he is joining the chorus of writers, including Landow (1994) and Joyce (1995), who see the same mirror between postmodern theory and literature created in electronic writing spaces. As Bolter explains,

> [I]n a curious way, hypertext is a vindication of postmodern literary theory. For the past two decades, postmodern theorists from reader-response critics to deconstructionists have been talking about text in terms that are strikingly appropriate to hypertext in the computer. When Wolfgang Iser and Stanley Fish argue that the reader constitutes the text in the act of reading, they are describing hypertext. When the deconstructionists emphasize that a text is unlimited, that it expands to include its own interpretations—they are describing a hypertext, which grows with the addition of new links and elements. When Roland Barthes draws his famous distinction between the work and the text, he is giving a perfect characterization of the difference between writing in a printed book and writing by computer. (qtd. in Tuman, 1992b, p. 24)

The intelligent work of Bolter, Landow, Joyce, and others has rightly identified many points of correspondence between post-structuralist theories and hypertextual practices. However, their work sometimes ignores those points where theory and practice do not correspond. We need to examine the so-called mirrors themselves, to admit our own cultural biases and theoretical limitations, so that we might see how we distort or miss altogether the ways digital fictions can lead us beyond current theories of how reading and writing work. Digital fictions are a useful site of study not least because they anticipate models and theories of rhetoric that will better represent the dynamics of storytelling in general.

Before we go further, let me define "digital fictions." I propose this term to encompass stories that are written on or by computers, read via a computer interface, and that are one genre of what Espen Aarseth (1997) calls more generally the *cybertext*. By *stories*, I mean narrative fictions; by *writing*, I mean to include all the coded or symbological acts of generating meaning, whether that symbology be invented by human, programmer, or program, and whether the result be text, graphics, music, or touch. By *reading*, I mean to include the more common terms of "playing," "using," or interacting with a computer's interface; and by interface, I mean any software and hardware (including monitors, helmets and gloves, simulated sounds and smells, or even a *Star Trek* holodeck). In short, digital fictions are stories written and read on a computer.

Digital fictions already come in several types, and no doubt will soon "morph" into many more. Interactive fictions, for example, are text-based stories whose structures are multilinear, playful, spliced, and combinatory. Interactive fictions (or text adventures) allow readers to engage the text in limited co-authorings: through the agency of a keyboard, readers type short sentences or phrases that appear on the screen and direct a computer program to select and return written responses. Hypertext fictions, on the other hand, are written today in several programs, including the widely-used Storyspace, but all are based originally on a prototype called Notecards, developed at the Xerox Palo Alto Research Center (PARC) (Joyce, 1995) and related to Theodor Nelson's (1974/1987a) early ideal of an interconnected web of knowledge. Hypertext fictions use notecards with embedded buttons to allow readers to make choices between alternative plot branches and to write in their own words, if they so choose, into the notecards and evolving story. MUDs, MOOs, and MUSHes are a third type of digital fiction, one that relies on the Internet to connect readers and writers in collaborative stories distinguished by other worldly settings and levels, the reader's selection of physical abilities and personality traits, and goals clearly stated at the outset of the session as sets of rules and objectives. (As explained later, the acronyms are all variations on the term "mulit-user dungeon" coined by Roy Trubshawin [1978].) Finally, computer games like *Riven* or *Myst* must be considered a type of digital fiction also, one that currently relies on a set of CD-ROMS with which a player interacts sequentially, selecting graphical elements and clicking on paths, parts of the world, or objects. This book centers its discussions on text-based digital fictions to enable us to draw on the body of scholarship that has been largley constructed on paper-based experiences of reading and writing stories.

While digital fictions to date have been criticized as a thin genre that is often dominated by shallow characters questing, hacking, and slashing across unlikely lands in a quest for some treasure, key, or goal, there is a real value in studying such popular culture, not least because of what it reveals about our whole culture's preoccupations. In digital fiction, we see men seeking women in the most hackneyed heterosexual plots; explorers seeking knowledge, liberation, or gold; warriors hoping to slay the dragon; and a whole set of tales, fables, and lessons, suggested behaviors or qualities, and story-outcomes that distill our culture's primary aims and motivations. Furthermore, if we look past their superficial content, plodding chronologies, and rote voices of these stories, we can foresee the possibility of a rich and radically altered version of narrative, a promise not yet realized but important for researchers who study stories in any medium or genre, whether popular, canonical, or other. Digital fictions help us researchers in rhetoric and narrative reconfigure our critical theories and models of textual interpretation. Digital fictions give us a means to understand better the larger relationships between reader and text, self and culture, and subject and object. And digital fictions give us a new tool with which to probe the rhetorical models offered by social constructionists and cognitivists; they grant a window into how *all* texts constrain readers and how our cultural contexts constrain message, form, and reception.

Digital fictions are stories in which the reader takes on the role of a central character and writes into an evolving narrative (to a greater or lesser degree according to subgenre), narratives which enact a post-structuralist notion of authorial intention, but paradoxically also neglect, to some extent, the possibilities of reader response. Author and meaning are endlessly deferred and sometimes even erased, textual stability is lost, and reading becomes more like orienteering or walking blindly through a maze than an activity of assembling a coherent narrative. Digital fictions provide an intriguing site for extending rhetorical and narrative theories that

encompass both the thudding drum of a machine weaving dreams and the dissonant chorus of readers responding to these narratives. While clearly tied to their
paper-based predecessors, the novel and the short story, the quality of digital fiction's rhetoric is, in some ways, more like speech than writing. Today's digital fictions remind me far more of myths and epics and far less of the depth and
complexity of most American and British literature. That is, the experience of reading digital fiction is more like listening to those oral performances that Walter Ong
(1982) describes as aggregative, associative, and formulaic, and far less like reading
the carefully laid groundwork of any novel by, say, Jane Austen.

However, digital fictions differ greatly from Ong's characterizations of oral performance precisely because they are not situated in the contexts of their tellers,
which is an important distinction. While digital fictions, especially Infocom's text-
based interactive fictions and some MUDs, rely on set expressions and formulaic
descriptions in their representation of fictive worlds and characters, the psychic distance between reader and writer can be increased by the computer's sometimes
hapless responses. In the terms John Gardner uses in his book *The Art of Fiction*
(1983), the continuous dream is interrupted, the illusion of engagement destroyed.
In the gaps or lulls between correct responses, at the moments of false steps, inappropriate remarks, and the many sheer misunderstandings between readers and the
machine's representation of that reader's mental models and expectations of the
story, our notion of digital fiction as an oral phenomenon, as "situated," as approximate to face-to-face communication, falls apart. When we see the difference in the
ways stories are presented and understood, in the ways a digital fiction is situated in
a particular "writing space" and a reader is situated in a very different "reading
space" (what Chartier [1994] calls *espace lisible*), we see that claims of digital fictions'
oral qualities are only half true. While digital fictions may undo some of the stability and fixity of stories written on paper, their new fluidity and interactivity do not
much match the range or expectations of their readers, or fit the formulaic patterns
of much oral discourse.

However, digital fictions do not quite fit into critical categories that see narrative
as primarily spatial, visible, linear, or systematically unfolding either. Jay David
Bolter offers the concept of "the writing space" in his provocative work on the ways
in which computers have changed the *techne* of writing, suggesting that computers
create an altogether new *place* for writing, as did the scriptorium, the printing press,
and other scribal "scenes." Like handwriting and printing, this argument claims, the
computer screen provides a writing space, one that is a more fluid textual space that
allows readers and writers to interact (see Tuman, 1992b, p. 20). Another important
critical theorist, Roger Chartier, has offered work on the reading practices of 16nth-
and 17th-century practitioners, developing our awareness of the ways in which
readers construct meaning within the "readable spaces" of manuscripts and codex
books. In his essay discussing the legacy of the critic Louis Marin, "The Powers and
Limits of Representation" (1997), for example, Chartier details some of the aspects
of the "reading space" important for us in understanding how readers in general

interpret texts and make meaning from them. In the remarks reproduced below, Chartier is addressing "...all whose operational space is a critical study of the place where works, their circulation, and their meanings and interpretations interconnect" (p. 102) and suggests that a number of critical questions intersect in our scholarly efforts to understand and acknowledge

> how an individual reader (or spectator) [who] produces meaning is always enclosed within a series of constraints. These are, first, the effects of meaning aimed at by texts (or images) through their use of enunciative mechanisms and the organization of their utterances; next, the ways the forms that present the work for reading or viewing dictate how they will be deciphered; finally, the interpretive conventions of a time or a community. (p. 102)

Chartier and Bolter's discussions of these two composing spaces—whether reading or writing—are rooted in a metaphor that sees literacy practices as visual, linear, and implicitly paper-based. However, they can be reconciled with digital textual practices by acknowledging the wider contexts of composing processes. Chartier's analyses of reading spaces and Bolter's examination of writing spaces can be coordinated in a larger discussion of *medial spaces*, those complex, layered information spaces within which we largely compose today.

Even as you read this page, my guess is that you, like me, are surrounded literally by other texts: newspapers, magazines, student papers, library books, advertising flyers, web pages, advertisements and e-commerce banners, professional journals, notebooks, reviews. We read and write in information spaces that are always changing. Most composing spaces today are richly saturated medial spaces, places rocked and shifted as the texts surrounding them retreat, respond, shuffle, desire, reject, collate, hinge, fall apart, and speak into each other in untold ways. When Bolter's writing space speaks to Chartier's reading space, the gaps in understanding are revealed; between the discrete symbols of digital discourse, between the units (numbers, words, sentences, paragraphs, *lexia*, sections) to which readers are expected to respond, there is a new, misunderstood space, one that yields a hitch or a pause as a reader unravels the knots of prose. It is important that researchers in rhetoric and composition pay close attention to the ways in which these coordinated composing spaces encompass and let escape the virtual histories of texts, or what Foucault calls the horizontal, fugitive flight of words, and to pay attention to their traces, migrations, and present incarnations.

THEORIES OF THE READING—WRITING CONTRACT

Consider yourself and your present reading scene. You are reading a book about writing that appears on a screen. This is a book that is about writing the readings that appear on a screen, and about reading the writings that appear on a screen.

This is a book that invites you to read about computers and stories and to write your own thoughts into the soft paper pages you hold now in your hands. (Get a pencil.) This is a book that invites you to reflect on your own habits of reading and writing and to speculate about how your habits change when confronted by terminal textuality and digital delights. This is a book that can be read in many orders, that can be read in many places, that can be held by many hands, that has a physical aesthetic that you should be thinking about, that itself may constrain narrative. Or at least your experience of this narrative.

Crack the binding. Rub the grain. Smell the rag content. Listen to the riff of pages under your thumb. Turn your book upside-down and shake it. Taste its glue. Examine the signatures and pull apart their threads, if you dare. Make visible a textual apparatus that is normally transparent. Take a window and make it a door. Check out this particular version of asynchronous communication and imagine it happening in real-time. Ponder the portability, deliberate about the durability, and consider the constraints of reading any book today.

In fact, although you probably are not used to thinking about it this way, you hold in your hands an information delivery system. Books are as much information delivery systems as are televisions, film projectors, radios, telephones, and computers, and as were clay tablets, papyrus rolls, parchment or vellum manuscripts, or even the damp walls of a dark cave. Furthermore, as Seymour Chatman elegantly outlines in *Story and Discourse: Narrative Structure in Fiction and Film* (1978), the different media of delivery systems support different narrative voices and story structures more or less efficiently. Different story delivery systems allow narrative discourse to take different shapes, to express different ideas poorly or well, and to convey shifts in time and location clumsily or smoothly. Computer technology, like most media, enhances or erases, creates and constrains, individual narrative techniques. Chatman's work offers an example of how film-based and paper-based fictions (my terms, not Chatman's) differ in their ability to summarize. Chatman outlines the differing techniques in film in a persuasive analysis he calls "story-space" in cinematic narrative, in which he discusses the devices of the "montage-sequence," and "peeling calendars, dates written as legend on the screen, and voice-over narrators" (p. 69). He reminds us of *Citizen Kane*'s newsreel summary of the main character's life and the disjunctive visuals in Clouzont's film *Wages of Fear*. Paper-based narratives in general are much more efficient in their summaries and in portraying shifts in time than are films.

Digital fictions, too, have particular strengths and weaknesses in their representations of time and space, in their conception of chronology and setting, plot, and engagement. The blended encounters that are the reader–writer compact reconceived by digital technology are not well modeled by the existing rhetorical triangle, although a revised rhetorical theory may still offer us the best hope of understanding digital textuality, of what these texts do with time, history, and memory.

The Rhetorical Triangle

The rhetorical triangle is an imperfect model of the metaphysics of communication, and reader-response critics, post-structuralists, and feminists are just a few of the theorists who most recently have questioned its ability to encompass what happens when we send and receive information and meaning. As a character in Luigi Pirandello's entertaining play, *Six Characters in Search of an Author* (1998), complains:

> But that's the whole root of the evil. Words. Each of us has, inside him, a world of things—to everyone, his world of things. And how can we understand each other, sir, if, in the words I speak, I put the sense and value of things as they are inside me, whereas the man who hears them inevitably receives them in the sense and with the value of the world inside him? We think we understand each other but we never do. (p. 20)

Pirandello's words remind us of the slipperiness of all meaning, the existential angst underlying our attempts to talk to each other, to discuss together what we are doing here or where we are going. The rhetorical triangle helps us name the participants in the communication, but it doesn't offer much of a foothold for understanding those exchanges that are flawed, hybrid, or blurred.

However, the hold of the rhetorical triangle has been tenacious, despite the repeated questions brought to it by theorists and artists. James Kinneavy offers us a thorough review of the origins of the triangle in *A Theory of Discourse* (1971). Kinneavy explains what every school girl knows, that the "so-called communication triangle" encompasses the "interrelationships of expressor, receptor, and language signs as referring to reality" (pp. 18–19). The enduring basis of the rhetorical triangle, according to Kinneavy, is that it visually represents the following important claim: basic to all uses of language are a person who encodes a message, the signal (language) that carries the message, the reality to which the message refers, and the decoder (receiver of the message). Kinneavy reminds us that it was Aristotle who made these elements the basis for his study of rhetoric, and precisely because of Aristotle's enduring influence, these factors have dominated rhetorical theory ever since.

Kinneavy (1971) also reminds us of the rhetorical triangle's usefulness to discussions by critics like Abrams and Richards, who were trying to establish a literary criticism that was more responsive to the world of texts, that looked beyond spoken word to that which is written down, represented visually, and often misunderstood. We might also note the ways semioticians, including Umberto Eco (1990) and Julia Kristeva (1992), have used the terms embodied by the rhetorical model to understand the "textualizing" of the world. And many cognitive psychologists have adopted this model as central to understanding reading and writing, although they tend to complement it with the languages of cybernetics and text processing. Kenneth Burke's (1969) dramatistic pentad no doubt also owes a debt to the communications triangle, as do several contemporary metafictions, including works by Jeanette Winterson (1991), Paul Auster (1990), and Jorge Luis Borges (1972). However, post-structuralist theories have in large part found the rhetorical triangle inadequate to the task of understanding diffuse identities and roles, the masked and multiple selves or blank subjects of postmodernism, the sometimes incomplete and fractured communication in multicultural communities, the splices and pidgins of multimodal discourse, and the occasional nonsense of distributed computer-mediated communication. We cannot find in the existing rhetorical triangle ample room for the representation of what Pfeil (1988) calls "the new, unrestricted, schizoid self, awash in its desiring flows, free floating in the warm, amniotic currents of the Kristevan or Barthesian semiotic, untethered by memory to any fixed sense of the self" (cited in Glass, 1993, p. 13). Again, while many contemporary critics have questioned the usefulness of the rhetorical triangle, not least because its three angles are represented by terms (reader, writer, and text, for example) that are unitary and bounded when identity itself is more likely to be fluid than fixed (see, for example, Barthes, 1977; Cixous, 1981; Deleuze & Guattari, 1987), digital fictions and their decentering of the reader and writer into congeries of composers provide a new and powerful site from which to renew our skepticism of this influential model.

The big problem, of course, is one that neither Aristotle nor Kinneavy foresaw: the dynamics of communication as they are shaken up and realized by the digital text in general. A model that would account for layered textual dynamics must better synthesize insights from both social-constructionist and cognitivist outlooks, must encompass the more visible and active readings invited by these fluid fictions, and must fully describe how writers, programmers, and software dovetail into complex and iterative composing processes, that are themselves fraught, unstable, and distributed. The stable, unwavering rhetorical triangle does not begin to describe this particular reading–writing compact. Digital fictions offer us an opportunity to synthesize existing critiques and rhetorical theories into a fuller explanatory model.

In 1983, Sandra Stotsky published a synthesis of current research on reading and composing relationships and suggested directions for future research. Stotsky presents a comprehensive overview of rhetorical models of reading and writing in the form of a taxonomy of the kinds of studies conducted, based on how readers and writers relate across the plane of paper texts. She summarizes the results of three types of studies conducted to date: correlational studies, studies examining the influence of writing on reading, and studies examining the influence of reading on writing. She closes her essay with a persuasive call for a different set of studies to explore the reading–writing relationship in greater depth, over longer periods of time, and using more descriptive methodologies. She asks researchers to conduct comparative studies (contrasting the performances of good and poor readers and writers), longitudinal studies, and case studies. Stotsky's excellent summary of reading–writing models is typical, in that it is a taxonomy based on research methodologies. However, it leaves the important influence of the epistemological basis underlying each study she cites largely unexamined, and she misses an opportunity to urge researchers to consider the ways our underlying epistemologies blind us to part of the reading–writing compact, even as they enable us to see other parts more clearly. Other taxonomies or overviews (see, for example, Kucer, 1985; Newkirk, 1986; Shanahan & Lomax, 1986) of how the reading–writing relationship has been previously conceived are limited by their being so embedded in research either on contextual influences or on textual processing that they do not mention models or theories based on other epistemologies or on other ways of conceiving the complexities of the relationship.[1]

Few researchers in reading or writing have satisfactorily attempted the work that Stotsky (1983) urges in her conclusion, the work of building deep and comprehensive theories that describe, over long periods of time, the complementary processes and relationships of reading and writing practices. Those contemporary researchers that have undertaken such important work are typically constrained by their position within research communities whose shared epistemology emphasizes either cognitive or social contextual understandings of the composing process and that act to exclude rival understandings. While offering important insights, ultimately existing models are inadequate to account for digital fiction because of the exclusivist epistemologies upon which they are based (whether explicitly called "realist," "cognitive scientific," "cognitive psychological," "information processing," or "Objectivist"; whether termed "social constructionist," "constructivist," "contextualist," or "relativist") and because they do not provide the synthesis of cognitivist–contextualist epistemologies, which is necessary to account for digital fictions. Again, a model that would account for these stories' layered textual dynamics must synthesize insights from both social-constructionist and cognitivist outlooks, and it is just such a flexible, synthesizing model toward which the following discussion ultimately aims.

Cognitivist Models of Reading and Writing

Many of the models of reading and writing generated by researchers in the interdisciplinary field of cognitive science are supported by a realist epistemology. This epistemology conceives of a reader's relation to text as similar to a unitary observer's relation to a fixed world:

> Ontologically, [realism] claims that much of the world does not depend on humans (or any other sentient entities) for its existence. Epistemologically, realism contends that humans are capable of knowing at least some aspects of the real world *as it is in itself.* (Hikins,1990, p. 22)

A realist epistemology sees the world as comprising a single truth, a definable text to be read (instead of sharing the social constructionist perspective, which sees the world as a text that we write collectively, idiosyncratically, and imperfectly). A realist epistemology allows researchers to distinguish sharply between subject and object, between separate identities, to establish taxonomies of behavior and discourse, and to contend that there are universal and describable processes underlying a reader's encounter with a text and a writer's conceptualization of a text. For example, Bracewell, Frederiksen, and Frederiksen (1982) propose their realist-based model of composing and comprehending discourse as the first step toward "a unified account of literacy" (p. 146), and James Glass (1993) rejects postmodern thought because its relativism and diffusive subjectivity are exactly what he hopes to get away from in his treatment of schizophrenic patients. This epistemological standpoint puts the "I" back in "identity" and resists the confusions of a multimodal, multivocalic, and multicultural world.

Realism views the finished text as unitary, static, and knowable. In Kucer's (1985) discussion of realist text-processing models, for example, he explains that

> readers are seen as passively decoding or abstracting an author's intended meaning from the text. Their role in the process is one of identifying each word on the page by matching its sound with the appropriate lexical meaning stored in long-term memory, and then linking the words syntactically. Writers, on the other hand, play a much more active role: generating, structuring, and encoding their meanings onto the page. (p. 318)

The central metaphor of a realist understanding of the reading–writing relationship is this view of the relationship as a process of coding and decoding a describable (and unitary) meaning. This metaphor underscores the cognitive view of reading and writing processes, which conceives of them as universal, goal-directed activities, which can occur on a continuum between novice and expert practices. This view holds the assumption that the two processes (reading and writing) are parallel activities of making meaning or solving problems; misunderstandings or misreadings of texts are understood as flaws in the process of coding or decoding this *a priori* meaning. These models do not permit easy discussion of the influences of cultural knowledge or other social constructs on text processing, although more recent work by Linda Flower (1994) does attempt this.

Studies that rely on this realist epistemology and its underlying assumptions of describable, universal processes of meaning-making and a clear, separable distinction between the knowledge embodied by texts and in their users, have been most prominently conducted by Bereiter and Scardamalia (1993); Flower and Hayes (1980, 1981a, 1981b, 1984); Rummelhart (1977); Schank and Abelson (1977); Tierney and Pearson (1988); as well as Bracewell, Frederiksen, and Frederiksen (1982). These studies build hypotheses about the particular processes of reading and writing through expert–novice comparative studies, self-observations, observations of schoolchildren's composition processes (such as Bereiter and Scardamalia's studies conducted outside the classroom environment), protocol analyses, and meta-summaries and analyses of earlier studies. While there are several important differences among the particulars of the text-processing models developed by these studies, a shared realist epistemology clearly underlies their discussions (their terms and their metaphors), their diagrams, and their methods of study, and those shared characteristics are what make it inadequate, in my view, for a model of the textual transactions of digital fiction.

To be fair, the cognitive view does presently acknowledge, to a limited extent, the influence of contextual knowledge on composing activities, influences designated as "task environment" in the Flower-Hayes model or the "content space" (broadly characterized as "beliefs") in the Bereiter and Scardamalia model. Bracewell and colleagues (1982) also recognize contextual influences as part of the "framing processes" a reader undertakes. Tierney and Pearson do not propose ways of accounting for context, but acknowledge that their account fails to "thoroughly differentiate how these composing behaviors manifest themselves in the various *contexts* of reading and writing" (emphasis added, 1988, p. 272). However, it is probably fair to criticize contemporary iterations of the cognitive view for designations of context that are insufficiently developed and constrained by the larger, epistemologically linked characterization of the whole process as a universal pattern of goal-directed problem solving.

When research based on the cognitive perspective explores the effects of context on meaning-making activities, it typically understands those contextual influences in terms of "schemata dissonance." Schema theoretical studies, a particular subgenre of cognitivist research, cursorily acknowledge the influences of the task environment on reading and writing, and they admit only the social considerations of *purpose* on composing activities. For example, Tierney and Pearson refer to schema studies that "have shown that if readers are given different alignments prior to or after reading a selection, they will vary in what and how much they will recall" (1988, p. 266). Likewise, Vipond and Hunt (1984) contrast kinds of readings that readers create according to whether they are reading "to learn or remember the material" (in other words, performing an information-driven reading), or reading to follow a story (which they call a point-driven reading). Cognitive scientists in general acknowledge the effects of reader's context and purposes in their models under the names *schema* (Tierney & Pearson, 1988), *frames* (Minsky, 1986), or *scripts* (Schank & Abelson, 1977), but in each case the term offers little more than a superficial label for the deep and profound effects of culture, gender, history, and the social positions of readers and writers encountering an evolving text or narrative progression in digital fiction.

Pat Sullivan (1995) offers a similar critique of Linda Flower's *The Construction of Negotiated Meaning* (1994) in her review of that book. She writes,

[In Flower's study], [t]he 'social' is reduced to context, context to situation, and situation to the immediate, temporally compressed circumstance in which Flower's students find themselves at the moment of inquiry…. Flower is asking all the right questions of social constructivism. But her project doesn't answer and can't answer the more pressing questions it raises for literary education. When the social is shorn from cognition, when gender, race, ethnicity, class, and ideology are rendered invisible to analysis, cognition is made to assume a burden of explanation greater than it can bear. (qtd. in Sternglass, 1997, p. 9)

One consequence of a theoretical stance that sees writing as a primarily cognitive process, one that occurs largely independent of cultural context, is a tendency to search for *gaps* and *problems* in student (novice) writing rather than for its strengths and successes, its underlying sets of negotiations of identity and place in the world. Deborah Brandt (1992) makes a related point when she questions the ways cognitivists interpret the texts produced by basic writers: "…composition studies would benefit from assuming more competence on the part of the people typically studied. Instead of looking for flaws in [students'] reasoning, we might look instead for the grounds of their reasoning" (p. 350). I believe the cognitivist perspective, which informs the composition of much digital fiction, similarly misses the opportunity to celebrate the aleatory and trust their readers' innate good sense.

In general, a realist epistemology underlies the programs and stories created by Infocom, Carnegie Mellon University's Oz Project, and many MUDs available on the World Wide Web today, which are discussed later. In fact, it is precisely within the clash of a narrowly defined fictive world that is fully programmed prior to a reader's inhabiting it, and the unpredictable, irresolute reader's encounter with that world, that is at the heart of much of a reader's dissatisfaction with interactive fiction. Writers and programmers consider too little the ways the layered codes, which constitute the often conflicting worldviews of programmers, writers, and readers, are themselves rhetorical, in the sense that they reveal at their material level that they are but languages that convey a narrow sense of the world. The brilliant work of Alison Adam (1998) characterizes so-called expert systems that demonstrate this same flaw, saying that the asymmetry between a human and a computer's interpretive powers leads to the "brittleness" of expert systems (p. 83) and, I would add, to the sorry quality of these digital fictions, which seem thin or narrowly imagined to their readers. That is, a realist epistemology underlies both the programs that compose digital fictions *and* many of the theoretical models that hope to encompass it.

For example, the popular, text-based interactive fiction, *Deadline* (1991), discussed previously by Sloane (1991) and Aarseth (1997), offers readers the role of a detective who must solve a murder mystery within 24 hours, but the story's opening screens demonstrate all too well how a realist reading–writing model inadequately encompasses the experiences of reading interactive fiction. After reading an overview of one's role as a detective solving a crime, the reader is invited to knock on a door and enter the house where a murder took place. A reader in *Deadline* may type a series of phrases that will allow her to go to the library and pick up a telephone, hear a dial tone, and dial a number, but she is unable to actually reach anyone by phone during the course of the story (although she is able to eavesdrop on a short conversation, if she picks up the receiver at the right time). If the reader-player types "Press 911," or asks to dial any number this reader has tried, for example, the story responds, "Pushing the number has no effect." Further, when the reader-player proposes to the story some unforeseen combination of objects, such as "Hit Baxter with the telephone," the story responds, "You rethink your planned action" or, in other situations, even executes a default reprimand: "This sort of shabby behavior is disgusting." In general during *Deadline*, when the reader-player types a response that does not match a response "understood" or "expected" by the program, the underlying programs provide a default answer that is sometimes frustrating for the reader.

A subtler version of this frustration occurs at a higher level in the story *Deadline*. When "you," the reader-player, starts the story-diskette, you are told that you are "standing just north of the entrance to the Robner estate." If the reader chooses to knock on the estate entrance (as "you" must do to begin the investigation of Marshall Robner's murder), the following screen invariably appears:

> Mrs. Robner appears, walking down a hallway from the north. "Hello," she says. "I'm Mrs. Robner. Please come in. I'm afraid I really can't help you much. This is surely a terrible waste of time, not to mention upsetting, having all these police marching around the house. This has been a trying time, as I suppose you can understand. As I told Mr. Coates and the other detective, you may look around but you must be out by 8:00 o'clock at the latest. Oh, I almost forgot ... Mr. Coates will be reading my husband's will at noon in the living room. You may attend if you wish...[2]

The reader is then told that Mrs. Robner heads away from "you" toward the kitchen. A reader familiar with other Infocom interactive fictions might choose to follow Mrs. Robner, might try to interrogate her, might sleep until the reading of the will at noon, or might explore and map the house. However, such an experienced reader would be accommodating (or constraining) her readings to fit her expert sense of the textual conventions (and boundaries) of this genre. A novice reader of interactive fiction, on the other hand, might attempt all sorts of interesting behaviors at the beginning of the story, such as shaking Mrs. Robner's hand, fingerprinting her, or asking her for a cup of tea and talking with her about the NBA finals. Of course, *Deadline* does not permit such interesting behaviors, and the reader who attempts them is told that certain words are "not in your vocabulary," or that "detectives are expected to know how to conduct an interrogation; please re-read your casebook for remedial instruction."[3] (This crack about remedial instruction echoes Brandt's [1992] concerns, previously discussed, of cognitivists who see flaws and problems rather than promise in basic writers.) In general, when an untested, novice reader musters a behavior outside of what the program has accounted for, she is firmly herded back to the known world, the world as it is constructed by its programs. In *Deadline*, in other words, the story's addresses to novice readers show clearly the realist epistemology that guides them.

A realist model of reading and writing would interpret the new reader's frustration (and his or her occasional ethical discomfort) as a result of a mismatch between the program's transcription of the underlying synthetic world (including characters, objects, and behaviors of both) and the reader's ability to decode that transcription. Instead of framing the problem of a frustrating reading experience in the way a social constructionist theory would (that is, instead of seeing that the story has an insufficiently rich field underlying it, a rough parser, and a built-in inability to support multiple interpretations), realist theories of reading and writing look for ways to better guide the reader's interpretation of the text, to help the reader achieve the expert behavior, which, in this case, would be executed by her perfect reconstruction of the buried text—and of the means, motive, and opportunity for Robner's murder. Realist models of reading and writing clearly do not provide the tools necessary for programmers and writers to create satisfying reading experiences, nor do these models fully account for the causes of readerly frustration and dissatisfying reading experiences.

Social-Constructionist Models of Reading and Writing

A social-constructionist epistemology, on the other hand, underlies a different set of reading–writing models and accounts for a different, but equally incomplete, way of understanding reading and authoring digital fiction. While my own sympathies clearly lie with the social constructionists, in large part because such a perspective better allows us to see the rhetorical dimensions of reading and writing, I have to admit the limitations of this epistemological standpoint as well. Broadly speaking, social-constructionist models posit that meaning is always socially or culturally grounded, and that any model that attempts to account for the complex literacy acts of making meaning through reading and writing must consider them as contextualized activities. In contrast to the cognitivist characterization of the reading–writing relationship, this relativist perspective

> argues that … symbol systems are socially grounded; that they are in place and are sustained by social and cultural groups … before you or I were born. The process of changing from a newborn into a fully functioning adult is the process of becoming the kind of conscious creature that our symbol systems make us into. (Brummett, 1990, p. 85)

According to a social-constructionist epistemology, *location* is one of the single most important considerations in understanding how meaning is made. How an individual is located physically, socially, sexually, culturally, and historically, by herself and by others, and how she is positioned according to class, gender, religion, sexuality, ethnicity, race, and nationality, among other influences, make location in all its complex variability come to the fore as an essential consideration in understanding how meaning is made, valued, and distributed by readers and writers. Social-constructionist models of reading and writing embody the claim that the locations of readers and writers will affect individual understanding, purpose, and strategies of making knowledge. Among those who have constructed reading and writing theories based on a social-constructionist methodology include

Bartholomae (1993); Cooper (1986); Heath (1983); Lunsford and Ede (1990); Sternglass (1997); Troyka (1995).

These contextualist models of the reading–writing process often explicitly call into question the epistemology that underlies the text-processing cognitivist models and much of contemporary research in artificial intelligence. They can be quite effective for accounting for a reader's frustration with a deceptively flexible text. However, social constructionist theories of reading and writing do not have the tools to describe the layered, Objectivist-linked texts that comprise the *programs* of these digital fictions. For example, in *Deadline* (1991), each character in the story has a specific script he or she follows. At particular times, each character executes a particular activity: Mrs. Rourke prepares food in the kitchen, George reads in his room, a will is read aloud, a phone rings. Furthermore, particular minor characters repeat activities over and over; if "you" (the reader) stay with Mr. McNabb, the Robner estate's gardener, long enough, you will see him repeat the following four activities in the same order: Mr. McNabb examines his work, mows the grass, picks weeds, and wipes his brow; then examines his work, mows the grass, picks weeds, and wipes his brow. (I would wipe my brow, too, if I had to mow, pick weeds, and examine my work every minute, in the same order, at the same pace, in the same degree of detail, for 12 hours straight. But my attention span has always been worrisomely short.) My point here is that the insights of social constructionism are inadequate to the task of describing particular links among layers in the materials of these programs. Furthermore, as synthetic characters peopling digital fictions grow deeper and more "life-like," as advances in the design of "artificial life" are made, their behaviors will still be algorithmically bound in ways that will probably not be describable by existing social constructionist theories.

Social constructionism, as described above, does not allow for constructed (programmed) worlds to exist independent of the observer or user's interactions. Instead of the world's languages or symbol systems creating ourselves and our sense of reality, the programs of the typical digital fiction thunder along, regardless of our presence or engagement. For example, the scripted behaviors of characters such as McNabb and George are predictable, repetitive, and not subject to change in the way real people are subject to the effects and influences of their surroundings. And George will be surly and McNabb a workaholic no matter how we might cajole them to behave otherwise. Characters and objects "existing" in the synthetic worlds of digital fiction are artificially situated, and the scripts of their behaviors are not explainable according to their contexts. Within the layers of programs that comprise the interactive fictions of the Oz Project, described in more detail in the next chapter, for example, there are clear, definable, and mathematically linked programs that guide the behavior and artificial "personalities" of characters—and that coordinate together only in rigidly predictable ways. A social-constructionist model cannot describe the unalterable links between a story's particular description of a place and a character's behavior within it. It does not account for the fact that Mrs. Robner is always going to answer the door in the same fashion; McNabb will always wipe his brow at the same moment; and unpleasant George will always play those same records, over and over. These characters operate in a hermetic world with predictable consequences, and social constructionism does not adequately describe the utter, literal predictability of these virtual worlds. (For a humorous example of real people trapped in an unalterable virtual world, see the science fiction *Realtime Interrupt* [Hogan, 1995], loosely based on the Oz Project, in which the protagonist becomes trapped in a world in which he lives through 25 years of a life, while outside that world only three weeks have passed by. The "Epilogue" to that story begins, "The irony of it all was that in those first two days, it was the *animations* that had behaved rationally and commendably" [p. 319].)

The coded connections between program layers typical of digital fictions are one aspect of the movement from a static paper text to a dynamic digital text and introduces a new dimension into our theorizing about the materials of textuality. The scripts of behaviors and locational changes of synthetic characters occur without real regard for the positionings or locations of their users. For example, in *Deadline* (1991), a paperboy will throw *The Daily Herald* on the porch at the same time during every reading of *Deadline*, and that newspaper will always contain the same article every time you open the second section to a description of "the Focus scandal." Of course, the sense you the reader make of that newspaper's account of the business scandal, and how insightfully you connect that scandal with Robner's apparent suicide, is idiosyncratic, interpretive, and subject to change. However, in a metaphorical sense, the story's engine keeps driving on, regardless of the idiosyncratic readings we bring to it.

The rote activities (or *scripts*) of *Deadline*'s (1991) minor characters like the paperboy and gardener are evidence of the program's underlying epistemological realism; and the programs that drive these two-dimensional behaviors are themselves an early draft of current work into creating artificial life. There is a long history, of course, for models and metaphors for human behavior that are mechanistic and insulated from contextual influence, from the medieval belief in God as watchmaker to contemporary models of android behavior. I read the Enlightenment's preoccupation with Francis Bacon's (1620) *Novum Organum* and its assertion of the universe behaving like clockwork, the ordered movement of celestial orbs imitating the wheels of a clock, as a clear, early example of an Objectivist epistemological stance. (I also read *Novum Organum* as an early instance of a worldview that does not itself recognize all the ways in which ideology and culture intertwine with claim, argument, "fact," model, and script.) Bacon's model of the universe was rewritten by Enlightenment thinkers to encompass what they saw as the mechanisms of human behavior (Kimbrell, 1993, pp. 238–239). (See, for example, the English physician William Harvey's 1628 model of the human heart as a pump.) However, for every historical claim of the world's basis in knowable mechanisms, there comes a counterclaim of humanity's difference, uniqueness, and unknowability, whether that difference is called soul, essence, or emotion.

In this century, for example, Kenneth Burke (1966) calls to task those who would hold such a view in his provocative essay, "Definition of Man":

> The idealizing of man as a species of machine has again gained considerable popularity, owing to the great advances in automation and "sophisticated" computers. But such things are obviously inadequate as models since, not being biological organisms, machines lack the capacity for pleasure or pain (to say nothing of such subtler affective states as malice, envy, amusement, condescension, friendliness, sentimentality, embarrassment, etc., *ad nauseam*). (p. 23)

More recently, an understanding of all human behavior as algorithmically-guided informs the research of computer scientists designing characters, agents, 'bots, androids, and computer avatars and guides. Maureen Caudill's (1992) discussion of efforts to design recent artificial life sees computer viruses as "the very first artificial systems that can truly be called alive" (pp. 202–203) because their sequence of computer instructions can replicate themselves and spread—in ways, she supposes, that might be helpful to NASA's consideration of self-replicating lunar mining colonies. In Steven Levy's *Artificial Life* (1992), he describes the efforts of computer scientists in MIT's Mobot Lab (Mobile Robot Laboratory) to design mobile robots to land in advance of a planned manned expedition on Mars in the year 2019. Levy explains the possibilities of using the experiments of Belgian scientist Luc Steels to guide the work of Patti Maes and others in the lab, resulting in something like "gnat robotics" or "swarm intelligence," wherein intelligent social behaviors would emerge from groups of autonomous agents (pp. 302–306). The self-replicating, self-regulating, self-building, and self-teaching computer-controlled entities under consideration today must be far more responsive to environment and rhetorical context if their behavior or banter is to be any more convincing than McNab in his garden in *Deadline* (1991).

While paper texts certainly support multiple and idiosyncratic readings, too, digital fiction's explicit gaps and the reader's engagement of those gaps make the dissonances, the tensions, the ways in which a text can vary according to reader, both more visible and less sensitive. Reliance on either social constructionist or realist models alone does not allow us to encompass the composing processes nor the reader responses that digital fictions—and the characters that people them—currently prompt.

A Synthesis of Cognitive and Social-Constructionist Theories of Composing

Deborah Brandt (1990, 1992) has offered researchers in literacy a way to synthesize cognitive and social constructionist understandings of reading and writing by offering us a view of literacy not as "a technical capacity that is introduced into various contexts" (1990, p. 103), but as a cooperative relationship of technology and context; she views reading and writing as "forms of metacommunicative knowledge" consonant with the demands of their pluralistic cultural contexts (p. 103). Her critique of the realist epistemology and "strong text" conceptions of literacy held in the work of Walter Ong, E.D. Hirsch, Jack Goody, Eric Havelock, and others is the first serious attempt of which I am aware to model the cooperative influences of cognition and context. Brandt's model shows that literacy is primarily an "intersubjective involvement"; that literacy is collaborative, or primarily a function of readers and writers understanding the activities and roles of their counterparts; and, finally, that "textual relationships are less logical than they are social" (p. 91). It is this last, key understanding that many of the authors and programmers of digital fictions fail to grasp. Brandt indicates a possible synthesis of Objectivist and social-constructionist epistemologies, and this synthesis is very important in modeling both literate processes in general and electronic literacies in particular.

Recent discussions of computer literacies usually subscribe to the "strong text" version of literacy and see computers as the latest in a long line of technologies transforming consciousness (Heim, 1987; Lanham, 1993; Ulmer, 1989). Cindy Selfe's discussion of "Redefining Literacy: The Multilayered Grammars of Computers" (1989) relies on a realist epistemology when she asserts that technology transforms consciousness (a claim she implicitly retracts in her later discussions of technology and ideology). Selfe, like Lanham and Bolter, sees computers pushing users to a new typography that will reconfigure genre, form, textual status, and eventually the cognition of the users themselves. Although Brandt's (1990, 1992) model ultimately does not go far enough to describe the layered, dynamic, collaborative processes of making meaning that characterize digital fictions and other electronic texts, adding her insights to current discussions of the influences of the computer on composing can help support a theory that will allow a fuller description of the processes of composing digital fiction, a description not weighed down by irreconcilable ideologies, unsupportable epideictic rhetorics, or implicit claims of the superior thinking of those who use computers.

Reading the work of Selfe (1989) helps us see one important point: that computers are requiring of their users and their instructors a new range of conventions that are drastically different from those required of and fostered by print literacy. Selfe contrasts computer texts with the characteristics of "the world of print," especially its linearity and spatial orientations, and discusses how the computer fosters an alternate layered literacy. Selfe follows this observation with the provocative assertion that computer users might internalize the new formal conventions of computer texts and, because of that internalization, reconfigure their understandings of the world, which I understand as a social constructionism in reverse, with the world creating the readers it needs. Bolter (1991a, 1991b), too, sees a relationship between the physical form of messages, their rhetorical form, and their reception as an important one to consider. However, in the end, in their assertions that technology transforms consciousness or styles and patterns of thinking, Selfe and Bolter are implicitly offering an electronic textual version of the "strong text"

Objectivism of Ong (1982) and Havelock (1986), which is frequently invoked by critics in composition and computers (see, for example, Costanzo, 1986; Ulmer, 1989, 1994), but is ultimately problematic because it is so reductive.

However, when we read Selfe, Ong, or Bolter against Brandt, a more accurate picture of the potential and problems of computer literacy emerges. Rather than as a new delivery system transforming consciousness, the digital text needs to be considered as a partner in a familiar transaction between makers and users of texts. Digital fiction in particular must be considered a new site for interpretation, one that gives us exciting insights into story, form, and making meaning, but that is not in itself a transformative medium. Again, at the risk of repeating myself *ad nauseam*, rather than focusing exclusively on the technology or delivery system of the transaction, we need to focus on digital fiction as an unfamiliar version of a familiar social exchange between writers and readers, between invented self and real self, between world imagined and world around us.

To understand this idea fully, and to combine the insights of Brandt and Selfe into a single model explaining how reading and writing cohere in this particular medium, we need first to rethink our model of materials and participants in composing interactive fiction and other digital texts. That cast is comprised of programmers and writers in the initial stages of composing, and readers or users at the other end of the transaction. At the center of these transactions is the delivery system (Welch, 1991), medium (McLuhan, 1964), or element (Heim, 1987): the computer screen and its dynamic arrangements of pixel-based print. However, the overlap and blurry interactions among these participants and parts defy clear categories.

In an oblique echo of the post-structuralist assertion that the author is dead, digital texts demonstrate that the notion of a stable text, if there ever really was such a thing, is drawing its last breath. Digital fiction demonstrates the new importance of the textual *materials* of communication, a *multimaterial* that is layered and deep and related to what Baudrillard (1983) and Eco (1990) call the hyperreal, the simulacrum, the false that indicates the actual. Baudrillard has developed his notion of the *simulacrum* in a number of his essays, beginning with his claim in "The Dual, the Polar, and the Digital" that "...we are presently living with a minimum of real sociality and a maximum of simulation" (p. 155), a digital world that coaxes us via "soft seduction" into "the playful erotization of a universe without stakes" (p. 156). In "The Political Destiny of Seduction," Baudrillard extends his explanation of the seductiveness of the simulacrum, calling electronic games "a soft drug" and tracing their evolution back to everything from old-fashioned card games to the ludic impulse of "modulating the [DNA] code, playing with it as one plays with the tonalities and timbres of a stereophonic system" (p. 159). As Baudrillard and other French post-structuralists have shown us, the center of the digital reading–writing compact is a material that is fluid, not stable, a plane dynamic in its illusions and subtle in its allusions. The central features of this new plane, this screen, are its depth, its malleability, its altered visibility, its new intangibility or untouchability, its element, and, in general, its new social dimension (its synchronous and mutual inscribings, and its levelings between readers and authors).

The new *depth* of the textual material is related to the layers of programming code that underlie the "final," pixel-based text that is visible to the reader. Beneath the visible interaction between reader and computer screen is a deep, hierarchically linked series of programs, scripts, instructions, or textual codes that "read" one another to determine which has precedence, which rule will fire, and which text will ultimately appear. A fictional character's relation to his or her synthetic world, for example, is governed by such sequences of rule firings, and the perceived *malleability* of an interactive text is, as we have seen, actually constrained by hierarchical rules and their implicit ideologies.

The new *visibility* of interaction between user and story also has several layers. On the one hand, digital fiction permits researchers to trace a reader's interaction with a story, to infer her mental representation of the progression, and to see how the reader's sense of actions and incidents are cohering. (Of course, the more a reader's mental representation diverges from what the programs next serve up, the more frayed any illusion of a narrative thread becomes.) However, the material of the digital text is visible in another important way: the computer screen is a more public space than the codex book, and the reading surface tends to be more vertical than horizontal. A person reading and writing at a computer screen is having a textual encounter that is public in a new sense, that is visible to any casual observer. This new publicness to her encounter with the fictive world may have effects on her readings that have not yet been explored. We read differently (more quietly, for one) in a library than in a home; we read differently in an Internet café than in our offices.

The *element* of the textual material is different as well. The element of these textual transactions permits a "monitored" exchange that is intangible and untouchable in new ways, and that subtly changes the processes and possibilities of symbolization. Heim (1987) distinguishes between the medium and the element of computer texts in the following way:

> The element ... is not a tool for symbolization but the significant backdrop or horizon on which symbols move.... Element emphasizes the conditions of symbolic experience and the implications of the mode in which things are represented. (p. 102)

The element of digital fiction conflates reader and story, subject and object, in a uniform, leveling inscribing across the vertical screen. Further, as Richard Lanham and others have eloquently explored, the element of computer texts allows a new variability and instability into the texts themselves and thus, then, into paper-based conventions of canonization, textual emphasis, and establishing authority.

The metaphor of layering, introduced by Cindy Selfe and others into discussions of computers and composition, describes to a limited extent the parallel processes of text-making and text-reading in this medium. However, the metaphor of layering alone doesn't capture the dynamism of the competing processes involved in the literate acts. The layered processes underlying digital texts are more like time-lapse photography of the creation of sedimentary rock. The layering is a shifting, accretive, and cumulative process, and the material of story is significantly shifted by its instabilities established, exploited, and destroyed. Text has a new flexibility and suppleness, and its layers blend and blur in a spontaneous concatenation of counterdiscourses colliding, melding, wandering, evaporating, and cohering. This is the element of the interactive text. One challenge to the digital fiction writer is to properly use this new element in all its possible forms, to account for textual fluidity and variant readings.

The most important new participant in the design and collaboration of these texts is the *programmer*, whose programming codes provide a useful entry point into a description of this key player. The programmer's materials are a computer, a computer keyboard, monitor, and central processing unit, and a knowledge of programming languages, such as LISP, invoked through a keyboard. The programmer's composing process is a process of designing and "building" worlds in layers of these programs, to a layperson's eyes working in a coded, algorithmic version of prose. The location of these programmers is most typically within a first-world technological context—either an academic institution or in a computer company, sometimes among hackers—and also within the beliefs and cultural groundings of their community. The programmer's creative process is one of coding and debugging programs' representations of cognition and reading, story, and character, all invoked in the form of rules and scripts, codes and programs. Those representations are usually based on her own limited sense of how knowledge is represented and created in "the real world," on the fictions and games she has played, on the conventions of the particular programming language, and on the constraints of the particular programming task she may be trying to achieve.

As you can see, the *materials* of this composing process are complicated in all the ways the social constructionists say it would be, but their models don't yet capture this variety. The programmer's choice of materials reflects the influence of the social, cultural, gendered, and historical groundings of her composing community. Her ideas for the narrative, her processes of negotiating with programmers and users, her access to computers, and her patterns of work all are likewise influenced by her own social, cultural, historical, and gendered positioning. The ways in which MUDs reflect their designers and writers, or the ways in which *Adventure* was based largely on its programmer's interest in Mammoth and Flint Ridge caves, clearly demonstrate the need to pay attention to the contexts of this new creative participant.

The *writer* of digital fictions is sometimes a different person from the programmer. The writer's composing material is typically paper or computer screen, and she may have occasional difficulties in making the transition between the two media. Her composing process is a collaborative process of mediating between the prose she writes for the reader, the programs and systems she anticipates underlying that prose, and her own predictions of how readers might read or misread, use or misuse, the text. To a greater extent than traditional authors, the digital fiction author must engage in an anticipatory composing process, and must imagine audience more fully. In this anticipation, the text endlessly recedes from her control. Heim (1987) describes the loss of "human presence" within the electronic text that results:

> The language of direct assertion gets poured into the electric element, where the logic of manipulative power reigns supreme. It becomes possible to treat the entire verbal life of the human race as one continuous, anonymous code without essential reference to a human presence behind it, which neither feels it must answer to anyone nor necessarily awaits an answer from anyone. The absence of personal presence so proper to the written letter will be not just absence but anonymity. (p. 213)

Not only is the participation of the programmer and the writer usefully described by looking at the different materials of their textual production (the programming code of the former and the prose of the latter), but the participation of the electronic text's *readers* or *users* are usefully individuated as well, although this may be hard to achieve, practically speaking. Such individuation is extremely difficult in the face of a digital text that blurs boundaries between self and other and creates jarring, seaming syntheses between reader and story, consumer and producer, world and fictive world. We should aim to unmask the digital text, to interrupt its inherent anonymity by close readings of its discrete elements and participants in the composing process, but such enterprise is difficult. The materials of computer fictions are process, not product: these stories have no necessary closure, no grand finale, no necessary resolution. The ephemera of digital fictions and their underlying participants, scripts, and codes allow users to grasp the never-ending story with both eyes, reading and rereading unstable stories, which they can never hold in their two hands.

If we look again at the opening screens of *Deadline* (1991), we can see a concrete example of how the rhetorical triangle does not describe the range of participants and their interactions. We can see how probing the story with an eye to its materials, composing processes, and locations of programmers and other participants might help construct a more comprehensive description. The screen I particularly want to look at again is the one containing the initial appearance of Mrs. Robner:

> Mrs. Robner appears, walking down a hallway from the north. "Hello," she says. "I'm Mrs. Robner. Please come in. I'm afraid I really can't help you much. This is surely a terrible waste of time, not to mention upsetting, having all these police marching around the house.... Mr. Coates will be reading my husband's will at noon in the living room..."[4]

The traditional rhetorical triangle would explain this communicative transaction as the writer's introduction to a reader of a particular character through the agency of a text. Such a characterization would miss interactive fiction's central interactivity, the reader's part in evoking this particular screen. The reader's response to Mrs. Robner, written into a scrolling text, will generate in turn one of dozens of possible responses about Robner, the room, the will, or the task of discovering the murderer, for example.

The traditional communication triangle would also miss the range of possible relations the reader-player might have with Mrs. Robner, as well as the layered rules and programs underlying this particular block of text and responding to the reader's input. Such a characterization would also miss the embedded instructions on how to progress through the text, or assemble the narrative, instructions that come in the form of Mrs. Robner's suggestion to the reader that Mr. Coates will read the will at noon and that are enacted by the reader choosing to write into the text an intent to visit the library at that time. Looking at the materials of this particular transaction, however, lets us see all these new relations as well as the central instability of the text (the reader-player has no obligation to attend the reading of the will, for example), the co-authoring collaborative roles of reader and writer (the reader could choose to ask Mrs. Robner about her husband's murder), and the process of negotiating the unfinished, evolving fictive text.

Digital fictions such as interactive fiction require a theory of the reading-writing relationship that helps define a rhetorical model of materials, processes, and locations of its participants and that synthesizes insights from both realism and social constructionism. Digital fiction makes visible the constant tension between participants who hold to these two competing epistemologies, a tension revealed through the clashes between a variable reader and a story developing over a vertical screen. A version of a cognitivist-contextualist theory of reading and writing might look something like the "feminist objectivism" of Donna Haraway (1991), which holds that situated knowledge is always dialectical and that acknowledges the constraints of both context and cognition. It might embody insights from Wittig (1992) regarding the productions of "the straight mind," substituting instead the covert, interdisciplinary, literally eccentric views of ourselves. Haraway argues for a "coyote discourse," a compromise between the social constructionists and the realists, or "a practice of objectivity that privileges contestation, deconstruction, passionate construction, webbed connections, and hope for the transformation of systems of knowledge and ways of seeing" (pp. 191–192). Or, such a synthesis of context and cognition might look like another animal altogether.

Cynthia Selfe's (1989) metaphor of the layered literacies required of computer users, informed by Deborah Brandt's (1992) insights into the social dimensions of literacies and by Donna Haraway's (1991) attempts to synthesize Objectivism and social constructionism, yields a new way of looking at digital fictions. I can see Selfe's metaphor igniting and becoming a dynamic model of the shifting, layered locatings of authors, readers, and texts interacting in the materials of digital fiction, if we just look closely enough at what we do when we read and write stories at a computer. Such close reading will lead naturally to an understanding of the problems of a lack of closure, blurred distinctions between subject and object, and meanings endlessly deferred.[5]

Finally, as digital fictions edge away from the models of their paper-based counterparts, the characters in their stories often becoming pale and mechanistic, the plots growing less plausible, and their narrators' flexibility and subtlety, especially in their handling of temporal discontinuity, becoming far too predictable, we must take care not to measure their progress only against the traditional tales they are not trying to be. While digital fictions in general are not nearly so rich nor as imaginative as are many more traditional fictions (reading Infocom's *Deadline* [1991] against Wilkie Collins's *The Moonstone* [1874] is cause to weep), they direct our attention to how a delivery system can affect plot, setting, and character, as well as to the quality of the overall reading and writing experiences. However, those of us raised on a diet of Miguel Cervantes and Toni Morrison will not find the same authorial voices nor qualities in digital fictions, nor should we expect to. If Seymour Chatman's (1978) central insight is right, and I believe it is, and different media constrain how a story is told, it is important to recognize how the computer suggests narrative voices and structures, rhetorical resources, and interactions. Such investigations are part of the larger questions about how our own contexts or locations affect what we read, how we read, who we read, and who we are when we read.[6]

And paradoxically, we need to temper this new recognition of participants, materials, and goals with a sense of how their textual precedents inflect their current incarnations. In both *Riven* (1997) and *The Edge of Intentions* (1992; a synthetic world inhabited by a few Woggles, which are round, expressive creatures invented by the Oz Project), we can see visible traces of pictographic writing; we can also see echoes of hieroglyphic drawings of gods and goddesses (Thoth and Isis) in the characters in graphical MUDs; and we will find general traces of the papyrus scroll in the textures and navigational problems of composing onscreen. In fact, we might see medial hauntings in every feature of the personal computer as it is currently designed (Sloane, 1999b). In general, one inadequacy of the postmodern response to literature is its small appreciation of the importance of *histories* of textual production and composition when we build models and develop categories of rhetorical analysis and textual production. By saying such, I know I position myself as a critic only half-dressed as a postmodernist, as a reader with her own inadequate appreciation for some of the fragmented, meandering, paratactic narratives of both paper-based and computer-based fictions, from Janice Galloway's *Foreign Parts* (1995) and Jeanette Winterson's *Written on the Body* (1994) to Paul Aster's *New York Trilogy* (1990) and Carolyn Guyer's (1993) hypertextual *Quibbling*. Although I am quick to appreciate the postmodern elision of soup cans and the Mona Lisa, to applaud the integration of pop culture and high culture in general, I am less comfortable assuming the post-structuralist critical posture that to a large extent disregards history or understands history as discontinuous, fragmented, and always suspect (Sloane, 1999c). Therefore, I do attempt to bring an historical understanding of literary experiments and innovations below.

PRINT PRECURSORS OF DIGITAL FICTIONS

zimzim uralalla zimzim urallala zimzim zanzibar zimzalla zam[7]

When Jonathan Swift's Gulliver traveled to Laputa, he toured the Grand Academy of Lagado, where he found professors engaged in "speculative learning," including one professor engaged in an experiment to allow "the most ignorant person at a reasonable charge, and with a little bodily labor," to write books "without the least assistance from genius or study" (1960, p. 148). No doubt many authors, including myself, hanker for such a device, and several computer hobbyists have written primitive programs that will suggest sentence endings, rhymes, or bits of haiku. In *Gulliver's Travels*, the professor shows Gulliver a frame, 20-foot square, "composed of several bits of wood ... linked together by slender wires." Each bit of wood is "covered on every square with papers pasted on them, and on these papers were written all the words of their language in their several moods, tenses, and declensions, but without any order" (p. 148). The professor explains to Gulliver that by turning the handle connected to that frame, he will be able to change the "disposition of the words," until he finds "three or four words together that make part of a sentence" (p. 148). The professor and his students turn the handle until many sentences are assembled, and they would then compile those sentences into a "book." Thus, scholarly texts were written in the Academy of Lagado in Laputa, with little mental effort and much reliance on chance.

More recently, throughout the 20th century, writers and researchers have experimented with techniques of generating creative writing that are not far removed from the Grand Academy's book-generating machine. Early Dadaist and Surrealist manifestoes, including Picabia's *Dada Manifesto 1918* and Andre Breton's 1924 and 1929 *Manifestoes du Surrealism* (trans. 1972), championed chance, lauded the ludic, and played with possibility in creating innumerable poems and other art. Dadaist experiments in poetry, including those invented by Marcel DuChamp, Hugo Ball, and Jean Hans Arp, let writers reassemble words and images cut out of contemporaneous texts and thus strip them of their familiar meanings and, they hoped, their bourgeois contexts. In another example, Eluard, Tzara, and Ball placed adhesive-backed "papillons" on various ceilings and walls in Paris, decontextualizing messages. Lake (1990) recalls:

> [T]hose small rectangular pieces of colored paper the size of a calling card that the Surrealists used to stick onto the walls in highly visible public areas, together with a small stack of cards about twice that size, each bearing a message such as "If you like love, you'll love Surrealism," "Parents, tell your dreams to your children," or "If you're not a priest, a general or an ass, you'll be a Surrealist" and—from a pre-zipper day— "Unbutton your brain as often as your fly." (p. 58)

Arp also freely cut words and phrases from the local newspaper and built them into poems. (Some of his wood reliefs were similarly made of "found" objects, including rotten wood and bits of flotsam and jetsam glued on a panel [Ades, 1978].) In his essay, "I become more and more removed from aesthetics," he explains the motives behind his Dadaist artistic techniques: "Dada aimed to destroy the reasonable deceptions of man and to recover the natural and unreasonable order. Dada wanted to replace the logical nonsense of the men of today by the illogically senseless" (qtd. in Ades, 1978, p. 16). Dada and its automatic writings, painting machines, and experiments with randomness are early versions of a postmodern digital aesthetic. It is an aesthetic that values chance, that celebrates the "natural" or spontaneous, and that valorizes play. Dadaism and subsequent experiments in art and literature (including Zurich Dadaism, Surrealism, and Italian Futurism) in many ways anticipated and rehearsed both the processes and products of contemporary computer writing. Writer Richard Lanham, in "Digital Rhetoric and the Digital Arts" (1993), likewise connects the Italian Futurist movement of the turn of the century to the "digitally driven 'theme parks'" (pp. 32–33) being built by Lucasfilm and Disney. Jay David Bolter also connects Dada and interactive fiction in *Writing Space* (1991b).

OULIPO

Forty years later in France, on November, 24, 1960, several writers who were interested in "combinatorics" in fiction, or *combinatory literature*, formed a group called Oulipo (*Ouvroir de Littérature Potentielle*, or *Workshop of Potential Literature*). These writers, too, in many ways predicted the participatory and aleatory texts that we call today digital fictions, developing mathematically determined techniques of generating poems and stories without the benefit of computers. Oulipian writers such as Jacques Bens, Georges Perec, Italo Calvino, and Raymond Queneau experimented with many random techniques of generating writing, techniques ranging from using dice to pick words to writing a novel without the letter "E." According to Warren Motte's (1986) analysis of this fascinating group, two goals guided Oulipian experiments: putting power in the hands of the reader and *play* (play with authoring and play with their readers). He writes,

> The Oulipian text is quite explicitly offered as a game, as a system of ludic exchange between author and reader.... Says [Jacques] Bens, "For Queneau [one of the best known Oulipians] ... there is no, or very little, literature without a reader." And Queneau himself demands the reader's participation, refusing on behalf of the latter any possibility of passivity toward the literary text: "Why shouldn't one demand a certain effort on the reader's part? Everything is always explained to him. He must eventually tire of being treated with such contempt." (pp. 20–21)

In general, Oulipians paid less attention to the experience of readers and more to the pleasures of enacting bizarre literary experiments.

In Jacques Roubaud's introduction to *The Oulipo and Combinatorial Art* (1998), he outlines the aims of Oulipo in similar terms, stating "[t]he aim of the Oulipo is to invent (or reinvent) restrictions of a formal nature (*contraintes*) and propose them to enthusiasts interested in composing literature" (p. 38). He continues by explaining that the collaborative work of Oulipo is carried out in part at its monthly meetings, where "...a strict and immutable agenda is followed, one necessarily including the item 'Creation,' that is, the presentation and discussion of new constraints." According to Roubaud, the Oulipian texts are "the literary consequences" of certain mathematical axioms designed by members of the group. When Jean Lescure invents the axiom "N+7," for example, he is inventing literature that replaces the noun in any literary fragment with the seventh noun following it in the dictionary (cited in Mathews & Brotchie, 1998, p. 198). (A great deal depends, of course, on what text and what dictionary is chosen.) In two examples offered by Mathews, we can see the sheer pleasure of this axiom applied first to Shakespeare and then to the Bible:

> To be or not to be: that is the quibble.

> In the bend God created the hen and the education. And the education was without founder, and void; and death war upon the falsehood of the demand. And the sport of God moved upon the falsehood of the wealth. And God said, Let there be limit: and there was limit. (p. 198)

Examples of other entertaining mathematical axioms produced by the Oulipians include "slenderising (*asphyxiation, lipossible*)," in which a text is contracted by removing all instances of a particular letter; "perverbs," in which two proverbs are crossed, as in "[a] rolling stone leads to Rome" (p. 65); and of special interest for our purposes, multiple-choice narratives and multiple-choice theater. Oulipians looked back at the literary experiments of writers like Jorge Luis Borges, Edgar Allan Poe (particularly *The Philosophy of Composition* [1986]), and Lewis Carroll and terms them "anticipatory plagiarists." (Luigi Pirandello's *Six Characters in Search of an Author* [1921/1998] might easily be cited as an example of anticipatory plagiarism.)

As Mathews and Brotchie (1998) recount, Francois de Lionnais first introduced to Oulipo the idea of a story whose evolution might be partly determined by its reader. Mathews recalls,

> At the group's 79th meeting, [Lionnais] presented the schematic plan of detective novel in which, early on, the reader would be asked: do you prefer a mystery story (go to page x), a novel of suspense (go to page y), a sado-erotic continuation (go to page z)? Similar alternatives were to appear regularly throughout the book. (p. 195)

Raymond Queneau soon after wrote his famous story, "The Appealing Tale of Three Lively Peas" (Motte, 1986), and we can read the Oulipians themselves as being in the position of "anticipatory plagiarists" when we look at the Choose-Your-Own Adventure books published in North America in the 1970s.

Another well-known Oulipian composition, Italo Calvino's *If on a winter's night a traveler* (1981; henceforth, *IWNT*) is one of the best examples of how the literary result of a mathematical axiom might approximate (on paper) the aesthetics of digital fiction. Structurally, Calvino's work of fiction is comprised of the first parts, or *incipits*, of 10 different novels, interleaved with 12 numbered sections of narration about the Reader's frustrated reactions to his experiences of trying to read the complete text of the 10 novels. The 10 titled incipits are characterized best as the first chapters of various kinds of pulp fictions: spy story, romance, mystery, action adventure, Oriental sexual thriller. Carl Malmgren (1986) credits Mary McCarthy and John Updike with the insight that "these ten narrative starts" all share features ("eros, mystery, suspense") of the detective-thriller genre (p. 10), although I think they might be better read as a range of "genre fictions."

The 12 numbered chapters, on the other hand, detail the character called Reader's frustrated readings with his inability—because of circumstances such as mistakes in binding, manuscripts lost or stolen, or books misplaced or mistranslated—to complete even just one novel and to consummate his relationship with the Other Reader, Ludmilla. These numbered chapters themselves are conventional in their formulaic love story (eventually the Reader and the Other Reader are wed), but they are unconventional in their constant comments on the activity and situations of reading, as well as on the contexts of the reader. The numbered chapters urge us to measure ourselves against the Reader, and thus engage in self-reflection. *If on a winter's night a traveler* (Calvino, 1981) clearly demonstrates a textual form in which layered artifice engages us readers in a frustrating, constantly interrupted participation, even as the Reader resolves his own tension by pursuing the most common heterosexual plot imaginable.

Calvino's novel foregrounds the author's artifice at every level, and the reader's process of negotiating the synthetic devices raises his or her degree of engagement, resistance, identification, and self-reflection. Several critics have outlined the combinatory aesthetic of Calvino's *IWNT* (1981), noting its roots in Calvino's participation in Oulipo, and Calvino himself has commented on the novel's artifice in his interview *"Comment j'ai ecrit un de mes livres"* (1983), translated and paraphrased by Warren Motte. In Harry Mathews and Alastair Brotchie's (1998) synopsis of the book, they explain:

> The book is made up of eleven numbered chapters (plus an epilogue) and ten intercalated first chapters of imaginery novels. The numbered chapters follow a pattern [of a semiotic square]. The intercalated chapters, in a gamut of styles ranging from the detective story to Japanese erotica and from East European realism to Latin American magic realism, obey other, partly unstated rules. You, the reader, are the book's protagonist, projected into a frustrating world in which you begin novels but… never proceed beyond their opening chapters. (p. 157)

Calvino's semiotic square is based on A. J. Greimas's model, and it is diagrammed by Motte and shows a layered representation of book, book within book, reader, and reader within book. Greimas's semiotic square is just one of several "ludic combinatory systems" experimented with by Calvino.

Calvino's literary experiments such as *IWNT* explore potential literature, "that is, a text constructed according to a rigorous system of formal constraint, a text in which a strong ludic current balances the serious intent, ... a text whose structure may be defined as combinatory" (Motte, 1986, p. 81). Calvino himself says, in "The Novel as Spectacle" (1986) that contemporary fiction writers

> now know the rules of the "romanesque game," [and so] we can construct "artificial" novels, born in the laboratory, and we can play at novels like playing at chess, with complete fairness, re-establishing communications between the writer, who is fully aware of the mechanisms he is using, and the reader, who goes along with the game because he, too, knows the rules, and knows he can no longer have the wool pulled over his eyes. (pp. 194–195)

In an interview about composing *If on a winter's night a traveler* (1981), Calvino described himself as "a more sadistic lover than ever ... I constantly play cat and mouse with the reader, letting the reader briefly enjoy the illusion that he's free for a little while, that he's in control" (qtd. in Malmgren, 1986, p. 106). However, the reader of Oulipian literary experiments is never really in control, and neither is the author. It is the law of chance that prevails in Oulipian texts, the rules of a game that result in a sort of awkward predestination for both the story and its readers.

Already an accomplished novelist when he was elected to Oulipo in 1973 upon the recommendation of his friend Raymond Queneau (whose *Les Fleures Bleues* Calvino had translated), Italo Calvino's subsequent literary experiments under self-imposed mathematical constraints are worth recording here. In addition to the one previously discussed, Calvino's Oulipian works include *The Castle of Crossed Destinies* (1977) and *Numbers in the Dark* (1995). *The Castle of Crossed Destinies* is remarkable for its wonderful premise,[8] but Calvino's story "The Burning of the Abominable House," published in *Numbers in the Dark*, is most worthy of our attention because of its background and provenance. In Esther Calvino's introduction to *Numbers in the Dark*, she explains that "The Burning of the Abominable House" was the result of

> a somewhat vague request from IBM: how far was it possible to write a story using the computer? This was in 1973 in Paris when it wasn't easy to gain access to data processing equipment. Undaunted, Calvino gave the project a great deal of his time, carrying out all the operations the computer was supposed to do himself. (p. 2)

Esther Calvino explains that he had planned this story to be published by *Oulipo* "as an example of *ars combinatoria* and a challenge to his own mathematical abilities" (1995, p. 2). Buried among his other previously unpublished work, among very short stories and essays that Calvino referred to as *raccontini* (little stories), "The Burning" is an entertaining and marvelous fragment that reminds this reader of Borges's "The Garden of the Forking Paths" (1972). In the course of the story—a mystery in which the narrator is hired by an insurance company to discover which of four suspects is an arsonist (and to reveal the chain of events that leads to the arson)—the narrator refers to his flow chart, orders of precedence, and exclusionary rules as he prepares his computer to run the data he has collected. The narrator confesses to his readers,

> Half I'm concentrating on constructing algebraic models where factors and functions are anonymous and interchangeable, thus dismissing the faces and gestures of those four phantoms from my thoughts; and half I am identifying with the characters, evoking the scenes in a mental film packed with fades and metamorphoses. (Calvino, 1995, p. 161)

The split perspective endured by the narrator here is related to the division between *roman* and *fabula* posited by the Russian Formalists (and discussed in Chapter 5, in this volume) and the implicit division between programs' models of reader's behavior and what readers actually do when they read. Calvino's *The Uses of Literature* (1986) is another good source of this Oulipian's thinking about literary games and mathematically constrained *raccontini*, especially his essay called "Cybernetics and Ghosts." In this essay, Calvino explicitly proposes *ars combinatoria* as a method of releasing the unconscious, of breaking the conscious mind's "ban" on mentioning something, of crossing "the barriers of prohibition" (p. 19). Calvino explains further,

> The unconscious is the ocean of the unsayable, of what has been expelled from the land of language, removed as a result of ancient prohibitions. The unconscious speaks—in dreams, in verbal slips, in sudden associations—with borrowed words, stolen symbols, linguistic contraband, until literature redeems these territories and annexes them to the language of the waking world. (p. 19)

Calvino finishes his discussion here with the claim that "[t]he power of modern literature lies in its willingness to give a voice to what has remained unexpressed in the social and individual unconscious..." (p. 19).

Oulipo's use of the computer was confined in the 1970s to generating "combinatorial literature" and using common data processing to play with textual "arrangement, placement, order: because these are the materials of Oulipian combinatorial research, what generally results can be called rearrangement, replacement, reordering, subsumed by the generic term *permutation*" (Mathews & Brotchie, 1998, p. 129). These possible "permutations" were great fun for Calvino and Paul Braffort, when they undertook to write collaboratively a narrative in the mid-1970s. As Mathews characterizes the narrative, the story was based on the same idea as "The Burning of the Abominable House," discussed above:

A house has burned down, consuming its four occupants. A charred notebook recovered from the ruins reveals that 12 kinds of crime have been perpetrated by the occupants on one another, but the record of who has done what to whom has been destroyed. (p. 130)

According to the writers, four categories of crimes have been committed (coercion, stealing of information, sexual assault, and murder) with three subcategories possible under each larger criminal type. As Braffort and Calvino calculated it,

[t]he four people present generate 12 potential pairings that, combined with the 12 crimes, open the prospect of 12^{12} or 8,916,100,448,256 possible sequences of events. A man who has insured all four of the victims (as well as the house) against various risks hires the narrator, a data-processing expert, to reduce this unwieldy figure to a few logical and probable alternatives. (The narrator soon realizes that the insurer has been a fifth participant in the activities of the 'abominable' house and that he himself has become a sixth, since the insurer is planning to kill him.). (cited in Mathews & Brotchie, 1998, p. 130)

Braffort and Calvino used an actual computer to sort out which of the 12^{12} scenarios would be ridiculous and thus eliminated all storylines that were absurd or patently impossible. As Mathews explains, "If A strangles B, he has no need to stab him; if A has killed B, B cannot kill A; etc." (pp. 130–131). In the end, Braffort and Calvino successfully used the computer in a new way, not as a combinatorial engine, but as a partner in the creation of likely stories.

ALAMO

ALAMO (Atelier de Littérature Assistée par la Mathématique et les Ordinateurs; a workshop for literature assisted by mathematics and computers) was started by Paul Braffort and Jaques Roubaud in July 1981. Frustrated by their early attempts to use a computer to create literature, they proposed to compose using a computer using *combinatorial, applicational* (involving substituting and filtering words) and *implicational* (using "generative components such as the principles of narrative logic") methods to write their stories. Not surprisingly, it was this last category that quickly was found to be the most difficult to implement; ALAMO found that developing these principles of narrative logic to be the same stumbling block that North American researchers were finding it to be. One temporary French solution was to invent "litware" programs (*litteraciéls*) that intended to direct the computer to "the structures of existing works" and to use simple rules like plot-branching diagrams as they transposed these structures to digital composition.

Other Print Precursors

Other 20th-century critics (Bolter, 1991b; Landow, 1992a) have lucidly traced the connection between some contemporary conceptions of textuality, authorship, and reading defined in contemporary critical theory (especially in the theories of Jacques Derrida, Michel Foucault, and Roland Barthes), and their realization within the contemporary electronic text. While Barthes does not explicitly discuss computer texts in *S/Z*, nor Baudrillard in his discussions of the *simulacrum* in *America*, nor Eco in his writing on the *hyperreal* (especially in his *Travels in Hyperreality*), all three of these theorists anticipate, explain, and demonstrate hypertextuality.[9] Their texts permit, and even invite, a nonlinear, aggregative reading process, often characterized as multiple, that is itself spun from a peculiarly guided and rigid ludic text, whose density and opaqueness is almost aggressive.

Many other contemporary writers have anticipated ways a text can invite the reader to inscribe the text in a series of literary experiments ranging from high art to low. From the Crossroads Adventure Series (Costello, 1987), a series of "gaming books" where "each adventure is a thrilling tale, with the extra suspense and satisfaction of knowing that you will succeed or fail by your own endeavors" (p. 10), to more sophisticated, self-reflexive narratives such as John Fowles's *The French Lieutenant's Woman* (1969) and Flann O'Brien's *At Swim Two-Birds* (1976), authors have enlarged the conventional relationship between reader and text by allowing the reader to direct the narrative progression, choose episodic sequence, and influence closure. Playwright Alan Ayckbourn has also played with audience intervention, with notions of crossing the proscenium, in plays such as *Sisterly Feelings* (1981). In all these books and plays, however, readers often choose between different readings in obvious ways, skipping pages, rolling dice, flipping coins, or adding up points to determine which section to read next. Thus, these interactive texts only in a primitive fashion predict the digital fictions under discussion here.

Choose Your Own Adventure books, written for children in the 1970s and 1980s, are a short-lived genre clearly related to these earlier textual experiments, as well as to the computer's first "text adventure" in the form of Woods's *Adventure* and the stories published by Infocom. Choose Your Own Adventure books, such as R.A. Montgomery's *Journey Under the Sea* (1977), begin with a recitation of setting, conflict, and the reader's role in resolving the conflict. For example, the following choose-your-own-adventure book, the second in a series by Bantam Books that by 1991 numbered over 100, begins like this:

> You are an underwater explorer. You are leaving to explore the deepest oceans. You must find the lost city of Atlantis.
>
> If you decide to explore the ledge ... turn to page 6.
>
> If you decide to ... dive ... into the canyon of the ocean floor, turn to page 5.

Like all the books in the popular Choose Your Own Adventure series, Montgomery's readers are offered choices at the end of each section, typically every two or three pages. The "ending" of this particular example can come in one of 42 different varieties; the pages you choose to turn to can lead to the discovery of Atlantis, or less happily, to underwater imprisonment, death from the bite of a poisonous fish, or your leading a desperate revolt against an angry Atlantean king. Other writers for the series, such as Jay Liebold, have created adventures around conflicts in foreign countries, as in his *Flight for Freedom* (1990; set in South Africa), and *Beyond the Great Wall* (1987; set in China). The Choose Your Own Adventure books as a whole are characterized by second-person narration, present-tense address, and multilinear narratives among which a reader chooses a path.

Other literary experiments range from concrete poetry to metafictions in contemporary efforts to play with textual conventions and readerly interventions into narrative. Writers of "found poetry," such as the Language Poets of Columbia University, plunder and mix texts as diverse as classified ads and *The Oxford English Dictionary*, assembling and reassembling words, definitions, phrases, and lines to form sometimes bizarre elisions and new meanings. The process of writing language poetry sometimes intends to blur traditional distinctions between reading and writing; as Craig Watson (1985) explains, language poetry is "a performance in which the reader is both audience and performer" (p. 160). Texts like Cortázar's *Hopscotch* (1975) and Coover's "The Babysitter" (1969) likewise invite readers to take an active role in assembling meaning out of the visibly spliced, disrupted text; these are texts that invite readers, to some extent, to construct their own meanings, although unlike Choose Your Own Adventure books, these narratives are linear (although interpretations tend to be multiple). Metafictions like Cortázar's and Calvino's invent a reader that has precedence over the author, letting the flesh-and-blood reader triumph over the ghost of the author and the apparatus of this particular reading machine, the book. Akin to Baudrillard's (1983) notion of the *simulacrum* or Eco's (1990) construction of a hyperreality, the triumph of the reader over both author and "bookishness" foreshadows the tandem gesture of digital fiction, a gesture in which author is submerged and reader aggressively engaged, deceived, and teased. These very different literary and artistic perspectives—Dadaists, Oulipians, Language Poets, and metafictionists—while diverse in content and divergent in motivation, share a respect for serendipity and a technique of *bricolage* that is close to the aesthetic of digital fictions today.

Composition theorists and writers have long been aware of the value of chance in the generation of creative texts, although they diverge in their views of the relations between chance and the unconscious—or between tools like mathematical constraints, Ouija boards, or automatic writing, and what those tools reveal of the subconscious self. While some writers, like Stephen Spender, Dorothea Brande, and Paul Valery,[10] see creative constraints in general or mathematical axioms in particular as enabling a writer to compose, expressivist composition theorists such as Peter Elbow (1991) more often take a view of nonlinear, raw, illogical discourse as a substance that must be worked or tamed by a human hand before it is presentable to an audience. Representing the former writers, Brenda Ueland, in a short section on writing instruction in her popular book *If You Want to Write* (1987), derides careful planning and outlining in the generation of stories; she recommends that a creative writer simply begin to write her story. In a section headed by a quote from William Blake, "The Tigers of Wrath are Wiser than the Horses of Instruction," she explains:

> No, I wouldn't think of planning the book before I write it. You write, and plan it afterwards. You write it first because every word must come out with freedom, and with meaning because you think it is so and want to tell it. If this is done, the book will be alive…. That is why I think English teachers and all short story courses put the cart before the horse…. In English courses, you study plot-construction and sharpen your anxious brows as the tailor does on the needle's eye, over all these necessities, before you begin your story. But you should tell the story first. Everybody can tell a story. (p. 168)

Dorothea Brande's fascinating text, *Becoming a Writer* (1934/1984), likewise dismisses formal knowledge of plot construction or characterization and instead relishes in outlining a lifestyle regimen for a beginning writer, specifying everything from where to write, when to take baths, and what kinds of tea to drink. She also suggests beginning writers practice sharp observations, finding the right turn of phrase to describe people and places, before they abandon their writing to the manipulation of the unconscious; she sees writers as moving between conscious and unconscious moments in their composing process. Gabrielle Rico's *Writing the Natural Way* (1983) explicitly picks up on some of Brande's ideas and rituals, and uses Brande's remark that "[t]he most enviable writers are those who, quite often unanalytically and unconsciously, have realized that there are different facets to their nature and are able to live and work with now one, now another, in the ascendant" (p. 77) as an epigraph. Picking up on Brande's idea that writers are comprised of two metaphoric selves, the artist and the critic, Rico says that two-sidedness in the creative process is related to the two hemispheres of the brain, which she terms "the Design mind" and "the Sign mind" (p. 77). Stephen Spender's famous essay, "The Making of a Poem" (1952), also talks about the rituals and habits necessary for the writer to connect with his (or her) unconscious as well as noting an essentially two-part writing process. He states,

> Schiller liked to have a smell of rotten apples, concealed beneath the lid of his desk, under his nose when he was composing poetry. Walter de la Mare has told me that he must smoke when writing. Auden drinks endless cups of tea. Coffee is my own addiction, besides smoking a great deal, which I hardly ever do except when I am writing. (p. 113)

Spender goes on to explain that the smell of rotten apples or the taste of cigarettes themselves are not a prerequisite for good writing, but they are part of maintaining the concentration essential to good writing, a concentration that permits writers to shift between two ways of seeing and being. Spender sees concentration as occurring in two alternating forms: the first he characterizes as "Mozartian" and more immediate; the second as "Beethovenian":

> The difference between two types of genius is that one type (the Mozartian) is able to plunge the greatest depths of his own experience by the tremendous effort of the moment, the other (the Beethovenian) must dig deeper and deeper into his consciousness, layer by layer. What counts in either case is the vision which sees and pursues and attains the end; the logic of the artistic purpose. (p. 115)

In their advice to beginning writers, expressivist composition theorists like Peter Elbow emphasize a similar method, one that asks writers to "freewrite" their drafts, and to allow uncensored thoughts and feelings to find their way onto the page. Elbow's work is extremely valuable for blocked writers, and influential and important for writers struggling to compose both inside and outside the classroom. However, the goals of Elbow and composition theorists like him (such as Donald Murray, Gabrielle Rico, and James Moffett) differ somewhat from Brande's. While Brande's technique claims to open a channel to the creative unconscious, Elbow's technique as described in *Writing with Power* (1981), helps student writers, especially blocked student writers, to draft competent writings for audiences sometimes hostile (such as some academic audiences). In that book, Peter Elbow suggests that writers use the cut-and-paste method of revising and explains how to construct a "collage" out of the cut-apart fragments of one's own writing. While a student of Elbow's might construct a "collage" that looks similar to one of Ueland's exercises in raw writing, the explanations Elbow gives for why student writers wrote as they did are very different. Ueland writes to go within, to plumb the depths of the unconscious and shed the light of day on individual truths. Elbow's students write, cut, and paste ultimately to satisfy distant audiences who may well not care at all about the writer's feelings, positions, and intents. (To be fair in my characterization of Elbow, it is important to note that his suggestions in *Writing Without Teachers* more readily acknowledge the role of the unconscious in generating prose. In that book, Elbow encourages writers to compose prose that expresses their own truths more clearly, and that assumes a sympathetic audience.)

For example, "The Open-ended Writing Process," a chapter in *Writing with Power* (1981), Elbow suggests a way for writers to "bring to birth an unknown, unthought-of piece of writing," a way that entails "maximum chaos and disorientation" (p. 50), presumably because within that disorientation is yielded the gold of the unforeseen, the genuine insight. Like many other writers of advice to poets and fiction writers, Elbow ultimately presents the composing process as occurring in two phases: writing in and writing out. He says,

> I think of the open-ended writing process as a voyage in two stages: a sea voyage and a coming to new land. For the sea voyage you are losing sight of land—the place you began. Getting lost is the best source of new material. In coming to new land you

develop a new conception of what you are writing about—a new idea or vision—and then you gradually reshape your material to fit this new vision. The sea voyage is a process of divergence, branching, proliferation, and confusion; the coming to land is a process of convergence, pruning, centralizing, and clarifying. (pp. 50–51)

The writing philosophy and exercises of Elbow's *Writing Without Teachers* are also very useful, and are closer in spirit to the earlier recommendations of Brande and Ueland, and the later books for creative writers by the compelling Natalie Goldberg.

Natalie Goldberg's immensely popular books *Wild Mind* (1990) and *Writing Down the Bones* (1986) offer other writing exercises that capitalize on accessing the unconscious and writing without criticism or censorship, that then turns to editing that raw material into something more understandable or clear. In *Wild Mind*, Goldberg states her rules for writing practice, which are certainly related to those already discussed above. She develops seven precepts that I think can be roughly divided into Rico's (1983) Design mind and Sign mind, Spender's (1952) Beethovenian and Mozartian concentration, or Elbow's (1981) writing out and writing in to new land. Goldberg's rules, described in much more detail in *Wild Mind*, might be summarized as follows:

1. Keep your hand moving.
2. Lose control.
3. Be specific.
4. Don't think.
5. Don't worry about punctuation, spelling, or grammar.
6. You are free to write the worst junk in America.
7. Go for the jugular.

One useful way to read this list of Goldberg's is to notice the oscillation or contradiction built into these rules; writers should lose control *and* be specific, for example; they should feel free to write the worst possible junk *and* they should go for the jugular. A rhetoric of contraries is embedded in this list, too.

But these expressivist theories and techniques are different in their methods than other creative writing forms, which rely on chance and different in their outcomes from the spliced, combinatory genres of teacher-writers like Wendy Bishop and Gregory Ulmer. These two authors dispense with Elbow's goal of communicating self to a sometimes hostile audience, and their compositions bear little resemblance to the powerful personal writing that Ueland and others claim wells up from the springs of the creative unconscious. Bishop and Ulmer see in the random elisions of the montage or collage a release of partial meanings and a chance to meditate, albeit obliquely, on how memory functions within the asynchronous assemblages of postmodernism. Reminiscent of an Oulipian *cento*, Wendy Bishop's "Found Poem Exercise" (1992) suggests that writers take "words already available in the material world and reshape them to make a statement" (p. 77). For example, she shows us a poem based on excerpts from her father's letters, written when he was stationed in Iceland during World War II, a poem she hopes demonstrates the power of the found line. And Gregory Ulmer's (1989a) story called "Derrida at the Little Bighorn" is another example of a digital aesthetic that dices and splices, in this case filling a form he calls "mystory," a genre he invents to bring into relation personal, popular, and expert discourses, written about the land where Custer fought and died, and where Ulmer himself grew up (and drove a snow plow). Ulmer urges writers of *mystories* to "use the punctum or sting of memory to locate items significant to you; once located, research the representations of the popular and expert items in the collective archive or encyclopedia (thus mixing living and artificial memories)…" (p. 209).

Ulmer's (1989) invented genre of "mystory," and Bishop's "Found Poetry Exercise" (1992), like the Oulipian, Italian Futurist, and Dadaist experiments before it, and like many of the computer texts written after it, demonstrates the signal gesture of a digital aesthetic. It is a gesture that is singularly postmodern: heteroglossic and fragmentary, occasionally nihilistic, disjointed, and facing outward rather than within. However, despite claims to the contrary, these predigital texts, these "anticipatory plagiarisms," are not paying much attention to their readers, either. The digital aesthetic celebrates the individual ludic response and deemphasizes shared readings and interpretations; blends a curious combination of the rigid and the flexible in its layered, iterative, interruptable texts; and shuffles its parts rather than synthesizes or aligns them in meaningful patterns. The concept, form, and aesthetic of digital fictions existed long before the delivery system of the contemporary computer was actually implemented. Through this brief overview of other literary and textual experiments, I hope I have made clear how the digital fiction aesthetic was realized for decades, albeit clumsily, on a less fluent platform—paper.

EARLY USES OF THE COMPUTER TO GENERATE STORIES

suvax1!dataio!uw-entropy!uw-june!uw-beaver!

My problem is
that I am stumped on a problem
in Space Quest by Sierra.

For those of you that have played the game
I am at a loss at how to get by the electric beams
in the caverns past the pool
of acid. I think it requires a mirror
to block the beams

but I have no idea
on how to get said mirror.

—Found poem, March 24, 1988

A few essays on the underlying structures of computer programs that produce "literature" (Kurzweil,1990; Lebowitz, 1992; Meehan, 1976; Yazdani & Lawler, 1987) are available. These reports, however, focus typically on analyses of the "output" of particular programs in particular games, and not on the collaborative process of writing the programs, their rules, and their scripts. For example, William Chamberlain and Thomas Etter (as described in Kurzweil, 1990, p. 370) have written about their program called "Racter" (named after "raconteur"), which generates nonsensical poems and stories. According to its programmers, Racter's prose, collected in a book called *The Policeman's Beard is Half Constructed*, is generated "in the manner of Dada artists ... who wrote poetry by randomly picking words from a paperbag" (qtd. in Caudill, 1992, p. 162). Maureen Caudill's (1992) characterization of Racter (published by Mindscape and available for the Macintosh) is that it was "not much more sophisticated than Eliza" (the famous psychology program that cleverly parroted back your own statements as questions demanding more explanation) (p. 162). She explains,

> Racter could carry on long conversations and even talk out loud using the computer's built-in speech synthesizer.... It was a bit like talking to a slightly schizophrenic literary genius who made wild leaps and connections, and even occasionally backtracked to previous topics...Racter had the ability to create stories in his own, somewhat bizarre style, but which generally made sense at some level—at least as much sense, for example, as Lewis Carroll's poem "Jabberwocky." (p. 162)

Three other early experiments in using computers to generate literature are important to mention: the 1972–1976 development of the first large-scale computer-based "text adventure," called Adventure; the 1982–1984 development of a computer program, Universe, designed to tell extended stories; and the 1985 British work of Mike Sharples and five 11-year-olds in using a program called FANTASY to write stories.

Crowther and Woods's Adventure

In 1972, while programmer Will Crowther was working at Bolt, Beranek, and Newman (BBN) in Boston and developing the assembly language for the routers used in creating the ARPAnet, he began to map the Mammoth and Flint Ridge caves in Kentucky for the Cave Research Foundation.[11] It is important for our study of the *scenes* of writing to note that Will Crowther, an avid rock climber and caver, was also a regular participant in Dungeons and Dragons, a role-playing game in which Crowther regularly assumed the character of "Willie the Thief." Crowther explicitly acknowledges this connection in his following remarks on the *Colossal Cave Adventure Page*:

> [T]he caving had stopped, because that had become awkward, so I decided I would fool around and write a program that was a re-creation in fantasy of my caving, and

also would be a game for the kids, and perhaps some aspects of the *Dungeons and Dragons* I had been playing.

After a divorce, and in an effort to grow closer to his two young daughters, Crowther began to build a very simple computer simulation of the caves in which he had climbed, a simulation based on his maps and one that ran on a Digital Equipment Corporation (DEC) PDP-10 computer, in FORTRAN. (His daughters reportedly much enjoyed the game.) From this one early game, Adventure, soon shortened to "Advent" by users, came a variety of digital fiction conventions in how to move through the story space (by typing "e" or "w" for cardinal direction; using spells for faster transportation) as well as inspiration for the content of many other early text adventures. After a month of testing, Crowther put his text-based story on ARPAnet for other computer users to read and play. Don Woods, a programmer working at Stanford University's Artificial Intelligence laboratory, saw Crowther's game on the ARPAnet, debugged it, and released it on the network around 1976 in a game that is remembered today as "Original Adventure."

Over the next three years, several graduate students at MIT's Computer Research Laboratory built their own "interactive fictions" based on "Original Adventure" and their own ideas. In 1979, some of these students formed a company called Infocom and wrote and marketed a trilogy of story diskettes they called *Zork* for personal computers (Addams, 1985). (The *Zork* trilogy was the first of dozens of text adventures and computer games produced by writers and programmers, and initially marketed with great success, at Infocom, which is discussed in the next chapter.[12])

Tale-Spin and Universe

Also in 1976, at Yale University, James Meehan was developing a story-generating program that he named "Tale-Spin," a program that told stories for children in the style of Aesop's fables and folktales (Meehan, 1976). Soon after, Michael Lebowitz, a faculty member from 1980 to 1987 in the Department of Computer Science at Columbia University, developed a simple, prototype story-telling program, Universe. Based in part on television melodramas, Lebowitz's story-generation program generated simple plot outlines about different sets of characters it invented. By 1984, Universe was generating short stories the authors and programmers likened to television soap operas (Lebowitz, 1992).

According to Lebowitz's own account, the Universe model of storytelling is indebted to work in artificial intelligence done by Meehan for Tale-Spin (1976) and Dehn's Author (1981), but had a different goal than either of these projects: Universe was an attempt to give a computer program "…enough information available to tell consistent, coherent, and hopefully interesting stories over long periods of time." (Lebowitz, 1992, p. 174). Lebowitz looked to the stereotypes of soap operas to fulfill this goal. Lebowitz also relied implicitly on research that construed writing as a cognitive process, citing the 1980 work of Flower and Hayes in his published writings, and mentioning ongoing research in several computer labs into the structural forms of stories, known as "story grammars." The terms in which Lebowitz describes Universe are also based in a cognitivist epistemology. He speaks of the importance, for example, of a story generation system "[p]roducing the information needed for understanders to be able to extract information involving...knowledge structures" (p. 175), rather than mentioning the central point of creating stories that have meaning for their audiences. The terms Lebowitz uses are utterly different from a social constructionist's view of the world. Lebowitz cites research into "conceptual schemata," "causal chains," and "thematic affect units" (de Beaugrand, 1982; Dyer, 1982), rather than terms used by social constructionists, most literary critics and composition theorists, or fiction writers themselves.

Rachel Blau DuPlessis (1985) once made the intelligent observation that many of 19th- and 20th-century romances have their women characters ending up either married or dead. She writes, "[o]nce upon a time, the end, the rightful end, of women in novels was social—successful courtship, marriage—or judgmental of her sexual and social failure—death" (p. 1). In an odd echo of that observation, the plots of almost all early text adventures lead their central characters either to marriage or to a career as a detective. Lebowitz's program demonstrates the first alternative:

> To illustrate how the story-telling process might go, consider the following example. Imagine the program ... had decided that John and Mary should fall in love (to satisfy higher level author goals)—for instance, perhaps Mary's husband, presumed dead, is about to return, which should produce interesting results.... If John and Mary are already known to be friends (and the reader knows this), then Universe can set a goal for something terrible to happen to one character, and recursively pursue that goal until a tellable event is decided on, say one character's child is kidnapped, at which point some story generation can begin." (1992, p. 177)

Perhaps because Lebowitz turned to soap operas for his model for plot and character, the synopses of the stories he would like Universe to generate, like the story idea described above, are based on heterosexual characters who desire to be together but are forced to overcome some obstacle to their union (Lebowitz, 1992). The myopic goals of an "extended story generation system" like Universe, I believe, are the result of a cognitivist perspective and epistemology that provides little framework for the wider social analyses of the complexities of context, culture, and minority discourse or viewpoint. Alison Jagger's (1989) work on alternative feminist epistemologies might be worth mentioning here, especially her insight that "feelings are often unauthorized modes of knowing," and that the so-called rational is simply "authorized feeling" (qtd. in Hunter, 1999, p. 237). Objectivist and realist epistemologies permit the unexamined story script to repeat itself *ad infinitum*, with television screenplays relying on conventions of pulp fictions, and programs like Universe deriving from soap operas and romances. A better composing practice, I believe, would be one that constructed stories and meanings based on alternative ways of being in the world, that acknowledged the contributions of feeling, being, and saying to the multiple ways that people construe their worlds.

Sharple's *Fantasy*

A different example of early story generation software is offered by Mike Sharples in *Cognition, Computers, and Creative Writing* (1985) and discussed by him again in his 1999 work. The former book details Sharples's work in a classroom of 11-year-old children using Logo, a derivative of LISP, to help students write poems and stories. Sharples (1985) designed "a language toolkit" for the children, a figurative toolkit containing three programs: PAT (named for PATtern generator), WALTER (for Word ALTERer), and NETTY (NETwork TYpes). Using a smaller program called FANTASY in place of this last, more general program (NETTY), Sharples and five of his students took part in a project exploring how computers might be able to help them write stories like Crowther and Woods's *Adventure*. The book's full appendices include samples of the stories children wrote with the aid of these programs, which I will quote briefly below.

Sharples's students first wrote stories by hand about the Edinburgh Wax Museum. The students had been told that they would tour the museum and that each one should pick a particular wax statue and write notes about it, which they would later turn into a story. I was not surprised to learn that all of the students elected to write about wax figures found in the Chamber of Horrors. By the end of the exercise, one student whom Sharples calls Dorothy, had written a particularly gruesome description of a man murdered by a hook, a composition that she called "Hook Victim." The handwritten version of her story begins,

> This man must be in pain there is a hook through his stomach. His tongue is hanging out. His eyes have turned white and have red lines through them. He would not give evidence against the person he was working for... (1985, p. 94)

Who could resist such wonderful purple prose?

The five students and Sharples began visiting a room in the Artificial Intelligence Department at Edinburgh University each week. One week, each student played a session of "Colossal Adventure" (see above) for about 25 minutes, until Sharples "prised [them] away from the terminals" (1985, p. 96). After they had played the game, Sharples led a discussion of story planning. Sharples and his students then made the following observations about the story plans of text adventures like *Adventure*:

> Each run [of the program] produces a new narrative and shows that not only can many stories be built around one environment, but also that the layout of the house

and the order in which its locations are explored can determine the player's interest and suspense: secret passages may herald treasure, or danger; the object of the search should be well hidden, far from the entrance and accessible only by a tortuous route; decoy signs and small pieces of treasure can heighten suspense. (p. 99)

Dorothy and another girl, Louise, next produced a predictable (and pleasurable) stew of clichés, lurid details, and high drama, in their first attempt at writing in the same genre on a computer using Sharples's program, FANTASY. Copying both the form and tone of Adventure, their first attempts at story are not much different from Infocom's first productions. Dorothy and Louise wrote, for example:

> You are in a bright coloured happy atmospheric room in it there is, two big lounging chairs bright fabric but damaged, a sofa to match chairs, a coal fire still burning, a glass coffee table smashed to pieces. Keys to the cellar lie beside it. Ripped victorian pictures are hanging on the walls.
> a wooden door leads west
> a wooden door leads northeast
> a wooden door leads south
> a wooden door leads east
> The following are also here:
> 1. — a chef
> Objects:
> You can see
> 1. — a page of a diary dated April 10th
> 2. — a note saying "Have a glass of wine." (Sharples, 1985, p. 99)

Finally, students were asked to write their own narratives based on their experiences using FANTASY. In their new prose version, Dorothy and Louise referred to a plan of the house they had made, drew a line on it indicating the "explorer's" progress through the rooms, and then followed this route in their story. With no doubt great pleasure, the two girls turned their main character into a detective and wrote a new version of their story, as excerpted here:

> The detective walked up to the wooden porch of the manor. He knocked at the large oak door, the door opened with an enormous creaking sound. An old butler appeared and asked "Whom seeketh thou this evening?" Suddenly! a giant black bat flew down from the lintel above the oak door. (Sharples, 1985, p. 100)

The lurid detail and high drama of these two girls' wonderful writing samples quoted here demonstrate the importance of combining knowledge of social context and cultural milieu with the mechanics of generating stories. In some important ways, Sharples's literary experiments are the most truly successful of the three discussed here. His students rely on conventions and commonplaces gleaned from their experience with computer games, local public meeting places (the museum), genre fictions, classroom practices, and the enticing pleasures of purple prose.

IMPLICATIONS

At the time I write this, digital fictions commercially available in the U.S. are generally the product of computer game companies or individuals and teams using the World Wide Web to disseminate MUDs, MOOs, and Web soap operas. (A number of basic text adventures are readily available on the WWW. Try, for example, the Interactive Fiction Archive.) Generally, in writing digital stories and games, members of a design team (often comprised of programmers, writers, and a producer) are assembled by a company and given the task of bringing a story idea to fruition. Don L. Daglow (1987), for example, provides an overview of the conventional design process of computer game designers such as interactive fiction composers. Peterson describes the six steps in a "standard design process" (a process he defines as distinct from the subprocesses of programming and implementing graphics and sound) and traces the process from generating the initial idea, to writing a proposal, to implementing and refining the design and explains how computer game publishers are likely to respond. A thorough review of the literature on the composing processes of authors of any computer software reveals that, as in the Daglow article, a large majority of articles focus on the latter steps in this process, such as on how to implement designs or prepare a game for a publisher, and ignore the former.

As I mentioned in Chapter 1, the best existing source of descriptions of the composing process of digital fictions are accounts written by expert designers for novices (Betz, 1987; Crawford, 1984; Lebling, 1980; Peterson, year TK). For example, in two separate articles, David Lebling describes his process of writing *Zork*, its underlying language (the MDL language), and its programs. Betz, on the other hand, describes his own programming system, AdvSys, written in C. These retrospective accounts by programmers and designers provide simple descriptions of the parsers, object-description facilities, and languages they used to build simple text adventures that are, most often, fairly thin games of adventure. The accounts often include discussions of data structure and control structure within their programs (Betz, 1987; Lebling, 1980), but they seldom go deeper into the process of construction, nor discuss the philosophies or epistemologies that guide their choice of subject, medium, or content of story. And they provide only overarching conceptual descriptions of the process of computer game design. Novice computer game designers might do well to start here for a description of the processes of writing a game, but in general these descriptions are cursory and attend too heavily to the technological parts of the composing process and too lightly to any underlying literary theory, or epistemology, for those of us interested in understanding how digital fictions reveal the cultures within which they were composed.

The only other accounts of the process of composing interactive fiction come from literary critics who have speculated on its form, "literariness" (Banks, 1985; Buckles, 1987; Costanzo, 1986; Randall, 1988; Ziegfeld, 1989), or significance, or who have written cursory descriptions of the layered programs and sets of instructions underlying interactive texts (Bolter, 1991b; Niesz & Holland, 1984). In their early article exploring the features of interactive stories, for example, Niesz and Holland include an example of the Basic programming code underlying one popular adventure game, but they do not discuss its consequences for the quality of reader engagement. In a similar vein, speaking about a higher-level programming concern, Slatin (1990) conjectures that the data structures underlying the computer's representation of knowledge are sometimes in dissonance with the reader's own constructed knowledge, in hypertexts. While both these articles are important for the ways they initiate discussion of computer games in literary journals, ultimately these brief descriptions and analyses are static, snapshot portraits that insufficiently describe the layered materials and dynamic processes of composing that characterize contemporary digital fiction.

To understand better the layered dynamics of computer-based storytelling, and to question more fully the problems raised by the realist epistemologies of some programmers coming into conflict with the social constructions of some unpredictable readers, we need to examine more closely what happens when the story does not fit the reader. The next chapter looks closely at two kinds of digital fictions, the Infocom text adventures, and the Oz Project's interactive fictions, examining how the materials of their production contribute to the quality of the reading experience they support and sometimes fail to achieve.

3

The Materials of Digital Fictions

THE SYNTAX OF WIND

I know for a fact
that piece of wet newspaper
(blurred, soiled leaf of the daily)
blowing down the alley
behind the Metropolitan Opera House
remembers how to fly.

The paper's damp crease
catches then shrinks back
to the street
some tired gust buffeting
its blurred sorrowing words.

It starts to rise
into the heart of this Dutch island sky
before it scrabbles back
to the mixed scree
of these weeping streets.

Rest, roll, scuttle, leap,
it flies under the purpling sky
the tall buildings bruised
by the light of the practice rooms

and the newspaper growing more moth-like
butterfly on a bicycle
as it jerks and climbs
into a soft square of light
only the bats can hear.

The violinists depart.

I jam my hands
into my winter coat pockets
and keep walking, remembering
the small town where I was born
an obligation never met
my shoes still in a closet up there.

I linger only long enough
to recognize the sight
of paper flying is itself
lyric and companionable,
sad, but no less a sign of life
than my daily intake of breath
rising through this pliant architecture
of body, limb and lung.

INTRODUCTION

There are many things one cannot do with contemporary computers, even things that our society would obviously like to do. For example, artificial intelligence has not provided machines with the capacity to write stories or create graphic worlds autonomously, though many technophiles dream of such machines.

—Jay David Bolter (1996)

...as a word is alone in the moment it is spoken
meaning what it means only then and meaning it only
once with the same syllables that have arisen
and have formed and been uttered before again and again
somewhere in the past to mean something of the same nature
but different something continuing and transmitted
but with refractions something recognized in its changes
something remembered from what is no longer there
and behind it something forgotten...

—William S. Merwin (1998)

...Disentangled from
The syntactical challenge she nips his ear ("A god himself gave him")
The introduction of Episodes. An eloquent foreground. A
uniform present entirely foreign to the story
Of his scar ("The woman now touched it...")

—Katherine Lederer (1998)

In the near past, writing was a bodily skill, visible and finite, undertaken to communicate within known cultural settings. From Gutenberg's decision to print the Bible to editorial discussions underlying today's newspaper, writing has always been situated within broad cultural contexts and preoccupations, not to mention within the context of an individual human being wrestling with her own soul. Even Dada's automatic writing- and painting-machines, James Merrill's writing poetry with a Ouija Board, the Surrealists' *papillons*, or early stick-based alphabets of the Greeks (Graves, 1966), depended on a link between body and letter—a connection that is largely severed by digital fictions in both composition and form. Our textual selves recede even farther away from the body when we read these stories. As the materials of literacy production have changed, as hands shifted from quill to moveable type to pen to keyboard to lying quiet in their laps as their owners speak or wink to a computer, the ways that bodies and their contexts are connected and revealed within stories grows progressively more removed from reality. The "somatophobia" that Kirby (1991) sees arising in feminist debates between essentialists and anti-essentialists is revealed also in the new human dependence on a creative machine, a computer assigned the task of telling our most intimate, bodily-based stories as well as the larger epics and cautionary tales of our time. When we look for the traces of an author within the bob and weave of an advanced story generation system, one like Carnegie Mellon's Oz Project, we must look into the materials of production themselves, into the gaps and silences of story and teller, to see the reflections of body, mind, and cultural milieus of their creators. While some would argue that *all* written fiction is separated from its composers by distances both spatial and temporal, I believe that digital fictions expand those distances, and in some cases invents new gaps (of meaning, engagement, and identification), especially when the prose, pace, and sequencing of stories is adjusted by computer.

Some of the earlier experiments in which a machine participated in the production of literary materials like stories and essays (Lebowitz, 1984; Meehan, 1976; Sharples, 1985) borrowed existing fictional formulae (such as the quest, the love story, the mystery, the soap opera, the fable) from which to construct scripts that the reader might read and cowrite. Many of Infocom's text adventures fit that description. Likewise, MUDs, MOOs, and their literary cousins online rely on existing scripts, but in their borrowings from J.R.R. Tolkien, Douglas Adams, Frank Herbert, and other speculative fictions already published, they are borrowing some of the dominant cultural narratives of our time, and recreating them online, at once removed, as it were, but still in response to real events and real people. Many of the earliest digital fictions echoed existing formulae and genres, but as the capabilities of artificial intelligence (AI), and its models, scripts, and thematic schemata, grew more powerful, there will be for the reader both the possibility of a more persuasive engagement and the danger of greater disappointment in the level of narrative engagement offered. In particular, the realist epistemology that continues to underlie recent digital fictions can make the reading experience progressively more alien, more distant, and less satisfying. (These dissatisfying reading experiences also derive from the very *processes* of reading and writing digital fictions, as discussed in the next chapter, but here we will trace the ways in which the *materials* of digital fictions, in their newly exaggerated loss of cultural context and meaning, so far have made disappointing, unresponsive digital fictions.)

We are dealing with a paradox here. On the one hand, the materials of digital fictions, as they are represented to a reader via a computer interface, are woefully inadequate in their representations of readers and their explicit expectations of readerly attitude, response, quirks, and behaviors. By using a composing process that includes a computer as an active partner, and whose human participants may be narrowly schooled as well, the texts presented on the screen are seemingly stripped of shared cultural context and meaning to a new degree. But are not all readers nearly unknowable to authors? Am I not just echoing Plato's whine in *Phaedrus* (trans. 1952), complaining that writing erases body and memory, displaces the speaker, and makes what is said not responsive to the needs of its audience? Once a story is written down, doesn't the storyteller always recede from the immediate social scenes of telling or reading?

To a limited extent then, yes, I am echoing Plato's criticism of writing. I make these claims afresh in part to emphasize that digital fictions are the latest iteration of an age-old dispute about how writers respond to their audiences, explicit or evoked. On the other hand, digital fictions are discontinuous with the literary tradition because only a new methodology, a new way of reading, reveals in the material gaps of these stories the degree to which their authors (programmers, writers, and designers) explicitly reveal their own narrow social contexts (contexts that are largely first-world, young, white, heterosexual, and male, based in universities and research laboratories with excellent computing facilities in the U.S.). Furthermore, digital fictions reconstruct the literary distinction between story and expression (or *roman* and *fabula*) so carefully prepared by Russian Formalists like Yury Lotman, Zinovy Zinik, and Todorov, and this newly distanced narrative form prompts narrative theorists to look into and between the materials of digital storytelling to find both object and meaning of stories.

Kenneth Burke's *Philosophy of Literary Form* (1957; discussed in more detail in Chapter 5 in this volume) helps us realize the paradox of digital fictions: that its layered materials reveal more than their writers intend of the cultural milieus of the authors; and its layered materials simultaneously reveal, within the ripped seams and mangled interstices and missed opportunities of its supposedly interactive responses, how little these authors actually know of their various readers. The computer, to date anyway, knows little of readers, too. Burke develops a method of "dramatic criticism" in this important text, one that helps us understand the dynamics of digital fictions. As Burke explains,

> Words are aspects of a much wider communicative context, most of which is not verbal at all. Yet words also have a nature peculiarly their own. And when discussing them as modes of action, we must consider both this nature as words in themselves and the nature they get from the nonverbal scenes that support their acts. (p. vii)

It is precisely the nature of these "nonverbal scenes," both during the composing process and while a story is being read, both in their implicit models and representations and explicit social milieu, that complicates the production and reception of digital fictions. As Burke continues his discussion of the ways in which language is a kind of symbolic action, and that all language, of course, can be moved into many contexts, he reminds us that "...when the character of the context changes, the character of the act changes accordingly" (1955, p. viii), an insight that many digital composers have neglected. Finally, Burke begins to detail the way linguistic acts, when contained within "critical and imaginative works [like plays and novels]," are always "answers to questions posed by the situation in which they arose." He explains that creative works offer answers that are "strategic" and "stylized" in response to specific situations; that the creative work operates on its readers by strategies, primarily a strategy that sizes up situations, names structures, and "contains an attitude towards" the world described (p. 3). Such strategies are not readily apparent in most contemporary digital fiction, probably because their models of reader and reading scene is barely developed.

Digital fictions like Carnegie Mellon University's Oz Project have tried to account for the ways language and stories change according to context by experimenting with programs that change rhetorical delivery (such as PAULINE), add an affective dimension to responses (Picard, 1997), or that create coherent narrative sequences (such as Sengers's Expressivator, 1999). However, Oz and other story generation systems would be better off rejecting the Formalist distinction between story and discourse altogether, and embracing instead the notion implicit in all of Burkean analysis of discourse: All language (and linguistic acts) is rhetorical, and all texts a form of argument. Claims and warrants change according to the context of argument. By adopting Burke's (1955) rhetorical perspective, and by jettisoning the Formalist distinction between story and discourse in our analysis of digital fictions, we are closer to a methodology that will allow us to analyze some of the disjunctions between digital story and reader. I find such a useful method by coordinating Kenneth Burke's understanding of rhetoric with some current work in semiotics and in discussions of iconic rhetorics.

John Deely's (1990) intelligent synthesis of some of the most difficult ideas and readings in semiotics (tackling the most important essays of Eco, Barthes, and others) reminds us of the central enterprise of semiotic theory: "[A]t the heart of semiotics is the realization that the whole of human experience, without exception, is an interpretive structure mediated and sustained by signs" (p. 5). In the course of his book, Deely develops his idea of a semiotic web, an idea he credits to the philosophers Sebeok and von Vexkull. Deely writes, "[a]s the spider spins its threads, [so] every subject spins his relations to certain characters of the things around him, and weaves them into a firm web which carries his existence..." (p. 14). It would be easy to read into Deely's notion of a semiotic web as an allusion to the World Wide Web, an apparent instantiation of this idea, but instead it is important to focus on Deely's notion of aggregative, partial, woven readings, similar to those suggested by Wendy Doniger in her wonderful book, *The Implied Spider* (1998). We must look for truths (in this case the truth of a poor fit between reader and story in digital fictions) in what does not translate easily between a reader's web and the reading web, between the metaphor of a reader as a spider picking her way across a text, and the metaphor of a text that offers a premade web, one that does not match the needs or the path of the spider. It is in the interruptions of the spider's web, within the spaces between its lines and inevitable geometries, that we can see how digital fiction does not work like other stories, perhaps because it seems to offer so much, and yet yields so little.

The central problem of interactive fictions like those produced by the Oz Project is that they have taken the challenge of storytelling to be one of *mimesis* rather than one of *rhetoric*. Like the Russian Formalists, the Oz group sees an important distinction between representation and expression; while they seem to grasp the basics of semiotics and recognize that language and textuality are a mere order of signs, they do not follow the Burkean insight that all signs are, by nature, rhetorical. All language is an argument. Every text acts on its readers in ways palpable, regulable, even moralistic, and always persuasive. Their job as programmers is not to reproduce "reality" as they see it; it is to recognize the weight, responsibility, and possibility of every word they use, and to calculate its possible placements (and hence, actions) by careful consideration of the audiences they might strategically address.

Critical theorists interested in the iconic rhetorics of theater or film (such as W.J.T. Mitchell, Peggy Phelan, and Teresa de Lauretis), and early Russian Formalist writings about painting, such as those written by Yury Lotman, provide some of the groundwork necessary to connect an analysis of visual signs with the Burkean insight into the ways language acts. In Lotman's (1993) creative and expressive discussion of the origins of mimesis (in which he speculates provocatively that rhyme and the genre of poetry derive primarily from echo, and that drawing itself originated in the act of someone tracing the outlines of a shadow in some cave), he discusses the function of objects like mirrors in mind and art:

> [T]he magic function of such objects as the mirror in creating another, *prima facie* world, which resembles the reflected one without actually being it, is just as significant for the self-cognizance of art as the metaphor of reflection or mirroring. The possibility of duplication is the ontological premise for transformation of the world of objects into a world of signs: the reflected image of an object is separated from natural practical relations (spatial, contextual, functional, etc.) and, therefore, can be easily included into representational relations of human consciousness. (p. 45)

Lotman continues his interesting discussion with an analysis of Jan Van Eyck's painting *Arnolfini Wedding* and the ways in which two-dimensional canvas space (and screen space) can be made three-dimensional through the creative use of representations of mirrors, soundtracks, and overlaps between screen space and sound space.

The key issue that Lotman (1993) helps us recognize is that the challenge to the painter (or filmmaker or programmer) is not one of creating a simple representation of the natural world (certainly, anyway, not since the advent of photography), but one of representing objects and experience in such a way that they *can be easily incorporated into representational relations of human consciousness;* or, to use Burke's (1955) terms, to create a fictive world in such a way that its structures motivate particular human responses and acts. Lotman writes, "[i]n order to exist ... an individual must add a semiotic Being to his physical Being..." (p. 52), an injunction useful to understanding both ourselves (and our interior representations of world) and the possibilities of created worlds, including computer-mediated ones. Finally, I would argue, that Lotman's latter category of Semiotic Being and its representation of the ways in which human consciousness can be altered by signs, might just as well be called Rhetoric. In fact, later in his discussion, Lotman implicitly rejects the Formalist distinction between story and discourse (or *roman* and *fabula*), saying that "[r]hetorical structure is not found in the plane of expression but in the plane of content" (p. 48). The men and women who wrote the programs, rules, scripts, and words that make up the interactive fictions published by Infocom or are currently under development by the Oz Project, have often failed to recognize two things: that their own Semiotic Beings are encoded and revealed in the traces of their stories, sometimes even in the interstices or ellipses of the programs themselves; and that their readers are projecting their own Semiotic Beings into stories, and that those stories must account for this semiosis.

Before we finally turn to considering Infocom's interactive fictions and the Oz Project's current compositions, we need to flesh out some of the ways the author's Semiotic Being (and somatic being, too, intended or not) is embedded in digital textuality, and to develop a vocabulary of the material dimensions of digital textuality that is useful to those of us who wish to study stories. First of all, when we read digital fictions, we see that reading, more than ever, has become a motion, an activity or engagement with a movable text, a visual field that has been newly unlocked. The moveable type, improvised for the first time in 1453, has leapt from behind the page to in front of it, and type now rearranges itself, dissolves, and is reconfigured before our very eyes. Has the flesh-and-blood writer, to improvise on a critical term used by both Wayne Booth (1983) and James Phelan (1989), likewise leapt from behind the page, from a state somatic to semiotic, from being to sign? And if so, how do we read those traces in the materials of these fictions?

One problem with contemporary models of the physical apparatus of computers, those that include all the software and hardware that underlie the production of digital texts, is that those models do not distinguish at nearly the right level of what computer scientists sometimes call "granularity." Current models often do not distinguish among computer types, types of documents generated, nor kinds of readers and writers. We need to heed better the ways in which *soma* or person writing story becomes the semiotic being of an author, represented both atomistically and digitally on particular computer screens. New models, of course, will themselves be signs (that themselves will be hampered by recursive, self-reflexive analyses of their writers' semiotic beings), but they may help to distinguish among the flesh-and-blood author, and her visible and invisible implications within the digital text. We need also to recognize the semiotic basis to our own biases and agendas when we feel discomfort with some digital fictions, tracing its origins to the ways in which our own semiotic being is imperfectly projected within the text. Ultimately, we need to construct models and understandings that result from "the sustained attempt to live reflectively with and follow the consequences of one simple realization: the whole of our experience, from its most primitive origins in sensation to its most refined achievements of understanding, is a network or web of sign relations" (Deely, 1990, p. 13). Inadequate critical attention has been paid to the ways a reader actualizes a digital text, as well as into how that text might be constructed to aid in particular "actualizations" (a term used by both Kenneth Burke [1957] and M.M. Bakhtin [trans. 1993] to describe how a reader responds to and constructs fictional texts, characters, or world). Paying attention to these new problems and giving attention to them at the right level of "granularity" is an important site of analysis in digital fictions, one that is discussed at greater length in Chapter 5. Suffice it to say here that Bakhtin's distinction between "inner" and "outer" form, between the form of an imaginary world (inner) or the material form of the work of art itself (outer) is relevant to the distinctions we are working on here.

Models of the writing process used by contemporary computer scientists and programmers, whether explicitly or implicitly, rely heavily on cognitive science and its realist epistemologies. The models we can infer from the programmers' accounts of the composing process mentioned in Chapter 2 are based on game theory, notions of reading as textual processing, and the idea of writing as predicting the vocabulary and syntax of reader responses so that they might be countered. The roots of the common criticism of interactive fiction as being "a narrative meets a crossword puzzle" is made plain by these models. When a storyteller meets a programmer who believes his job is to represent a univocal and unilateral world in programming, so that the text might be processed with little effort by an ideal reader, the result is predictable, in all of the discouraging senses of that adjective. On the other hand, literary theorists and rhetorical critics have not necessarily modeled writing in ways more successful, when confronted by digital fictions. These theorists and critics either describe the hardware and software (outer) in place of proposing a full-fledged theory, or build a model of text-processing (inner) that looks like a schematic diagram or the back of a television set.

For example, Kalmbach's interesting exegesis of textual production using computers includes the following breakdown of the components of a document.

> A document consists of text, display space, a container, and an interface. The text is a document's contents. In paper documents, this content can include words, graphics, and typographic color. In electronic documents, this content can also include sound and video. The container is what holds that text (a book, a magazine, a newspaper, a brochure, or a CD-ROM). A container is usually a physical object, but in the most recent forms of distributed hypertext (such as the World-Wide Web), the container of a document is created virtually through the act of browsing Web pages. Linking text and container is display space, that is, the visual space in which text is revealed to a user. Display space may be a page, a spread of two adjacent pages, a panel in a brochure, or the screen of an electronic hypertext. (1996, p. 13)

While useful and interesting as a taxonomy of the new parts and the new division of labor that computers permit, Kalmbach's divisions are (most likely as they are intended to be) mundane, practical, and, for the most part, tangible, or at any rate, literally divisible. The emphasis here is on texts and their various containers, implicitly suggesting a textual-processing model that is based in cognitive science, and that misses both the semiotic web and rhetorical resources of digital texts.

Writer Espen Aarseth (1993, 1997), too, ventures a number of useful theories and models, but his models, like many others under discussion, are firmly embedded in a realist epistemology. For example, if we look at Aarseth's Figure 3.1 and read the discussion that follows, we can see Aarseth's explicit connection with the

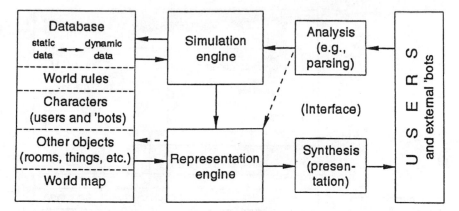

FIGURE 3.1. The components of a generalized, roleplaying cybertext (Aarseth, 1997).

ideas and theory that underlie one of the first models of the cognitive process of writing, Flower and Hayes's (1980) design.

According to Aarseth, components of "role-playing cybertexts" are configured as "internal mimetic machine[s]," which have "very different mechanical structures." Aarseth states that his model is not to be viewed as "a one-to-one mapping of actual components," but should instead be understood as "a generalized conceptualization" (Aarseth, 1997, p. 103) of what happens with a story generation system. He explains, "Th[is] model is not limited to single-user adventure games or text-based games but can also describe multi-user dungeons and graphical games such as Doom." He continues,

> Notice the four groups of components: the data, the processing engines, the front-end medium (interface), and the users; note the way information flows in feedback loops among them: going left on the upper level and then right on the lower, with the two middle layers like an artificial heart pumping information between the user and the database. This model is best suited to describe indeterminate cybertext. In determinate cybertext (e.g., Adventure), the three functions—simulation, representation, and synthesis—might be better described as a single component. (p. 104)

If we compare Aarseth's model with that of Flower and Hayes, pictured in Figure 3.2, we can see the ways in which both are inflected by cognitive psychology, cybernetics (in both language and diagrams of "feedback loops" and "protocols") and schematic design. Neither model really gets below the surface in understanding literary concerns like meaning, or understanding reader–writer relationships and reader–character relationships (or soma and semiotics), much less the relations between the flesh-and-blood writer and the slippery signs with which she conveys meaning. Both these models are limited by their chosen compass and their theoretical underpinnings.

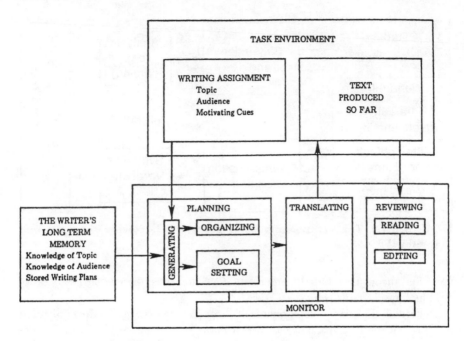

Figure 3.2. Flower-Hayes model of the writing process

To extend models and analyses like Kolmbach's, Aarseth's, and Flower and Hayes's, we need to take a perspective both feminist and semiotic, more socially inclusive, as it were, and develop a set of terms that might better probe and understand a particular category of digital fictions, such as interactive fictions. I develop such a set of terms below, which might contextualize Aarseth's model by detailing elements both prior to the development of "world rules" and "databases" and within the choices made by the "engines" of simulation and representation. If we apply the elements of Figure 3.3 to a particular story generation system, we can see how the realist epistemology underlying it constrains and distorts a reader's pleasure in narrative.

MATERIALS OF COMPOSING	MATERIALS OF READING
PROGRAMS	ETHICS
WORLDVIEW	WORLDVIEW
RULES	RULES
NARRATIVE DESIGN	EXPECTATIONS OF STORIES
SOMA	SOMA
INTENTIONALITY	INTENTIONALITY
	GOALS

VISIBLE READINGS AND VISIBLE WRITINGS
WRIT *in silico*

**POINT OF
SEMIOTIC AND FEMINIST
ANALYSIS**

FIGURE 3.3. The semiotic beings of writer and reader as represented on a screen of interactive fiction.

INFOCOM AND DEADLINE

You are a thirty-year-old *auto* worker in *Detroit, Michigan*. Ten years ago you married a fellow worker. You now have two children. A year ago, your factory closed. Neither you nor your spouse were able to find other employment. Your unemployment insurance has run out. Although your savings are gone, you do not qualify for welfare. You've already sold your lakeside cabin. Now the bank is threatening to take away your house, the car dealership to repossess your car, and the furniture store to confiscate all your furniture, including the TV set. To top it off, your baby needs an operation! You may now begin your adventure. I will be your eyes and hands. Direct me with commands of one or two words. If you need help type HELP. To see how you're doing type SCORE. GOOD LUCK. (Loader, 1989, p. 69)

Jayne Loader's (1989) spoof of interactive fictions (excerpted above), included in her disturbing and vivid collection of short stories called *Wild America*, directs readers' attention to the ethical dilemma of reading stories like those produced by Infocom. Her chilling indictment of interactive fiction in her book's title-piece, "Wild America," viciously lampoons one of interactive fiction's most troublesome features: its overt, heavy-handed insistence on a reader's participation in acts at best amoral and at worst unethical and criminal. In Loader's satire, "you" are an unemployed autoworker living in Detroit with an angry spouse, a sick baby, an empty savings account, and no hope of getting a job or welfare. Through a swift and unstoppable series of killings, thefts, a drug deal, and an encounter with an undercover cop masquerading as a prostitute, "you" are arrested, thrown into jail, and assigned a final score as "a menace to society." Loader's story makes it clear that "you" never really had a chance. The shared moral responsibility for event and sequence in interactive fiction is developed in Loader's story as a readerly encounter with an oppressive script full of trick requirements and an unrelentingly materialist culture, a narrative experience that critiques the consumerist contexts of our contemporary readings, even as it seduces us into pseudoparticipation.

Loader's (1989) story satirizes one of the central features of the experience of reading interactive fiction: the genre raises an ethical problem that is a key part of all readerly transactions with digital fictions, including virtual realities, multimedia hypertext fictions, MUDs, MOOs, and interactive fiction. Readers or users of all interactive digital texts bear a more overt and direct responsibility for the effects of their participation, which can range from assault and battery to MUD-rape and murder. Loader's story resoundingly critiques the ethics of engagement invoked by current interactive fiction and demonstrates the mixed promise of involvement evoked by an illusion of participation or empowerment and a reality of coercive engagement. In fact, it is precisely this *illusion* of participation, which Loader so efficiently skewers, that embodies one central difference between reading interactive fiction and reading conventional fiction.

All current computer-based interactive fictions reduce reading to a scavenger hunt to some extent, and the participatory reading that Loader lampoons relates this scavenging to the blind pursuit of the trappings of the American Dream: the Chrysler, the motorboat, the television, the Schwinn bicycle. However, Loader's (1989) story is most important for the question it raises about the ethics of participatory readings not only within particular treasure hunts, but in the world and lives represented within digital fictions in general; she highlights the central question of the relationship between the "you" that moves through the interactive fiction and the "you" who exists outside the text and guides "your" representation. Loader challenges us to examine how reading interactive fiction gains an ethical charge because of the problematic relationship its second-person address evokes between the reader and the "you" in the digital text. The invitational form of interactive fiction and its explicit opportunities for the reader to make responses compound the effects of second-person, present-tense narration on any reader's engagement with story.

According to Wolfgang Iser's (1978) model of reading outlined in *The Implied Reader,* reading is an imaginative activity of contrastive interpretation undertaken by individual readers. The reading process is "continually on the move," as the reader attends to the implications of sequent sentences, perpetually adjusting the virtual dimension of the text; Iser says, "This virtual dimension is not the text itself, nor is it the imagination of the reader; it is the coming together of text and imagination" (p. 279). Reading is a dynamic, transcendent, meaning-making activity negotiated through the gaps or indeterminacies of a text by the reader. I follow Iser in believing a reader proceeds by a system of comparisons between her own experiences and that of the texts, looking at a novel as "a set of reactions, [that] the reader is impelled to counterbalance..." (pp. 34–35). Iser is often invoked in discussions of interactive fiction because his discussions of how gaps in a text function seems to describe the visible gaps in these stories (see, for example, Aarseth, 1997; Niesz & Holland, 1984). However, by confusing Iser's implicit readerly gaps with interactive fiction's explicit ones, and by misunderstanding traditional fiction's subtlety and flexibility of representation with interactive fiction's far more brittle and thin extension of invitations within those gaps, these latter critics are missing a better application of Iser: to see how interactive fictions ultimately disappoint their readers. As Iser himself explicitly states again, "the virtual dimension is not the text itself." A close study of interactive fictions rewards researchers by revealing the grave, yet literally invisible, disconnection between reader and writer as they meet across an interactive fiction like those produced by Infocom.

Infocom was perhaps the most prolific publisher of interactive fictions (IF), publishing more than 20 titles between 1982 and 1988, including such well-received stories in mystery, fantasy, science fiction, and "tales of adventure" as *Deadline, Wishbringer, A Mind Forever Voyaging, Leather Goddesses of Phobos, Suspect, The Zork Trilogy, Nord and Bert,* and *Infidel.* These commercially available interactive fictions, known as "text adventures," were distinguished by their second-person narration, their multilinearity, and by the gaps visible in their texts (signaled by a prompt and a blank section of screen into which the reader would write). Interactive fictions in general are distinguished also by the range of responses and roles of the reader permitted: readers of IF in general engage the text as a character most often engaged in questing, sleuthing, rescuing, wooing, or solving, and who has an extremely limited vocabulary at her disposal.

In the history detailed by Johnny Wilson (1991), the principal founders of Infocom met at MIT's Laboratory of Computer Science in the mid-1970s, where two of the founders, Dave Lebling and Marc Blank, inspired in part by Crowther and Woods's Adventure, designed a mainframe adventure game. To overcome the difficulties posed by the two-word parsers of existing text adventures, Blank developed ZIL (Zork Interactive Language), "a 'parser' which allowed the program to find associations between sentences and, hence, better understood what the player wanted to do." According to Holden's account, on June 22, 1979, Al Vezza, a professor at the MIT laboratory and three of his star pupils, Berez, Blank, and Lebling, formed Infocom to market *Zork* (as it was now called) for the personal computer. *Zork* was soon followed by the company's second hit, *Starcross,* a work of science fiction that came packaged in its own flying saucer. Infocom eventually published a number of text adventures, published a newsletter ("The New Zork Times") and enjoyed commercial success up until the company was bought by Activision in 1986. Soon after, Infocom began to produce poorly received programs like "Infocomics," morale plummeted among the original, self-described "Infocommies," and soon, Wilson reports, Infocom "was only a label." The company published over 30 titles before they were through.

Early Infocom writers readily attested to their interest in Adventure in particular, science fiction in general (Lebling wrote *Starcross* in homage to Arthur C. Clarke and Larry Niven), and other genre fictions like mysteries. They based their stories on their own worldviews and experiences, building one game, *The Lurking Horror*, for example, as a "homage to H.P. Lovecraft and MIT." The locations in that game were based on real places at MIT (a concept echoed 10 years later in Amy Bruckman's MIT MediaMOO). Today, die-hard Infocom hobbyists and text-adventure aficionados continue to play the original Infocom games (republished most recently as *The Lost Treasures of Infocom*) and to invent their own. (See, for example, "Gumshoe," an interactive mystery [1996] by Mike Oliphant, available on the Internet.) Many of these "text adventurers" presumably feel as does Marc Blank, who said in a recent interview that while all games have some strengths, text adventures had more "imagination" than games with graphical interfaces marketed today:

> [W]hen it comes to point-and-clock [sic] interfaces or interfaces where you're either picking words or picking objects, I think the one thing that gets lost is the sense that you could do anything...and it might work. (1996, pp. 83–84)

Blank explains that in text adventures he believes there is more of a sense of "open-endedness." In this same interview, Blank also notes that he wrote the text adventure *Deadline* because he loves mysteries and he thought, "...most people, when they read mysteries, are constantly trying to think ahead," and to anticipate what they might do to solve the mystery. He said the mystery genre seemed "to lend itself perfectly to an open-ended text adventure."

If we problematized a traditional detective fiction like Edgar Allen Poe's *The Murders in the Rue Morgue* (1841) or Wilkie Collins's *The Moonstone* (1874) by giving it a consistent second-person narration and a randomly sequenced series of events; if we complicated our reading process by engaging in it as a character who intervenes repeatedly in the story, we would get a text quite a bit like Blank's *Deadline* (1991), discussed briefly in Chapter 2. Infocom writers explicitly proposed *Deadline* as an updated version of a traditional detective novel:

> Up until recently, the tools of the detective's trade consisted of little more than a sturdy pair of shoes, a notepad, and a well-oiled revolver. But such traditional standbys have gradually given way to the computer, which by virtue of its precise and logical intellect provides the perfect complement to the keenly intuitive mind of the detective. In fact, it is now possible to conduct an entire investigation without leaving one's computer terminal.

In 1982, when Infocom published this interactive mystery by Marc Blank (identified as "Chief Architect" on the packaging),[13] the story's advertising copy summarized the game: "A locked door. A dead man. And 12 hours to solve the mystery." Moving beyond the limited vocabularies and puzzle-oriented adventure games typical of mainframe-based digital fiction prior to 1982, Infocom's *Deadline* (1991) was innovative, in that it cast readers in a particular role and facilitated dialogue, albeit stilted, with a "responsive" story and characters. It is my project here to examine the effects of combining multiple viewpoints, multilinearity, and second-person, present-tense address in a text adventure, effects that shift the reader–text relationship playfully and radically. (In earlier versions of this work [Sloane, 1991], my use of the term "multiple viewpoints" may have been unclear [see Aarseth, 1997], so let me explain quickly that I mean to refer to a dimension of *Deadline*'s narration, and not to the secondary texts, akin to Genette's *paratexts*, included in *Deadline*'s packaging, as Aarseth supposes.) In *Deadline*, the reader plays a detective who has been called to investigate the apparent suicide of Marshall Robner, a wealthy industrialist, and to establish that his suicide was in fact murder. After a series of interrogations and the collection of clues, the reader must arrest the right suspect to end the story. The reader is given 12 hours (according to an onscreen clock that advances one minute after each response is typed) to accomplish these tasks.

After the reader loads the disk into a computer, the story begins with "you," the reader-detective, standing outside the door to the Robner estate. Although the reader may indeed proceed on literally thousands of different readings of the story, he or she in fact must perform only eight discrete actions (by writing them into the story) to find the evidence necessary to arrest the right suspect. Specifically, the reader must find a set of papers in a safe, analyze fragments of a teacup for traces of "LoBlo," show a calendar notation to the dead man's son, and surprise the housekeeper so she drops a theater ticket on the floor, among other actions, to solve the mystery. Again, one source of the story's suspense (perhaps the only real source) is that the clock is running all the while the reader attempts to solve the murder.

The packet of materials accompanying the story diskette and designed to aid "you" in "your" investigations includes a letter from Marshall Robner's attorney, Warren Coates, and initial findings of earlier investigators. Elsewhere in the accompanying secondary texts we can read about how to analyze physical evidence, make arrests, or interrogate suspects. The reader is advised of the formula underlying many of the tidy investigations of contemporary murder mysteries, and is told: "Since guilt must be established beyond a reasonable doubt, it is important to demonstrate the three crucial elements: means, motives and opportunities." In addition to the lists of workable verbs, maps, and lab reports, the packet included with the *Deadline* story diskette includes transcripts of interviews with the central people in Robner's life: his business partner, son, personal secretary, housekeeper, and wife. Finally, in a section entitled "How to Use Computers in Detective Work," the rookie detective is given advice on "doing the legwork," "handling evidence," and "dealing with suspects and other people." These packaging materials and packet are necessary to initiate a novice reader into an unfamiliar site and activity of reading: creating the illusion of interacting with a computer-based story. More experienced readers, of course, know these conventions. In Infocom's version of the familiar phrase, "as every schoolboy knows," the directions state:

[E]xperienced players seldom type more than a few words at a time. They usually pare their responses down to words that work: active verbs, nouns that name characters or manipulable objects, and some discriminating adjectives. Language thus becomes an instrument for probing fictional environments.

A "successful" reader would solve the mystery of Robner's murder by exploring the house and grounds, interviewing residents, and establishing the means, motive, and opportunity within the 12 hours allotted her. She would interact with the house, the characters, and objects in the story by using phrases or commands suggested in the accompanying instruction manual in a crude and explicit resolution of the textual gaps presented on the screen. Specifically, the reader would refer to her or his list of "Commonly Encountered Terms in Criminal Investigations" and use verbs such as "accuse," "analyze," "arrest," "follow," "fingerprint," "search," or "wait."

During the course of *Deadline*, the reader (or user) might interview the house-keeper or analyze medicines suspected in the poisoning of Mr. Robner. The reader might rummage through a medicine cabinet, find a bottle marked "Sneezo" and then type "Analyze Sneezo tablets." The text that next appears would say: "Sergeant Duffy walks up quiet as a mouse. He takes the bottle of Sneezo brand decongestant from you. 'I'll return soon with the results,' he says, and leaves as silently as he entered." In all these Infocom stories, the reader takes the role of a central character, whose duty is to solve a particular problem or set of problems; the narrative progression hinges on the reader performing this duty, and the program-mer and program have anticipated a certain set of user responses. In interactive fic-tions like *Deadline*, the reader's linguistic input is limited to statements of simple syntax and a vocabulary of about 1,400 words.

A hypothetical expert reading of *Deadline* would proceed as follows, taking place in real-time for about six hours from beginning to end: Even before loading the story diskette, the expert reader reviews the materials accompanying it, including the laboratory report stating that Marshall Robner died of an overdose of the drug Ebullion in his upstairs library. After loading the diskette, and then reading the first screen in which "you" are entering the story through the door of the Robner estate, "you," the reader-detective, meet Mrs. Robner. After reading her canned explana-tion of the parameters of the reading (when the will will be read and how long "you" the detective have to solve the murder), you would decide to explore the grounds and every room of the estate, drawing a map of the estate and listing your findings, taking removable items from each room. For example, the reader might decide to begin her "investigation" in the living room (executing this decision by typing "go north" and then "go west.") She would continue by typing phrases, such as "look around" or "examine," which allow her to explore the dining room, kitchen, pantry, and maid's quarters, and all the other rooms on the ground floor. This expert reader moves between rooms by typing in the names of the cardinal directions, while simultaneously, as most readers quickly learn, sketching a plan of the whole estate on a pad of paper.

After reading the descriptions of the living room and all the other rooms on the ground floor, and after looking at the objects contained in each room, this expert reader might attempt to interact with each object in the rooms, picking up the telephone, sitting on the couch, counting the silverware, or kicking a chair. Again, as any expert reader knows, she would collect all objects she or he finds, carrying books, tickets, and a wooden ladder with her throughout her search of the house and grounds.

After typing dozens, if not hundreds, of phrases into the story to allow her to thoroughly explore all locations, the expert reader finds a number of clues throughout the house that lead her to make the required arrest of the murderers by 8:00 pm. In the upstairs library, for example, she finds a partially erased message in which Robner threatens his partner, Baxter, about "the Focus scandal." She also finds a notation on Robner's library desk calendar saying "new will complete, call Coates." Armed with these two clues, the expert reader shows them to every character she meets. For example, she enters George's bedroom and shows them to him. (Robner's son spends most of the story ensconced in his room listening to an unlikely mix of music such as bluegrass, Bulgarian shepherdess songs, and a Hebrew prayer service.) After the reader types "show calendar to George," George will grow frightened and angry, and eventually open the safe in a secret room connected to the library. An alert reader (and one who has the wit to type "hide on the library balcony") follows George and catches him in the act of opening the safe. In that safe, the reader will find and read papers implicating Baxter in a business scandal involving Robner. Hence, Baxter's motive is revealed.

The successful reader not only hides on the library balcony but examines it, and finds signs of a ladder having leaned there. She goes outside (by typing a series of directions to bring her downstairs and out the front door) and asks Mr. McNabb, the gardener, about his roses; McNabb then shows the reader fragments of a ceramic teacup in a rosebed. She asks Sergeant Duffy to analyze the ceramic fragments and learns that they are tainted with LoBlo, a medication which raises the toxicity of Ebullion, the drug that killed Robner. When the reader next shows the report to Dunbar, the housekeeper, she gets frightened and mad and drops a concert ticket. If "you" ask Dunbar about the ticket, she admits she went to the concert with Baxter the previous night. Finally, the reader who has found these clues and executed these rote interrogations next arrests Dunbar and Baxter.

The story rewards this successful reader with a summary of evidence, explaining that the means of the murder was tea laced with LoBlo, that the motive was that Baxter was embroiled in an unlucky business deal with Robner, that Dunbar was in love with Baxter, and that the opportunity for murder was there for Baxter when he dropped off Dunbar after the concert the previous night. This summary of events in an expert reading of *Deadline* does not sufficiently describe the reader's race against the digital clock, which advances after each response she types, nor capture the frustration of a reader's engagement with a program that responds only with and to a limited vocabulary, and that does not allow the reader to use words it uses, responding with sentences such as "The word 'heirloom' isn't in your vocabulary," when a description of a room has just included that very word.

Deadline demonstrates the salient narrative features of Infocom interactive fiction: its multiple points of view; its gaps; its multilinearity; its second-person, present-tense address; the limited vocabulary of words it recognizes from readers. By comparing *Deadline* to traditional detective fictions like those by Poe or Collins, we can see how early interactive fictions yielded a reading experience that was thin and inadequate. First of all, Infocom's interactive fiction's nonlinearity is not underwritten by a coherent structure such as the straightforward chronology of Collins and Poe, the cohesive ties of experimental fictions of writers like Borges or Coover, or even the "combinatory aesthetic" of Calvino. A reader in *Deadline*, for example, could spend 12 hours shuttling between the library and the balcony, hoping to surprise George as he retrieves key papers from the secret safe, but that would be a frustrating rather than a playful reading.

This lack of coherent narrative structure is compounded by a lack of attention given to the story's rhetorical resources. Interactive fiction's second-person, present-tense address is not in any obvious way a part of some larger strategy of playing with the reader. The frustration that you the reader and "you" in the text do not concur as far as actions taken, sentences spoken, or choices available is a frustration compounded by a parser's limited understandings of the reader's typed commands. Even worse, as discussed briefly before, the gaps made explicitly available within the text on the screen for readerly intervention often do not coincide with the gaps in the individual reader's mental representation of text. There are dissonances between the semantics of text and the semiotics of that text's representation of the reader, and between the text's plodding, chronological notion of narrative progression, and the reader's revelations. In short, a reader's semiotic being is distorted. Third, key movements or conversations readers may wish to make or have with fictional settings or characters are constrained by the range of interventions and the limited vocabulary the program has accounted for and allows. Finally, because of the reader's illusion of control over the narrative, he or she has a new ethical culpability for event and outcome, which the reader might chafe against even as she engages in the text. The presentational device of the computer and the new control over narrative direction it lends the reader heightens her engagement in the story, fostering a quality of involvement. While that new quality of involvement can be exhilarating as well as frustrating, it has serious consequences for the reader's sense of responsibility for progression, action, and closure in narrative. It is in their very resistance to the brittle nature of an interactive text that makes these readers experience increased responsibility and occasional ethical discomfort.

Digital fictions in general make readers' resistance to particular stories explicit. In interactive fictions such as *Leather Goddesses of Phobos* and *Zork Zero*, in MUDs based on battle or quest, or even in the hypertext fiction *Afternoon*, readers are asked to participate in acts they would find personally repugnant, for example, committing adultery or killing other players. Because the reader resists vigorously the "you" or the self that fiction implies is you, the reader's participation is often reluctant, ambivalent, or culpable. Because she must often commit unconscionable acts to keep the story going, she may assume an attitude of expediency that grates before it becomes familiar, when she learns to kill other characters or loot whatever will advance her cause. The reader executes these acts through typing, talking, and interrogating, and through changing the pace and restructuring the sequence of events; thus, the ethical dimension of her participation in reading fiction is heightened. An individual reader identifies more closely (and with more problems) with the activities required by a multilinear, multiperspectival narration and second-person address in interactive fiction than in conventional fiction also because of her participation in making the text.

As Jayne Loader's (1989) satire suggests, in contemporary interactive fictions, both male and female readers can feel trapped in rigid, fatally scripted texts that silence dissent, force conformity, or compel other unpleasant textual collaborations for which they may feel responsible. Although these stories are uniformly advertised as participatory stories in which "You, the reader, determine what happens,"[14] a more critical reading reveals that, in actuality, in many of these stories the reader does nothing more than attempt to stay alive in a scripted microworld. In Infocom's interactive fictions, a reader who offers a rogue reading or a critique is silenced by the parser's claim of "incorrect" language or syntax. In these stories, inappropriate vocabulary or syntax leads always to stasis or death, revealed to the reader by textual responses such as, "There is no verb in that sentence." Worse, inappropriate action commonly leads to the game's response: "You have died," followed by the unlikely resurrection, "Would you like to play again?" In *Zork*, if a reader does not ax a troll to death and thus forward the narrative progress, then she dies instead. These extreme examples of a frustrating readerly engagement typical of much current interactive fiction is ultimately linked to the distance between a program's representation of reader, implicit or explicit, and that reader's representation of self. The link is cut between semiotic being and real self. While *Deadline* avoids much of the misogyny and joyous hacking and plundering mentality of many interactive fictions, *Deadline* has the common frustration of a parser that "comprehends" input with a limited range of replies and that inadvertently creates instabilities in the discourse between reader and Reader.

To summarize, the three narrative techniques of interactive fictions—multiple viewpoints, multilinearity, and second-person, present-tense address—conspire within the field of a new presentational device to create a heightened involvement and ethical implication in the process of reading. A new relationship evolves between the reader and the Reader that is even more pronounced within stories when graphics are added. Although current limitations in the technology create some of this ethical discomfort, the ethical problem will paradoxically only deepen rather than disappear when the technology allows a more seamless relation between reader and text. That is, if digital fictions become better at representing the reader's language and physical body, unless there is a corresponding broadened sensitivity to the reader's desires or being, that reader is going to feel even guiltier when the story requires her to perform some unconscionable act.

Reading interactive fiction is to engage freshly with fictional texts and a new system of rhetorical and medial enhancement and constraint, which at the time of this writing still feel a bit haphazard. Reading *Deadline* foregrounds reader responsibility for progression, a responsibility that might exist in all readings, but, in interactive fiction, is explicit. In contrast to the invisible engagement of paper-based stories, interactive fiction engages readers in performative readings that are visible. (Readers of conventional fiction do respond visibly as well, of course, in the form of reviews or critical articles, in conference papers or casual letters, but it is clear that paper-based stories do not invite intervention and direction to the same extent that computer-based ones do.) As interactive fiction narrows the gap between the reader and the story, the gap between the flesh-and-blood reader and her representation in the text grows more visible and problematic. The interventionary, performative readings of interactive fiction, combined with the narrative techniques discussed above, create a new narrative experience, one that is troubling and confounding.

Because these stories are written on and for computers, the text the reader reads on the screen is a text that is driven by and enacted by several layers of programming code. These layers contribute to the "feel" of the reading, both to its freedom and its constraints. While the reader may have the illusion that she may go anywhere, say anything, and interrogate anyone, in fact when she attempts to "read against the code," she will be frustrated, *killed*, or impeded in her progress through the story. This dynamic interchange between textual freedom and textual constraint is, of course, enacted in all textual exchanges. As Iser (1978) reminds us:

> Thus begins a whole dynamic process: the written text imposes certain limits on its unwritten implications in order to prevent these from becoming too blurred and hazy, but at the same time these implications, worked out by the reader's imagination, set the given situation against a background which endows it with far greater significance than it might have seemed to possess on its own. (p. 276)

However, reading interactive fiction is different because this traditional dynamic is heightened. Readers who choose to read against the code find themselves unable to do so. Thus, unfortunately, many commercial interactive fictions drive readers into behaviors that many of them would find personally unethical.

Describing the composing processes of developers of digital stories and story generation systems, such as the Oz Project discussed below, may help illuminate how the authors' manipulation of the layered materials of these stories contribute to the quality of reading them.

THE OZ PROJECT

"But it wasn't a dream, it was a place!"

—Dorothy, in *The Wizard of Oz* (1939)

Members of the Oz Project, located primarily in Wean Hall within the School of Computer Science at Carnegie Mellon University, are today engaged in an interdisciplinary effort to create dense, rich interactive fictions that will provide participants "with the experience of living in a dramatically interesting simulated world that includes simulated people." Dr. Joseph Bates, a Research Professor in the School of Computer Science at Carnegie Mellon, directs the Oz Project research group, a group made up primarily of graduate students in computer science as well as faculty and students in the departments of English and Drama. Bates says that the reason he embarked on this project was that he "wanted to build [his] dreams and have someone else be in that world" (personal communication, December 9, 1990).

The following description of the Oz Project is based on my own experiences as a graduate student at Carnegie Mellon University, wherein I studied artificial intelligence and narrative theory in a seminar taught by Bates (one devoted primarily to discussion of issues in interactive fiction), as well as discussions with Bates and other researchers during several subsequent visits. In addition, I am summarizing two papers presented at recent conferences by Bates, several CMU CS technical reports, e-mail entries posted by members of an Oz Project internal discussion group, and my own observations, including one intensive two-day period in December 1990, and my readings of two recent theses.[15]

The immediate and long-term goals of Oz are complementary efforts to create a medium beyond "static stories" and to create stories that are active and interactive. The goal of the Oz Project is to create "constructed yet unpredictable worlds" and to provide users with rich experiences of these worlds, most immediately through a text-based interface and, eventually, through a multimedia interface. In more general terms, Bates sees the Oz Project as "a place to study mind—the analysis and synthesis of mind." The interactive fiction project at Carnegie Mellon plans to use existing artificial intelligence technology to improve the state of the art of interactive fiction and to build dramatic worlds that users can engage in in a variety of ways. As Bates stated in a June 14, 1990, e-mail message addressed to members of his research group:

> My long term goal for Oz is to provide modern IF [interactive fiction] technology in a sufficiently well packaged form that individuals or small groups can build worlds.... [O]ur main goals should be the development of science/art and the accompanying technology, the eventual packaging of our technology for individuals, and keeping our research group open to ideas and comfortable for all who want to pursue this research.

Specifically, members of the project team are pressing forward on these areas of research by building together a prototype of an interactive mystery novel *(Tea for Two)* and dealing with questions of modeling as they arise. Their goals are to accumulate a large "library" of settings, characters, and plots (and other "meta-knowledge" that will direct the arrangement and editing of this library), which writers and artists can recombine and tailor to create new works of interactive fiction. They see possible applications for this technology in entertainment and in training in business.

The goal of Oz within the next few years is to move beyond text-based interactive fiction systems and to create "synthetic realities," that is, three-dimensional simulated environments enhanced by computer-generated sounds and graphics and encountered, perhaps, as virtual realities accessed via a helmet and a "data glove."[16] In these three-dimensional simulations, narration will be replaced by animation; text generation will be replaced by speech generation; and parsing will be replaced by speech understanding. In short, the researchers of Oz see their efforts moving beyond a pure text interface and advancing to replace the text interface with facilities for speech, animation, and gestures, guided cooperatively by program and user. Bates's organization of the "Workshop on Interactive Fiction & Synthetic Realities" at the 1990 Association of American Artificial Intelligence (AAAI) meeting was the first effort toward building a community of researchers to collaborate on making such synthetic reality systems a virtual success. Additional meetings of this new community of researchers and theorists have been held as a number of symposia sponsored by the American Association of Artificial Intelligence: Bates organized a Spring Symposium on Believable Agents at the AAAI-94 meeting at Stanford University, and an Interactive Story Systems: Plot & Character Symposium at AAAI-95. In 1997, an AAAI symposium on Socially Intelligent Agents was held, and in 1999, a fall symposium on Narrative Intelligence was held, chaired by Phoebe Sengers, a former Carnegie Mellon University graduate student.[17]

To realize their long-term goal of realistic and dramatic computer simulations, researchers at Carnegie Mellon University are currently involved in many daily tasks of modeling and programming "large numbers of world parts, such as physical objects and settings, parts of minds (planners, plans, kinds of social knowledge), sets of linguistic rules, and components of narrative and dramatic theories" in Common Lisp, with substantial use of the Common Lisp Object System on Mach/Unix workstations. While interested in the narration of these worlds, the primary focus of their current research is to build "the simulations behind the interface, which we call the deep structure of virtual reality" (Bates, 1990, p. 1). Members of the research group participate in modeling different parts of the programs that make up Oz by collaborating and corresponding over the electronic mail network that links their offices. The subject of their discussions is the ongoing production of an Oz synthetic reality and its pure text-based interface, physical world simulation, character models, a natural language generator and understander, and a theory of drama, all written in the programming language, Lisp. As Smith and Bates explain in an early technical report (CMU-CS-121):

> The world graph [of Oz] indicates rough 3D arrangement, plus relationships between objects.... Plot enforcement is currently embedded in the behavior of objects in the world and in the rules driving the characters (in the form of scheduled actions, for example). (1989, pp. 9–10)

To help his research team's daily work, Bates has divided the work necessary to realize the Oz Project's ambitious long-term vision into six sets of questions or problems. The six sections of inquiry defined by Bates are outlined as follows:

- physical world simulation;
- the minds of simulated characters;
- the user interface (and narrative voice);
- theory of drama;
- the world-building environment; and
- artistic use of the system.

Oz Project graduate students and recent graduates (including Mark Kantrowitz and Peter Weyhrauch) are engaging the central issues of these six areas by modeling everything the reader needs to maintain a rich illusion of participation in a story and for the artist (or writer-programmer) to have a sufficient "library of parts" with which to produce rich stories.

Building "rich, deeply modeled underlying worlds" with which the reader-user will interact involves writing several layers of instructions for the computer. At the lowest level, the level of "the real machine," a programmer composes a program in a machine language, "the long strings of 1s and 0s that are all the hardware can really understand" (Johnson, 1986, p. 16). This built-in program is called an interpreter or a compiler and can "write things on the screen and cause the other hardware (e.g., the chips of the memory and processor) to behave in selected ways" (J. Bates, personal communication, April 10, 1991). In the Oz Project, programmers run a higher-level program called "the Lisp system" that, for all intents and purposes, transforms any "real machine" into a machine that can run Lisp programs. (In general, Lisp programs not only perform reasoning tasks, "but are actually intended as theoretical models of how humans perform those tasks" [Anderson, Corbett, & Reiser, 1987, p. 2]). Once within the Lisp system, these programmers run another, higher-level program called Oz:

> Oz includes a framework for running a collection of other programs (called the 'agents' of the world). These agents are written in other languages, usually called the 'architectures' of the agents. These programs do not deal with their external world in terms of terminal screens. Instead, they think they are truly in a world—they have eyes and ears and hands. The agent programs manipulate the eyes and hands, and

therefore go through a general process of sense, think, act. (J. Bates, personal communication, April 10, 1991)

Bates's model of the Oz architecture can be understood as a high-level description of a system of hierarchically related programs operating together on several levels to collaboratively create a rich simulation of a world populated by deeply simulated objects and characters. At present, the reader interacts with these layered programs through a computer keyboard, a computer screen, and a text-based or graphics-based interface.

Each of the six areas of inquiry currently engaging researchers at Oz subsumes many smaller problems or areas of research that inform the ultimate shape of the layered materials of narrative. According to Bates, the work to simulate the physical world is ultimately intended to "provide just enough of a physical reality to let authors construct interesting characters and stories" (personal communication, April 1, 1999). (Note the epistemological assumption that an author rearranges or builds from parts of the natural world.) Oz uses the Lisp programming language to model the descriptions and behavior of objects (which for Bates and his team includes bodies of characters) and to provide a commonsense model of the physical world, relying explicitly on an Objectivist paradigm of world, person, and event. The goal of this part of the project is to provide rich and varied models of all classes of objects (including animate objects, such as people) in the physical world. The process of composing simulated objects in the physical world involves writing Lisp code, debugging that code, and then testing the object through a user's interaction with it, a user some literary critics would call "the ideal reader." Many of the daily discussions posted on the electronic-mail discussion group of the Oz Project involve debugging these models or posing questions and debates about how these evolving models of objects and characters should coordinate and work.

Simulating the minds of independent characters within the model of the physical world is more challenging than modeling relatively static objects. Currently, Bates uses two frameworks for designing the "minds" (that is, the computer programs that simulate mind) of characters, although these models are expected to change quickly. One is a goal-driven reactive planner called HAP, and the other is based on the Prodigy planner.[18] Other systems may eventually be linked to Oz's model of the minds of characters, including systems under development by Allen Newell at Carnegie Mellon University and John Laird at the University of Michigan (the developers of Soar), and Doug Lenat at the Microcomputer Consortium (MCC) in Austin, Texas (see Adam's discussion of Cyc, below). In brief, the ultimate goal, and the daily activity, of these researchers involved in this aspect of Oz is to represent explicitly, and deeply, the beliefs, goals, plans, and emotions of synthetic characters, "who will be able to discuss their mental lives (if they so choose)."

Ultimately, the programs that underlie these simulations of physical objects and characters are tested through a reader's interaction with them over a computer terminal. The user interface, which "connects human agents to the simulated world," is the second area of research currently being explored. The Oz interface is based on "Glinda," a natural language generator designed by Mark Kantrowitz. Kantrowitz characterizes Glinda as the "natural language generation module" of Oz, or an implemented natural language text generation system that uses the propagation of features during generation to license generation rules. These rules control the selection, organization, transformation, and combination of elements from the semantic and pragmatic representations input within a uniform, multilevel linguistic framework (Kantrowitz, 1990).

Kantrowitz's work hopes eventually to approximate Hovy's experiments in rhetorical transitions. Specifically, the work on natural language text generation in the Oz Project is linked to "Pauline" (Planning and Uttering Language in Natural Environments), a project completed at Yale University as Eduard Hovy's Ph.D. thesis in 1987. Pauline is a text generator capable of saying "the same thing in many ways to achieve various effects."[19] At present, Bates's group uses a general purpose bottom-up parser with a simple grammar and ad hoc semantic and pragmatic analysis. They are considering using instead a word-based parser because they think it might be more appropriate "for processing short, syntactically limited, possibly ill-formed input,"[20] which they find typical of readers of interactive fiction.

Next, one of the most important problems that Bates and his researchers are tackling is how to develop a computational model of how drama and stories work, the "metaknowledge" mentioned at the beginning of this discussion. Developing the narrative and dramatic theories that will be implemented in Oz has been aided by "live" improvisational experiments in drama, conceived and coached by Margaret Kelso, among others, and informed by the work on dramatic theory begun by Brenda Kay Laurel in her 1986 dissertation, "Toward the Design of a Computer-Based Interactive Fantasy System." Laurel relies on Aristotle's *Poetics* in her dissertation as a means of understanding and generating plot, character, spectacle, and creating an automated playwright. Laurel's encapsulation of Aristotle is one source of Oz's working theory of drama and the source of their conception of plot structure as comprised of complication, climax, and resolution, or as literary critics might characterize the novel, establishing conflict, resolving conflict, and relaying dénouement. Although interested in the possible applications of Aristotle to Oz, Bates says, "it is enough to know that the author constructs the text by hand through much effort ... although he may not follow any particular theory such as Aristotle" (personal communication, February 27, 1994). The Oz Project is currently debating rival theories of dramatic presentation and narration, and this is one area that is changing quickly. A central issue in discussions is how to reconcile the creative tension between scripting plot and allowing the dynamic interventions of the reader/user to have real effect on quality and sequence of event.

The current model of Oz is negotiating gingerly between the two poles in this tension, a negotiation that will eventually have important ramifications for the reader's experience of the narrative progression. Careful discussion and implementation of a particular theory of drama will precede a reader's satisfying engagement with her "body representation" or "you" on the computer screen. The proportion of readerly control, selection, and arrangement of event, sequence, and quality of encounter will shift according to which dramatic theory is ultimately chosen to guide Oz's constructions; the degree to which the reader experiences ethical culpability or even general responsibility for event will no doubt shift as well. The Oz Project is also currently choosing among several ways to codify plot and to suggest a route through the text for the reader.

Finally, beyond these important questions of modeling physical worlds and characters, plot, and arrangements of story, designing a satisfactory narrating device in the form of a natural language text generator, and developing an adequate theory of plot and drama, Bates is particularly concerned that the technology that he is building be used by artists, and that its development be guided by the needs of artists and writers building worlds. He hopes to have the population of Oz users grow as the system develops, and he hopes they will assist in constructing a substantial library of world parts. Bates's goal here is to have artists help us all "learn the potential of interactive fiction as a new art form and to guide the development of Oz toward reaching that potential." In the next several years, at any rate, collaborating in this regard with the members of the Oz Project will mean artists learning to program in Lisp as well as learning how to build complex systems.

"Dramatic Presence," by Margaret Kelso, Peter Weyhrauch, and Joseph Bates, offers an excellent overview of the Oz Project's research and goals. The essay gives an example of what they hope "interactive drama" will look like. (By interactive drama, they explain, they mean "the presentation by computers of rich, highly interactive worlds, inhabited by dynamic and complex characters, and shaped by aesthetically pleasing stories" [Kelso, Weyhrauch, & Bates, 1992, p. 3]. After offering the following example of "interactive drama," presumably the opening screens of a mystery based in Egypt, the essay continues by offering an example of the Oz system architecture at work:

> Dusk in Cairo. You are walking down a dusty street, on your way to a museum. You wish to discover the origin of a symbol found in a book belonging to your father the archeologist. Your father had told you, before he died, that this book contained his life's work. Suddenly, you hear footsteps. A man grabs the shoulder of your leather jacket. He says he is Horace, a friend of your father's, and if you come with him, he can help you. You stop in Café Tut—he is charming and surprisingly knowledgeable about your father. You absorb his every word, until you suddenly get an eerie feeling. Horace is asking strange questions about the book. Your father's book. You then notice a suspicious gun-like bulge in his suit jacket. You slowly get up, mentioning the restroom, and then bolt out of the cafe, barely evading Horace's hands as you jump into the nearest taxi. "Quick, get me to the museum," you scream over the sound of the screeching tires. You relax as you see Horace getting smaller though the rear window of the cab. "Yes, Sir," the gold-toothed cabbie replies with a smile, heading quickly in the wrong direction. (p. 8)

The writers of this article follow up this example and explain the complex interactions between reader and the computerized drama or plot managers under development, which they equate with "destiny." They explain, "[e]ven though the interactor is choosing what to do, say, and think, there is a destiny, created by the author of the interactive drama. This destiny is not an exact sequence of actions and events, but is subtly shaped by the system, which embodies dramatic theory and principle, in order to create a cathartic experience" (Kelso, Weyhrauch, & Bates, 1992, pp. 4–5). The first animated version of Oz, a group of four simple cartoon characters called Woggles, allows users to interact with the system through keyboard and screen, as well as through sonar sensors and a mouse. "The Edge of Intention," the simulated, interactive world of the Woggles, was first exhibited at the AAAI-92 Arts Exhibition in San Jose.[21] For both the textual and animated worlds under development at Oz, researchers are attempting to create dramatic characters presented in meaningful, rich, and persuasive ways. Oz foresees interactants being able to use speech and sounds to navigate through these fictive worlds.

CRITIQUING OZ AND INFOCOM

The recent brilliant work of feminist Alison Adam in *Artificial Knowing: Gender and the Thinking Machine* (1998), deconstructs two large-scale American AI systems, Cyc and Soar, and ties their research funding and agendas, scientific points of view, and ideas and goals to what she calls mainstream epistemologies that emphasize individualism, a monolithic and knowable world, and propositional knowing, and that tacitly reflects a norm of masculinity. In both method and conclusion, Adam's work is of crucial importance in understanding the ways gender is inscribed in computational models of world and mind, in the very materials of AI itself. Her discussion of Soar (another Carnegie Mellon University creation) is the most intelligent analysis of the implications of IF-THEN pairs in the production rules of AI programs yet written. Linking the early work of Allen Newell and Herbert Simon, *Human Problem Solving* (1972) with the predisposition of AI researchers today to write programs like Soar, Adam shows how Soar explicitly uses Newell and Simon's language of goals, scripts, and plans (and, I would add, implicitly maps the Flower and Hayes early models of the composing process). As Adam states, "This [the Newell and Simon view co-opted by recent AI research] assumes that actors will break down the problem into smaller problems by setting up subgoals to overcome difficulties in almost any domain of reasoning. For instance, this approach cannot deal with the human propensity at times to take an imaginative leap in order to solve a problem; what is sometimes called 'lateral thinking'" (p. 123).

Adam's summary of her philosophical critique of AI demonstrates how that critique is constructed against "the cognitivist programme—the computational metaphor of mind" (1998, p. 61) and reasserts the importance of views of philosophers "…from at least Mary Hesse (1970) onwards, [who] have long since abandoned the notion that there are independent observations of the real world to be had, arguing instead that all our observations are mediated by our theories of the world" (Adam, 1998, p. 86). Adam's work is extremely important in building an understanding of why many AI projects—which attempt to model the architecture of mind and the representations stored there, like secondhand furniture in the attic—are fatally flawed from the start.

A reader's sense of the scripted rigidity of interactive fiction and her problematic ethical engagement of stories like those by Infocom and Oz is a result of the shifting materiality of these texts, and especially of the ways that that materiality is inflected by an Objectivist epistemology. As Bates (1990) composes against the interactive fiction genre as it currently exists, and as he works toward richly modeled, "subjective" interactions between story and user, he is implicitly reacting against earlier interactive fictions that were more tightly linked to an Objectivist view of user, text, and world. Nonetheless, the Oz Project may be simply substituting a new version of that epistemology, one just presented in ways richer, deeper, and more complicated, but ultimately still problematic.

Commercial interactive fictions rely on an Objectivist epistemology that posits a universe univocal, monolithic, and describable. Readers of interactive fictions, of course, chafe against this characterization of the world, and some readers experience an ethical discomfort in their scripted encounters. An Objectivist paradigm still underlies the Oz Project's implicit model of the reader–text interaction, and that paradigm ultimately limits the activities of the readers of Oz's stories and prevents an adequate illusion of participation. This Objectivist epistemology is operating within these stories in the theories or "metaknowledge" that they use to guide their plots, characters, and processes of composing as well as in the literal layers of overlapping programs (the binary digits and the layered computer programs, rules, scripts, propositions, and instructions). An analysis of the layered composing process underlying a reader's experience of Oz's interactive fictions reveals an Objectivist understanding of reading that operates much like that which is attached to models of Infocom's commercial interactive fictions. This Objectivism operates by ignoring the various locations of the specific reader (in Infocom's implicit construal of one ideal reader, for example) and conceiving of the process of reading as one of coding and uncoding a single true text. Despite the flexibility, complementary divergence, and overlap of the Oz Project's layered programs, the epistemology underlying Oz still privileges a singular model of reader and reality, one that theorists in composition and rhetoric, as well as Alison Adam, have repeatedly shown to be patently false.

This Objectivist epistemology is also apparent in the Oz Project's implicit theory of drama and in its conception of the relationship between story and discourse. The Objectivist epistemology, as summarized below, clearly informs the composing process of the Oz project:

> as a set of shared commonplaces in our culture, [Objectivism] takes the following general form: The world consists of objects that have properties and stand in various rela-

tionships independent of human understanding. The world is as it is, no matter what any person happens to believe about it, and there is one correct "God's-Eye-View" about what the world is really like. In other words, there is a rational structure to reality, independent of the beliefs of any particular people, and correct reason mirrors this rational structure. (Johnson, 1987, p. x)

Bates (1990) reveals the Objectivist epistemology underlying this "metaknowledge" not only in his presentation of world but also in his conception of narration as a transparent presentation of world. Oz, like Infocom's interactive fictions, shares the limitation of seeing language as transparent, neutral, and, in essence, nonrhetorical; language is just another set of symbols that can be matched easily to a preexisting, singular world. In one CMU CS technical report, Smith and Bates (1989) try to utilize some of the techniques of filmmaking, seeing the essential relationship between constructed world and telling that world as one controlled by simple editing. The notion of words constructing worlds is utterly lost. In Smith and Bates's adaptation of "basic cinema techniques" to explore how they might be translated into narrative techniques in interactive fiction, he and Smith discuss how to transform the following techniques in filmmaking: lap dissolve, close-ups, repetitions, flashbacks, and zoom-freeze. Smith and Bates explore particularly the means filmmakers use to connect a world model and the narrated version of that world (yet again, a dualistic split between story and narration that is related to Chatman's (1978) distinction between story and discourse). In their conception of the possibility of a cinematic technique in interactive fictions, they reveal their epistemological predisposition to construe knowledge as universal, the world as monolithic, viewpoint as camera angle, and discourse as the straightforward reflection of reality. Their models do not adequately allow for the notion that worlds are coconstructed in a relationship between the individual (a problematic concept itself) and the world around her. The ways Oz and other interactive fictions implicitly conceive of the relation between text and reader misses the insights that language speaks us as much as we speak it, and that all human discourses are idiosyncratic, partial, and dynamically composed versions of a multivocalic, multicultural, and multimodal world.

An Objectivist epistemology is also operating within the very material of these presentations of story. The binary, digitized programs that comprise the lowest-level subtext of interactive fictions is a material that limits subjective interactions between fiction and user, between objects in the story and reader predilection. A simple example of the inflexibility (or difficulty because of sheer possibility) of programming objects can be heard in the words of an interactive fiction programmer as he discusses the difficulties of modeling rope in his story (Sloane, 1991). David Graves, an interactive fiction programmer at Interactive Fantasies, and Tim Brengle, a writer, were arguing over the relative dramatic benefit of any given "story element" versus the difficulty of implementing it in software. Graves explained:

For example, in a puzzle-based game you need a strong software model of the physical world. Some things such as modeling rope can get very complicated. A rope, for example, can have two ends that are located in different places, such as different rooms. Things can be tied to one end or the other with all sorts of complicated physics implied to the reader. Allowing the reader to express his own creativity in terms of using the rope becomes very complicated. At this point, the programmer may ask the writer, Is the rope essential to this part of the drama? (personal communication, April 1991)

Presumably, if the writer says yes, then that rope will be modeled after the programmer's sense of what rope is and does, as that sense is constrained by the requirements of the game. Because of the way computer programmers thus constrain their models of objects in the physical world, the reader's experience is constrained in ways more visible and more frustrating than in conventional fiction. A reader could not macramé a basket from that rope unless the programmer has foreseen that possibility and allowed for it in his world model. And the nostalgia associated with macramé today, for example, would not be conveyed at all. Readers of interactive fiction in general are constrained from idiosyncratic or novel interactions with objects and characters, and stories suffer as a result.

How detective stories, such as the Oz Project's detective fiction, Mike Oliphant's "Gumshoe," or Infocom's *Deadline*, fall flat, I believe, is in their limited recognition of the range and depth of the rhetoric (and dialectic) possible in interactive fiction. These stories too clearly rely on an epistemological basis and knowledge of rhetorical range that simply does not live up to the requirements of a convincing story. Researchers like Rosalind Picard might urge programmers to build applications that better represent emotions, moods, and human affective expression; however, she relies, too, on the naive notion that words alone, without a context, can relay feelings. Researchers described in Picard's *Affective Computing* (1998) search for the set of human physiological signals (heart rate, skin conductivity, mannerisms, and gait, for example) that best intimate human emotional reaction. Picard confuses the sign for the thing, not realizing that thing itself does not exist outside of language.

In recent years, the Oz Project has been relying more on the possibilities of animated fictions, studying not only the techniques of cinema, but the tricks and tips of Disney animators, past and present. (Picard [1998], for example, mentions the influence of Disney animation on Oz productions). Joseph Bates and Scott Neal Reilly (see Reilly, 1996) worked together to construct characters (including a cat with the fetching name, Lyotard) that represented clearly distinct emotional states. As Picard (1998) explains, within the broader architecture of the Oz Project is "an underlying emotion generation system" called Em that is based on the widely used "OCC" cognitive model. (This OCC model for how emotions work was published in 1988 by Ortony, Clore, and Collins in the book *The Cognitive Structure of Emotions* and is popular among artificial intelligence enthusiasts because it offers a framework and analysis of emotion that is very easily implemented in AI programming languages like LISP.) I would argue that the implementation of systems like Em are additional evidence of AI's failure to grasp the complexity and context-dependence of human qualities, language, and feelings.[22] Picard explains that the OCC model evolved from the idea that "they believed AI systems must be able to reason about emotions" (p. 195). Another researcher, Aaron Sloman, a philosopher at the University of Birmingham in the UK, conjectures that we have three "architectural layers" in our brains—a reactive layer, a deliberative layer, and a self-monitoring layer—all three of which "can be categorized loosely according to their evolutionary age," a model that Picard generously views as another potentially important possibility for AI modeling of emotion (pp. 211–212). According to Picard,

> The OCC model addresses the problem of representing emotions not by using sets of basic emotions, or by using an explicitly dimensioned space, but, by grouping emotions according to cognitive eliciting conditions. In particular, it assumes that emotions arise from valenced (positive or negative) reactions to situations consisting of events, agents, and objects. With this structure, Ortony, Clore, and Collins outlined specifications for 22 emotion types.... Additionally, they included a rule-based system for the generation of these emotion types. (p. 196)

The Oz Project's broadest architecture is intended to integrate emotion with the overall goals, intentions, perceptions, and language of their computer-generated characters (or "believable agents"). Scott Reilly's 1996 thesis outlines the default hierarchy of emotions in EM (see Figure 3.4).

Explicitly relying on the OCC model of 22 emotions in the underlying architecture of Em, Reilly's model of affect emphasizes "cognitive appraisal for emotion generation" (Picard, 1998, p. 200), which, said another way, emphasizes thinking first and reacting emotionally second. In Picard's and Reilly's discussions of the ways Em implements emotions within the larger architectures of Oz, they explain the ways Em's rules affect cognitions and behavior of characters in the fictive world:

> In Em's default emotion system, the emotions have intensities that are influenced by the importance of the goal that generated them. Each emotion also has a threshold, and only when its intensity exceeds this threshold does the emotion influence any outward behavior. Em also explicitly models emotion decay, where each emotion has its intensity lowered every clock cycle, until the intensity is zero. (Picard, 1998, p. 202)

Reilly, like other researchers profiled by Picard, implicitly relies on a view that emotion is a cognitive activity, a kind of negative or positive feedback registered in the brain. As Picard (1998) herself writes, "[W]hen it comes to synthesizing emotion, different components are likely to require different mechanisms, like in the human brain, where we know fear blazes its own fast path through the limbic system, while emotions like hope are believed to be more cortical" (p. 225). So, Emily Dickinson got it wrong after all. Hope is not "the thing with feathers/That perches in the soul,/And sings the tune without the words,/And never stops at all..." Hope is cortical.

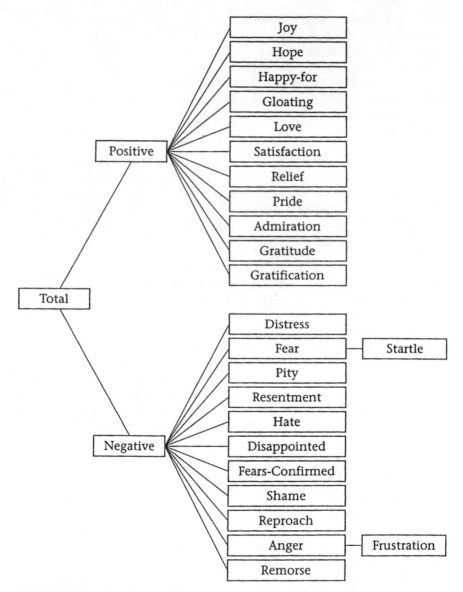

FIGURE 3.4. The default hierarchy of emotions in Em. Reprinted by permission from Reilly (1996).

One innovation of Reilly's model or emotional architecture is the way in which it permits agents to generate new goals and behaviors, depending on the level and typology of emotion "experienced" by the agent (in other words, by the ways in which temperament is encoded):

> For example, in an office situation, one character might become so angry at another that she generates a goal to get revenge. Another character might be so happy that he generates a goal to go dancing. (Picard, 1998, p. 202)

This innovation is an important advance into modeling emotion, and Reilly's thesis ultimately complements recent work by Phoebe Sengers, as well as promises one of the best innovations of the Oz Project as a whole. (Sengers's 1998 thesis, *Anti-Boxology: Agent Design in Cultural Context,* suggests a new agent architecture, "the Expressivator," which "provides support for narratively comprehensible agents," and which creates "behavioral transitions" to "link atomic [presumably isolate modules] behaviors into narrative sequences" (p. iii). Sengers has undertaken interesting work in "socially situated AI," a subfield she named to work on the problem of agent interaction as well as internal agent structure. In her recent thesis, Sengers proposes

> taking seriously the idea that the social and cultural environment of the agent can also be, not just a distracting factor in the design and analysis of agents, but a valuable resource for it. I coined the term "socially situated AI" for this method of agent research. (p. 94)

Sengers is attempting to bring the insight of cultural theory to play in the analysis of agent design, and the dynamics of that design as it interacts with its physical and social environments.

However, this interesting work to date by Reilly and Sengers does not solve yet another AI problem of modeling thought and emotion through behavior. One of the mundane problems faced by scientists who explicitly follow the computational theory of mind or feeling in their AI research is the simple problem of timing and reaction, or determining when a computer must sort through goals and subgoals, plans and scripts, before it finally fires back a response. As Adam (1998) cautions in her discussion of situated robotics,

> Rather than the impossible task of decomposing the world into bite-sized concepts and recomputing the model every time it changes (described as the "frame" problem in AI), we should look at defining the problem in relation to the world-for-the-agent which can change even if the world-in-itself remains the same. One of the virtues of doing things this way is that robots [or other agents in AI] need not be designed to plan their actions before executing them, which necessarily makes them slow to respond to the unexpected while they rethink their plans of action, a style of interaction sometimes termed the "Hamlet syndrome." (p. 145)

So far, the members of the Oz Project team, including Sengers and Reilly, have not yet accomplished building emotional, believable characters that act in real-time in convincing and engaging ways. (Of course, when Joe Bates and his team do accomplish such a goal, they will have passed the Turing Test.) But they have made some very interesting steps toward such a goal.

One of Reilly's most interesting literary experiments at Carnegie Mellon University was a digital fiction much like *Deadline* or the Oz Project's own early mystery, *Tea for Two*. However, even in Reilly's innovative mystery, which relied on some of the concepts that underlie Em, like most text adventures to date, falls short of offering the narrative enjoyment of mysteries by P.D. James, Josephine Tey, Barbara Vine, or even Edgar Allen Poe. While writing a detective story certainly has wide appeal among computer scientists, researchers, and cognitive psychologists, none that I have seen realizes the suspense and dramatic tension of the conventional mystery's linear plot, accrual of detail and discoveries, psychological tension, red herrings, climactic moments, and satisfying dénouements. While the cognitive scientist's language of mechanisms, protocols, plays, and goals would seem to translate well to a computer's construction of stories, in fact the implementation of such language (and the concepts it embodies) reveals itself as inferior to nearly any dime novel, for many of the reasons already discussed. Nonetheless, in its innovations, Reilly's research represents an important departure for the Oz Project.

Detective stories in particular may be paradoxically difficult to make digital and interactive. As Walter Ong observed in another context, "[d]etective-story plots are deeply interior in that a full closure is commonly achieved inside the mind of one of the characters first and then diffused to the reader and the other fictional characters" (1982, p. 149). Perhaps the real problem of relying on an Objectivist paradigm for the programs and architectures of the Oz Project's fictions is that in its rush to explicitly model the components of world, agent, and feeling, its gestures are coded always in the anterior, the prior, the world of making sign fit thing, and are rarely if ever coded with an eye to how they might be received, actualized, or made interior to the reader. How are these architectures or structures internalized by the reader? How do they motivate her? What rhetorical strategy is fostered by this particular character, sequence of events, phrases? The illusion of engagement is repeatedly disrupted because these questions are not adequately considered in the computer generation of stories.

IMPLICATIONS

In the past, reading was a matter of responding to a locked visual field, a habit of responding silently, within one's own skull and body, to a prefigured text. (One did also respond aloud, of course, under one's breath or to friends in casual conversations, but today, unless one is a professional reviewer or an academic, the traditional engagement with text is more private than public.) More often than not, traditional readings did not allow an active, visible rendering of the reader's presence in the text. Reading was a matter of the eye, not the hand or pen, and early interactive fictions are important precisely because of how they change that traditional alignment between reader and read. The materials of interactive fiction change the nature of the relationship between readers and stories so that reading becomes a public and responsive act of visibly inscribing self on text.

To return to a theme raised earlier in my discussion of Infocom's stories, the dissonance between implicit and explicit textual gaps in digital texts represents one aspect of a reader's unsatisfying experience of interactive fiction—as well as prefiguring some of the failings of an Objectivist paradigm. Gaps operate on two opposing levels in interactive fiction: implicit and explicit, or semantic and textual. The dissonance between these two kinds of gaps occur when, during the process of reading, the reader's questions about the progress of the text do not coincide with the gap inviting the reader to respond, and when the reader's interior experience diverges from what the representations in the text visibly ask. When the implicit gaps in the reader's understanding are in dissonance with these explicit gaps on the screen, the illusion of participation is ruptured, and a reader is left struggling palpably to make sense of the text. Interactive fictions fail to truly make accommodations for the variety of reading responses and various understandings of the world readers bring to texts. By offering only trivial options to readers, the text fails to live up to its claim of interactivity.

Debates about the problems of an Objectivist epistemology currently rage in a variety of fields, and insights from these other fields aid in a critique of the composing processes and materials of digital fictions. In contrast to these systems' codification of a single world inhabited by predictable creatures and knowable architectures of kind and meaning, opponents of the Objectivist epistemology in other disciplines suggest an opposing need to consider the context or background knowledge of the person (user, reader, or writer) engaged with the story. Within the field of artificial intelligence, particularly, the Objectivist epistemology has been criticized in several articles about the computational model of mind (Dreyfus, 1992; West & Travis, 1991), but nonetheless computer scientists return to it, both for its convenience and the mirage of its comprehensiveness. These critiques explain that the central metaphor of artificial intelligence is the flawed conception that intelligence is "a kind of mechanism—a subtle and complex processing of information." (Johnson, 1987, p. 16).[23] Two important critics of the present computational metaphor of mind, David West and Larry Travis, claim that a "methodological Cartesian dualism" is a necessary precondition to conceiving of computers as deep simulations of thinking, and that such dualism is by its very construction flawed. This Cartesian dualism within mainstream artificial intelligence models sees that "our brains themselves are machines" (Kurzweil, 1990, p. 214). Or, as Kurzweil states more succinctly, "while certainly very complex, our brains are clearly governed by the same physical laws as our machines" (p. 13). Picard, Reilly, Bates, Flower and Hayes, and other cognitive scientists are likely to take a similar position. Opponents (such as Dreyfus) of the current artificial intelligence models of mind, while quick to criticize sharply the materials and goals of interactive fiction, are much less clear in their suggestions of alternative metaphors or methods for understanding and modeling mind.

The debate between Objectivists and social constructionists in general is furthered by the heated discussion between artificial intelligence's champions and founders (Newell & Simon, 1972; Pylyshyn, 1984) and its critics (Dreyfus, 1992; Haugeland, 1985; Putnam, 1983; Weizenbaum, 1976; and others). While it is not my intent here to enter substantively into this general debate, artificial intelligence's working model of the process of reading is certainly relevant to an examination of interactive fiction, especially in its failure to model context-dependent reader response. This failure is made explicit in computer science's concepts of scripts, plans, and goals (here summarized by Kurzweil [1990]) and the discipline's general disregard for effects of context that cannot easily be modeled in present architectures.[24] Kurzweil writes,

> If we consider carefully the process of reading and understanding printed language, it becomes clear that we are dealing with a multiplicity of talents: at the character level, pattern recognition; at the word level, the syntactic analysis of word sequences; and at the higher levels, the decoding of semantics, the retrieval and updating of our knowledge base, and an understanding of "scripts" about the subject matter being written about, to name only a few of the intelligent processes involved. (p. 145)

As is typical in current artificial intelligence models of human behavior, neither Kurzweil (1990) nor Schank (1990) consider the much larger levels of cultural, social, and historical contexts operating in our understanding of printed language. Even the apparently promising alternative metaphor of "connectionism" offered briefly by West and Travis (1991) and discussed at greater length by Obermeier (1989), fails to make the much larger and more important step to acknowledging the effects of context on the way neural networks model knowledge.

Finally, although interactive fictions like *Deadline* (1991) claim to be open to many readings (*you* write the story, *you* solve the mystery, *you* interrogate the characters) and readers (*you* are the detective), as Adam (1998) discusses in reference to symbolic AI projects like Cyc and Soar, the knowledge architectures that underlie games like Infocom's and story generation projects like Oz implicitly assume a subject who is a masculinist rationalist idea. Even when these games or stories claim that the subject (or reader or interactant) is not explicitly defined, still they deny "the possibility of a genuinely pluralistic discourse..." (Adam, 1998, p. 179). What Adam sees in Cyc and Soar, I see in Oz and Infocom. The primary researchers and graduate students of the Oz Project are predominantly well-educated, middle-class men, and our culture's notion of masculinity cannot help but infuse their standpoints and models, no matter how much each individual participant might work hard to overcome stereotypes and gender conditioning.

Although clearly an advance over commercially available interactive fiction, the knowledge structures and architectures of the layered programs of Oz, as formulated by Bates and his research team, still fail to provide sufficient accommodation of the rich variation in human understanding, gendered and otherwise, a failure I would link, again, to the limiting influence of the Objectivist epistemology underlying its conception—and materials—of fiction. A epistemological model different from Objectivism would help projects like Oz to provide more satisfying fictive worlds for their users. Such a new epistemology would explore more comprehensively how interactive fiction's stories, and their digitizations of plot, character, and participants, can adequately engage and represent different readers.

Readers of interactive fiction need representations of reality and of themselves within the fictive world that are polycentric, polysemantic, and polysemic and that allow for the idea that mental representations of text and world are dissonant and conflicting. Programmers of interactive fiction need a crash course in semiotics, and need to consider more seriously the insights of cultural studies, social constructionism, and reader-response theories. Instead of relying on an Objectivist epistemology to inform their models and systems, interactive fictions should be grounded in an epistemology that acknowledges no single "ideal" reader and that recognizes that neither self nor knowledge is unified, universal, or context-independent. When we read and write digital fictions, we need to engage with models of reader, story, and world that open up to us and explicitly accommodate our idiosyncratic understandings; we need stories that live up to their explicit invitations to engage our imaginations. When we finally encounter truly interactive stories that will accommodate the anxieties, idiosyncrasies, and pleasures of users embarked on itinerant readings, we will have jettisoned the computational model of mind and the Objectivist paradigm it codifies. We might even contribute to the critique of faculty philosophy, begun by Mark Johnson in his influential *The Body in the Mind* (1987) and continued by Mark Johnson and George Lakoff's *Philosophy in the Flesh* (1999), in which we see we can build no metaphor nor have thoughts and ideas that are not themselves directly tied to our body's ways of being in the world. The new digital fiction must more actively seek to accommodate multiple interpretations, plural worldviews, and bodied interpretations, especially interpretations not foreseen by either writer or programmer, but that are actively invoked by readers engaged by particular rhetorical strategies.

The key point for contemporary programmers and composers of interactive fiction, then, is that the richest texts are those that have the most depth, offering a variety of roles for their reader-characters to "play," and granting a wide range of options to the reader to influence sequence and event, to allow her to honestly (or dishonestly and every version of reliability in between) converse with the story and characters. From a viewpoint both feminist and semiotic, the stories that follow these guidelines will be the best interactive fictions because they will provide room for the greatest range of response amongst a group of readers. These new interactive fictions will function as semiotic phenomena that will offer many avenues of interaction for all readers, that may match a living Reader with her Semiotic Being seamlessly and compellingly.

Today, most commercially available interactive fictions are impoverished texts that at best raise ethical questions, and, more typically, disappoint their readers. The tasks that they ask of their readers are not emotionally engaging nor fully satisfying in any way. I encourage designers of interactive fiction to move away from these diminished models of reading, reader, and text, models I see as limited because they are linked to Objectivism, and toward stories that are rich not only in their density and subjectivity, but that are novel in the subjects they explore, flexible in their creations of the relation between reader and reader-representative, and unconventional in the roles they offer readers and the stories they tell. Such rich stories will naturally evolve, I believe, as designers make the move toward building story generation systems that rely on a synthesized, more comprehensive epistemology, one that understands the influence of context not as simple variable or calculated permutation, but as the source of metaphysical complexity, linguistic invention, and personal meaning.

MATERIALS AS CRITICAL CATEGORY

...the question is not whether we will ever build machines that will think like people but whether people have always thought like machines.

—Raymond Kurzweil (1990)

Writing material is not neutral; it can shape and influence the development of scripts in matters of general appearance, the way individual signs are formed, and also as far as the direction of writing is concerned. It also frequently exercises a decisive influence on the shape of the "book" (palm leaves used predominantly in South and Southeast Asia dictate an oblong shape, for example). Moreover, once a particular convention has been established it will often remain, even progress further in the same direction, long after it has been replaced by an entirely different type of material (the oblong shape of paper manuscripts or copper plates in India, etc.). The material also predetermines to a large extent the instruments necessary for writing, and vice versa. The stone-cutter needs different tools and his tools create shapes different from those made by pen or brush on the soft surface of paper or papyrus.

—Albertine Gaur (1984)

Historian Albertine Gaur's (1984) insight that there is a direct relationship between the materials of writing and the messages conveyed (and the genres created) is a crucial understanding that has been noted in passing by both historians of writing and rhetorical theorists. Henri-Jean Martin has recently detailed a fascinating account of the development of writing, noting its roots in patterns of royal divination and economic record-keeping, and questioning the relations between writing and its material contexts. Martin explicitly notes the connection between the materiality of texts and the messages they convey:

> Writing systems are not disembodied, and written messages from past times are objects that speak more than one language. Dug out from the soil, discovered in tombs, or transmitted from generation to generation, they often seem odd to us and a

far cry from our modern books. By their very aspect they remind us that the shape of written signs depends on the material on which they are written. When signs are written with care they attest to an interest in proclamation and durability; when they are cursive they show that a society was familiar with writing. When they are laid out without separations they remind us that our modern page layouts are recent acquisitions. When they are written on scrolls the text unfolds like a film. (1994, p. 43)

In general, we can learn from the historians of writing, some rhetorical theorists, and many critics of symbolic AI, that we must attend to the materials of writing if we are to understand fully the intersections of context and substance, of rhetoric and world. Such a materialist analysis is necessarily political as well, since we must also understand how some particular contexts of power, gender, and economics intersect with who gets to write what story on which surface. Whether we note that the shift from papyrus to parchment was driven in part by Europe's desire to escape an Egyptian monopoly on the production of writing materials, or that the Chinese emperor Fu Hsi contributed to the origins of writing in his practice of divination by casting yarrow stalks, we need to acknowledge that the stories printed on top of a medial plane are just one of the most visible stories buried in the materials of discursive exchanges.

Telling stories is an essential part of being human, and creating narratives about ourselves and our worlds is an activity that has taken place in almost every conceivable setting: around campfires, in monasteries, in outdoor rituals, in caves and cafeterias, in libraries attached to temples and palaces, and, more recently, in university computing labs around the world. Telling stories is an activity that has been transacted also across a wide variety of media: from terra-cotta tablets to palm leaves; from wooden cups to Druid tree-alphabets; from cloth textiles to Mide songboards; from bones and bamboo to papyrus and pixels. When we read, for example, the images of the Phaistos disk[25] against the digitized graphics and fiction of *The Blue Penny Quarterly*, an e-zine distributed on the World Wide Web, we are comparing two different instances of one of the oldest activities on earth: storytelling. The Phaistos disk and the online literary quarterly are different not only in the actual *material* of their story delivery systems, but also in their oblique record of differences in technological ability, attitude toward natural resources, and shared cultural perspectives of what should be recorded, who should do the recording, and how that record should be disseminated. There are widely divergent attitudes, too, toward the relative importance of portability and durability of story, of the relations between hands and reading and writing, and the importance of remembering. When we explore representations of story as they exist in clay and cyberspace, when we want to understand fully the repercussions of medium on mimesis, we must attend to the *materials* of story transactions.

In her 1989 article "Cognition, Context, and Theory-building," Linda Flower proposes building theories based on observations, which become the basis for a comprehensive knowledge of writers and their situations, and observations that add to the specific knowledge that is a necessary component of "grounding and testing a developing theory within its own framework" (p. 284). Flower acknowledges the earlier work of Lauer and Asher on building theories of composing and "the rhetoric of inquiry" as she forges her own two-pronged approach to developing appropriate models: she encourages our community of researchers to engage in a *method* of building a theory from empirical observations; and she encourages our community away from divisive, insular models of composing processes and toward a *model* and an "interactive theory" that will evenly account for the constructive, cooperative, and mutually mediating influences of cognition and context on the acts of writing. Flower suggests that observation-based theory building will strengthen our ability to make claims about what happens when people write:

> Observation-based theory is built from the union of two sources of evidence: it springs in part from an intuition or argument and in part from the complementary evidence of close, systematic observation and data. (p. 297)

Flower's (1989) path away from false dichotomies of cognition and context and toward an understanding of how they might together influence writing processes is a necessary corrective to some of her early, and still important, attempts to understand what writers do when they compose. Flower and others have implicitly called into question the information-processing models upon which both text adventures and Flower's earlier theories are based. I applaud her efforts to construct a combined cognitivist-constructionist model that acknowledges the powerful and profound influences of social context as well as cognition on the collaborations and layered materials of composing ideas, stories, and knowledge on paper and screen. While Flower and Hayes do not ultimately achieve the synthesis to which they aspired, their attempts are a useful beginning. Ultimately, however, the materials of text adventures and the actions and underlying architectures of graphical agents like the Woggles demand a new theory of writing, one that is both descriptive and prognostic, that bases its claims on close readings of work like that done by the Oz Project, as well as divines where existing models of the composing process might be expanded.

Interactive fiction performs visibly, on a screen right before "your" eyes, a dynamic illustration of the post-structuralist preoccupation with the fragmentation of subject, the death of the univocal author and the objective text, and the competing, dissonant contexts of reading and writing acts. The visible contests between the interactive fiction reader (as she constructs the story) and author (as facilitated by a dynamic text and its underlying layers of instructions) add to the mounting evidence in favor of post-structuralist—and feminist—interpretations of text-making activities. Interactive fictions, like those produced by Infocom, demonstrate vividly that within freedom lies responsibilities. The failed contests between the novice-detective of *Deadline* (1991) and its resistant text that will not yield crucial clues when addressed in the wrong syntax, for example, demonstrate visibly the dissonant contexts between readers and authors. In fact, close readings of interactive fictions like *A Mind Forever Voyaging* (1991), *Nord and Burt* (1991), or *Plundered Hearts* (1991) contribute to the post-structuralist critical enterprise of redefining the rhetorical triangle.

One specific insight into the experience of reading and writing that interactive fiction in particular pressures us toward in considering a newly configured rhetorical model is, again, this primary insight that the *materials* of discourse matter. These stories are brittle or rigid despite their seeming openness because of the epistemology encoded in the materials of their discourse. They inadequately consider the varied locations of their readers, as evidenced by the rigid gender identifications of "you" in *Leather Goddesses of Phobos* (1991), the reader's rigid characterization as a sentient computer in *A Mind Forever Voyaging* (1991), and the reader's frustratingly limited range of actions available in the *Zork* trilogy. However, while writers and programmers may do well to reconsider their system design in light of some of the alternative epistemologies of social constructionism, feminism, or even postmodernism, such epistemologies are also an inadequate basis for a theoretical model that would encompass most facets of writing. The rhetorical model that encompasses interactive fiction must be built on both realist and social-constructionist epistemologies and more, both to capture the dynamism of the layered materials underlying writing, as discussed in this chapter, and to encompass the kinds and processes of readings engendered by digital fictions, like the hypertext fictions discussed in Chapter 4.

Interactive fiction changes our sense of reading because it makes the histories, intents, and designs of its programmers palpably visible. Its textual form puts pressure on the rhetorical triangle because the roles of author and the reader overlap and become mixed. In addition to its pressure on the spatial metaphor of the rhetorical triangle, interactive fiction exerts pressure on the traditional temporal relationship suggested by the existing lineaments of the rhetorical triangle. On one level, this seems a simple observation of the synchronous composing processes of reader and author of digital texts. But a closer examination of this medium's built-in capacity for dynamically linked coauthorings shows that the new temporal relationship between readers and writers has important consequences for authorial control over order, sequence, and content, and that has grave consequences for our models as well. What anterior, what posterior?

To summarize, models of communicative transactions between readers and writers in the past have been based on how those relationships are transacted over the paper text, particularly across the plane of the pages of a codex book. Because interactive fiction shifts the location of the communicative transaction to the computer, with unpredictable consequences, earlier models do not fully account for this new version of a traditional rhetorical relationship. In the "end," digital fiction requires a model of rhetorical transactions that describes both the Objectivist theories underlying its programs, architectures, epistemologies, and knowledge structures and the social constructionist theories that provide the best current explanation for a reader's various frustrations with the digital. Walter Ong (1982) reminds us that Homer was likely to think of words, too, not as quiescent phenomena, nor as simple signs or visible renderings of the oral. Instead, says Ong, Homer would have referred to the signs and symbols of writing "as 'winged words'—which suggests evanescence, power and freedom: words are constantly moving, but by flight, which is a powerful form of movement, and [by] lifting the flier free of the ordinary, gross, heavy, 'objective' world" (p. 77). But when we come back to reality, nay, to our respective realities, what do we do when we cannot find the world? When all that we have to connect ourselves with others is our words? And when others attempt to impose their language on us in ways that are hard to resist?

We should understand text adventures like those discussed here, as providing a new site for an old discussion of how readers and writers interact within the shifting boundaries of texts in general. The symbols writ "in silico" on a computer screen are themselves evanescent and mysterious, as are all the writing spaces, materials, and interstitial rhetorics such screen space reveals. Within the parts of this screen space, within the contrasts of the soma that exists and the soma imagined, the text that exists and the text that might just as well be there, we researchers can observe a visible clash between two competing epistemologies, social constructionism and Objectivism, and, through the dust raised by that clash, see how these digital fictions radically reconfigure hypotheses about reading and composing meaning.

4

The Process of Composing Digital Fictions*

COMPUTING FICTIONS

—I look up the etymology of Iris and find
this unreliable center of an eye
is kin to wire, garland, seaweed, sinew,
flower, a goddess tuning out and in
to build stories from hollow and root.

My closed eye turns to considering
the difference between garland and sinew,
flower and eye, the etymologies of being
so clearly tied up in seeing

and the zero finds the one
and a current lights the still air
and a wind rises littered with sticks and seeds
and the eye opens again.

---

* The first thinking I did toward some of the ideas presented in this chapter was in a paper called "Exploring the New Narrative for Computer Fictions: E.M. Forster and the Interactive Story," which I delivered in a panel sponsored by the Writing Division, National Broadcast Educators' Association, April 13, 1996, Las Vegas, Nevada.

QUESTIONS ABOUT READING AND MEANING

I need to get a laptop. This pencil is too slow.

—Andy Volk, college junior

"The only exact knowledge there is," said Anatole France, "Is the knowledge of the date of publication and the format of books."

—Walter Benjamin (1955/1988)

You may move through the story by pressing the Return key to go from one section to another. Should you lose your way in In Small & Large Pieces, *pressing Return repeatedly will eventually bring you to a table of contents, helping you to regain your bearings.*

—"Getting Started" (1994)

I hope to meet you someday, FTF.

—Michael Joyce, personal communication, 1998

to the bacteria, tumblebugs, scavengers, wordsmiths—the transfigurers, restorers

—A.R. Ammons (1993)

What is it about hypertext fictions that makes some readers find them so fundamentally dissatisfying? Why is it that *writers* of hypertext fictions are often the only *readers* who find the genre appealing? Why do some critics rage so vehemently against hypertext stories, seeing in their ascendancy the demise of meaning, narrative, the literary canon, even Western civilization itself? When hypertext fiction writers like Carolyn Guyer and Martha Petry discuss their work in the magazine *Writing on the Edge,* for example, their words express a degree of satisfaction and sheer pleasure in the stories they have made that is rarely expressed by their readers. (Robert Coover's 1993 essay in *The New York Times* is one notable exception.) In their "directions" to their hypertext fiction *Izme Pass,* for example, Guyer and Petry write:

> This is a new kind of fiction, and a new kind of reading. The form of the text is rhythmic, looping on itself in patterns and layers that gradually accrete meaning, just as the passage of time and events does in one's lifetime. Trying the textlinks embedded within the work will bring the narrative together in new configurations, fluid constellations formed by the path of your interest. The difference between reading hyperfiction and reading traditional printed fiction may be the difference between sailing the islands and standing on the dock watching the sea. (pp. 82–83)

While Guyer and Petry go on to explain that "[o]ne [method of reading] is not better than the other" (p. 83) within their own hypertext fictions, their preliminary directions to the reader, and the critical postures they assume in their own valuations of hypertext fictions, these writers implicitly express a preference for hypertextual discourse. Guyer and Petry share with many other hypertext fiction writers (including Michael Joyce, Stuart Moulthrop, and M.D. Coverley, for example) an intensely felt engagement in this new textual form, one that Coverley (1998) says "morphs" from genre to genre, one that Guyer says allows writers to compose "rich fields of complexity," (qtd. in Joyce, 1995, p. 89) and allows readers to explore parallel lives in multilinear, achronological fictions. My guess is that the more commonly held critical dissatisfaction with hypertext fictions springs from disappointment in a form that was, in fact, never intended to satisfy what traditional readers and critics wish to read. Instead, hypertext fiction should be read as the latest in a long line of artistic experiments, a lineage that includes metafictions, Dadaist compositions, Oulipian games, and *ars combinatoria*, as discussed in earlier chapters. On the other hand, on those rare occasions when readers express their satisfaction with hypertext fictions, that satisfaction directly corresponds to the heightened pleasure they feel upon discovering textual innovation and the new reading process such innovation requires. As Joyce and Moulthrop discuss below, sometimes that new reading process requires an entirely new way of understanding self and world, a change in perspective that is, in essence, a paradigm shift. In short, when we weigh the negative critical and readerly responses to hypertext fictions against the stated creative intentions of these fictions' authors, we can more precisely locate the source of their critics' discomfort.

The plaints and grumblings of traditional readers like Sven Birkerts as they encounter hypertext fictions like Stuart Moulthrop's *Victory Garden* (1991) are centered primarily on the traditional concerns of literary criticism, including taste, value, and propriety, and an Arnoldian conservatism that seeks to reconstitute traditional alignments of education, art, the subject, and the obligations and duties of an educated citizen. These concerns are not new. They are concerns addressed by the Edinburgh literati of the 18th-century Scottish Enlightenment, and later developed in the curricula of American universities in the late 18th and early 19th centuries, and only most recently challenged by clashes between the literati and digerati in the late 20th century. Literary critics like Sven Birkerts (1995) are asking about questions of taste, canon, and propriety, and are applying traditional notions of the sublime, grandeur, structure, and form to digital texts because those texts offer a new site for an old battle: the debate about what constitutes the individual, or, in the language of Zavarzadeh and Morton (1991), the crisis of the subject. In particular, the negative critical valuation of much of the creative work of hypertext authors composing today derives from applying a critical apparatus and posture designed to elevate the taste and propriety of print reading habits, American middle-class views and values, and a free market economy that privileges the status quo.

I posit that hypertext fictions in fact are the latest version of a critique posed against dominant cultural values, values implicit in our publishing industries, processes of disseminating texts, and patterns of reception, not to mention in our traditional rhetorical models and ideas of author, authority, and what we *do* when we read. Birkerts (1995) and critics like him offer their blanket rejection of digital fictions because of their ideological biases more than from an honest dislike of a new form. The ways in which hypertext fictions implicitly attack realism, shake up usual categories, reject the conventional, and decenter author and authority may indeed shake up the *status quo*—and the hierarchies of class and habits of consumption that dominate today. Birkert's nostalgia is actually entrenchment, a yearning for the days when the subject was intact and hierarchies static, when the art of writing fiction was the art of telling a truth that readers like Birkerts could recognize as familiar.

I also read Birkerts's (1995) criticism as originating in a fear of change, as part and parcel of the audience response that greeted the first performance of Stravinsky's *The Rite of Spring* with riots, the reviewers that complained furiously about Pirandello's *Six Characters in Search of an Author*, and of the critics that savaged some of DuChamp's earliest pieces of art. I read Birkerts's criticism as a screed against the unfamiliar, the unexplained, and the new in artistic or literary experiment. When Gianfranco Baruchello and Henry Martin tried to explain their notion of art as experiment in their marvelous *How to Imagine: A Narrative on Art and Agriculture* (1984), they defend the plays, assemblages, and paintings that grew out of contact with their farm outside Rome as works that fall outside conventional definitions of art—but that still very much are art. They write,

> [The idea of denying the need for a public] may seem strange and confused, it may even seem impossible in our particular here and now and through the ways of looking at the world we're accustomed to…. When people say that something isn't art, what they mean is that nobody's being amused by it. That's really such an empty way of looking at things. People are blind to all the metaphors that are really fundamental to art. But a process of growth, or a procedure of survival, a procedure of perception, a procedure that also offers some sort of remedium to psychic suffering … all of this has an extremely powerful pertinence to art… (pp. 144–145)

Baruchello and Martin (1984) call their Roman garden a kind of art, Jenny Holzer's intriguing compositions of words, granite, and neon are certainly art, and all the hypertext fictions published today by Eastgate Systems, from Jane Yellowlees Douglas's *I Have Said Nothing* (1993) to Kathy Mac's *Unnatural Habitats* (1994), are literary experiments in a long-standing artistic tradition. Contemporary Luddites who view hypertext fiction as a genre oblivious to audience, as one that ignores its readers and their needs, belong to audiences who do not want to work at constructing meanings or to challenge the status quo.

Instead of applying critical categories better suited to an analysis of traditional creative work, we need to ask what habits and expectations of reading stories are actually under attack by the genre of hypertext fictions. If we can uncover the critical positions that underlie claims of hypertext fiction's worth and worthlessness, we will be closer to understanding what is actually at stake in our discussions. My guess is that ultimately implicit in the devaluation of hypertext writings is a knee-jerk reaction against the post-structuralist critique of the subject, and a nostalgia for individual unity, social realism, and traditional aesthetic values. Zavarzadeh and Morton's (1991) essay on the ways the concept of individuality has been questioned for centuries in the Western literary traditions reminds readers that we can see opposing critical positions enshrined in our contemporary humanities curriculum. They write,

> The contradictions of [today's] curriculum ... are themselves the result of power/ knowledge relations deriving from the historical struggles of various social groups over signification, over the constitution and circulation of the "real" meaning of the subject in culture. These historic struggles, whose effects coexist in the dominant curriculum, have given it a layered and residual character. The curriculum's bourgeois moralism, for instance, clashes with its aristocratic aestheticism, while both of these elements conflict with its feudal historicism. (p. 2)

I would argue that Birkerts and critics like him fail to see in the galvanic text that is hypertext fiction that there exist layers of previous questions and critical positions, just like the humanities curriculum described above is constituted of layers and residues. By connecting hypertext fiction with theories and stances that question the unity of the Western tradition and the authority of canonical literature largely distinguished by masculinist perspectives and agents, Birkerts (1995) cannot help but prefer *A Midsummer Night's Dream* to a 20th-century *Afternoon*. Birkerts's criticism is at its root a stark complaint against an art form that does not explicitly include him in its audience, at least not in shared values, familiarity of form, nor dominant ideology.

By examining some of the critical attacks on hypertext fictions, supplementing that examination with a historical perspective on the evolution of hypertexts, and complementing both these bodies of information with a closer look at some of the words of the authors themselves, we will arrive at a better understanding of why hypertext fictions fall short of what some readers like Birkerts expect of them.

SOME CRITICAL RESPONSES TO HYPTERTEXT FICTIONS

Critical responses to hypertexts in general are of three types. First, some critics respond to it from positions as cognitivists or textual studies theorists interested in the mechanics of presentation. These critics see hypertext fictions as a new test site, and hypertext's version of the reading–writing compact as an opportunity to make visible and test empirically the ways in which information is effectively conveyed via differing "visual arrays," and that will allow researchers to trace connections between world event and narrative event, or biography and autobiography. These researchers (including Flower, 1985; Flower & Hayes, 1980, 1981a; Goldman, 1996; Scardamalia et al., 1992; van Dijk, 1987) understand reading as "text processing" and endeavor to examine (inferentially, one can only hope) the mental models that readers construct as they read. Second, some critics see hypertext within a larger social and cultural context, seeing in the spread of hypertext a confirmation of larger patterns of politics, hierarchy, and diffusion of power (for example,

Janangelo, 1991; Johnson-Eilola, 1997; Joyce, 1995; Selfe & Selfe, 1994), and they approach hypertexts from the position of cultural studies, Marxist critique, or the desire to historicize technologies. Third, and most important for our purposes, some critics (Luddites, one might claim), focus on the supposed dangers and possibilities of the delivery system itself, letting the computer overwhelm the narrative event, studying the radio instead of the melody. Critics like Sven Birkerts fall into this latter category.

The first group of theorists, the cognitivists, make some interesting observations about how differing visual arrays affect text comprehension, patterns of memory "decay," and mental models of text and meaning. Chris Haas and John Hayes's (1986) oft-quoted essay on the problems of location in text falls into this category. They analyze the way readers locate words or passages, noting the increase of errors when readers read text on the screen. The work of Flower and Hayes (1980, 1981a, 1981b), which uses think-aloud protocols to discover the processes by which readers and writers construct meaning, also fits here. However, more particular to our discussions of hypertext fiction are the findings of cognitive psychologists like Goldman, who study the breakdown of linear processing and its implications for readers confronted by hypertext on a screen. Goldman builds on the earlier work of Lashley (1951), a study that develops the notion that "the linear order of language was a central feature of the linguistic system that made it different from understanding nonlinguistic input" (Goldman, 1996, p. 9). For example, imagine how you "read" a painting in contrast to how you read a book. Goldman calls our familiar process of reading a book "the input order of language" and demonstrates that the physical form of a book itself insists on a linear process of assembling a preconceived (authorial) order. In Goldman's terms, when readers are confronted with graphical displays of information as in some hypermedia, "there may be preferred scanning strategies but there is no natural or inherent starting point for processing and the visual array is far less suggestive of a linear processing strategy" (p. 9). (Ironically, critics like Jay David Bolter find the idea that "[e]lectronic writing is both a visual and verbal description" [1991, p. 25] as one of its great promises.) At the same time, Goldman mentions the occasionally contrarian action of the eye confronted with linear texts. She mentions, for example, that studies have shown that flipping back through a book is a more common process than reading ahead, and that in conventional readings on paper, a reader derives meaning by considering relationships between adjacent and nonadjacent words, constructing mental models that account for all that has been read so far. Goldman ultimately explores the effects of hypertext on these developing mental models.

Cognitivists like Matsuhashi (1981) and others have focused on readers' "scanning strategies," and the challenges that the convergence of visual and verbal elements in hypertext poses to them. (Hypertext authors such as Kaplan and Moulthrop also implicitly reject the distinction between print literacy's capacity for description and hypertext's capacity for depiction [see Tuman, 1992a, 1992b, p. 127].) The studies and questions of the cognitivists are certainly useful and interesting, especially to systems designers and those working on interface configurations. However, by their concentration on the apparatuses of delivering stories, these critics overlook some of the wider connections among readers, writers, and cultural contexts.

The second group of critics, the cultural studies mavens, are those who are most interested in the cultural and social implications of hypertexts and who work in the field of cultural studies and critical pedagogies, including critics such as James Berlin, Raymond Williams, Myron Tuman, and Johndan Johnson-Eilola. Often of a leftist political bent, important writers like Johndan Johnson-Eilola (1997) see in hypertexts a confirmation of hegemonic relations, powerful alignments of technology and corporate sponsorship, and ideological traces within the interfaces of the machine (see also Selfe & Selfe, 1994; Sloane, 1999a, 1999c). Post-structuralist theorists like Frederic Jameson (1991) see in the growing global electronic networks an accompanying, invisible network of power, policing activities, and corporate hegemony. And cultural critics like Myron Tuman (1992b), too, see online literacy as imbued with cultural ideas and values:

> Vast hypertexts and computer networks are after all the very modalities of late capitalism, and we as consumers are ideally situated in this matrix when we have total access to (the right to purchase) any individual item we want and no sense whatsoever of how this vast system consumer network operates; for example, who or what controls it. (p. 136)

Given the explosive growth of e-commerce, online auctions, and a new Web-based service economy (for example, homegrocers.com, travelocity.com, and amazon.com), Tuman's (1992b) early insight resonates loudly today. For critics like Johnson-Eilola (1997), hypertexts are a catalyst for jettisoning some parts of postmodern literary theories, especially those parts that can be seen as amoral, ungendered, apolitical, and murky to such a degree that those of us who have embraced postmodernism in the past find ourselves tumbling into the muddy morass that is all that is left when we assume some relativistic beliefs. In groping for a new critical position that observes the functions of ideology and power but does not yield to their imperatives, cultural critics and teachers like Johnson-Eilola prompts us to look beyond postmodernist ideas and toward the perspectives and pedagogies of cultural studies. We need to learn that although we may agree with Foucault that all discourse is contained within larger systems of power, that all ethical truths depend to a large extent on who holds them, we do not mean by this relativism that there are no truths, words, or behaviors to which we might rightly (and ethically) subscribe. The position of cultural critic allows us to expand definitions of composing, to address a wider set of texts and writing situations, and to understand words and behaviors as situated knowledge, or partial truths. However, such a focus thus broadly construed does not help us fully understand the simple question of why some readers are so disappointed by hypertext fictions.

The third group of critics, the Luddites, tends to focus on ways in which hypertexts are disappointing books, and Sven Birkerts is one of the strongest adherents to this position. In the critical discussions surrounding the flash and dash of hypermedia performances like Carolyn Guyer's *Quibbling* (1993), Stuart Moulthrop's *Victory Garden* (1991), and, more recent, *Hegirascope 2.0* (1997), for example, we can heed the familiar notes of the New Critics and the Postmodernists squaring off, and hear loud echoes of the "strong" school of researchers into the dynamics of orality and literacy. Sven Birkerts, an engaging and persuasive critic of "electronic books" and the shallowness he believes they engender, is a reasonably good representative of a New Critic lunching with the devil of hypertext fictions. Birkerts's book *The Gutenberg Elegies: The Fate of Reading in an Electronic Age* (1995), in general an elegantly written, introspective account of Birkerts's own history as a reader and a writer, explores how one man's taste and habits as a reader have been constructed by his encounters with books at various sites (bookstores and libraries) and various forms (audiobooks and hypertext fictions, as well as more conventional codex books). Birkerts's book expresses his deeply felt concerns about the "electronic millennium's" various erasures; he sees electronic books as contributing to our loss of inwardness, introspection, subjectivity, and even soul.

For Birkerts (1995), hypertext fiction offers a clear example of how all electronic media constitute a contemporary incarnation of a sanitized, efficient devil that distracts us from ourselves. Birkerts develops his thesis that by extension, electronic media distances us from our whole culture and cultural possibilities, from great human questions, and really, from any possibility of ever becoming truly wise. Birkerts's book is a beautifully stated Luddite treatise that for this reader, anyway, fits the genre of such treatises a little too neatly. Although Birkerts disavows the intention, he looks back wistfully at a golden age of books; his whole presentation is steeped in a nostalgia for the classical tale and ideas of syntax, form, and expression that are multiple and multifarious, more complex, and deeply layered. (None of these adjectives, of course, precludes hypertext fiction, although Birkerts assumes they do.)

Although Birkerts (1995) wistfully details the social scenes (bookstore, library, home, school) of his own development as a reader, he does little work in analyzing how these scenes are imbricated in larger social orders and institutions, and are constitutive of dominant cultural beliefs. I suspect Birkerts has never read his Althusser, here elegantly summarized by Zavarzadeh and Morton (1991):

> The insertion of the subject into the social formation provides the individual with a post of intelligibility from which—as a "mother," a "successful man," a "learned scholar," a "skillful surgeon," and the like—he *sees* the world in a manner supportive of the dominant social relations; consequently he consents to the proposition that the existing order is not only the way things are, but also the way they ought to be. The subject, in Althusser's view, is the set of relations through which the social order of late capitalism reproduces itself. (p. 6)

Birkerts's meditations on self and meaning in their nostalgia yield to a kind of *essentialism* that is itself entrenched, blinkered, and firmly wedded to the familiar. We can see these general claims operating in Birkerts's book by looking at the following example.

Birkerts opens his essentially nostalgic essay, "Hypertext: Of Mouse and Man" (1995), with a short narrative of his own first encounter with hypertext fiction, a copy of Moulthrop's *Victory Garden* (1991), which he characterizes as "stylistically uninspired" (p. 151). (We might usefully contrast novelist Robert Coover's [1993] characterization of the same piece of work, in which he calls *Victory Garden* "...indispensable. No one has ... played so intransigently with the myriad possibilities and obstacles of this new art form" [p. 11].) Birkerts says that when he first read Moulthrop's story, he had the following reactions:

> A kind of paralysis swept over me. I was reminded of Julio Cortázar's *Hopscotch* [1975], where the reader learns that he can follow the chapters in a number of different sequences. But this was stranger, denser...I felt none of the tug I had felt with Cortázar's novel, none of the subtle suction exerted by masterly prose. Still, I did not give up. I tipped up and back in my chair, clicked and clicked again, waiting patiently for the empowering rush that ought to come when worlds open upon other worlds and old limits collapse. (p. 151)

Birkerts follows these querulous complaints about his dissatisfaction with *Victory Garden*—and hence, by his extension, all hypertext fictions—with an argument that is even more clearly predicated upon nostalgia for a familiar social world, in this case the shape of exchanges between reader and writer to which he has grown accustomed, roles that he is used to playing in particular ways. Birkerts continues,

> [M]any...[writers] say to me, "Words are still words—on a page, on a screen—what's the difference?" There is much shrugging of the shoulders. But this will never do. The changes are profound and the differences are consequential. Nearly weightless though it is, the word printed on a page is a thing. The configuration of impulses on a screen is not—it is a manifestation, an indeterminate entity both particle and wave, an ectoplasmic arrival and departure. (pp. 151–152)

Gradually shifting his metaphor from the sexual to the parapsychological, Birkerts (1995) blames the missing "suction" and "tug" on a hypertext's weightlessness, its ectoplasmic substance a mere fluid that floats away from a reader, that reader becoming like an astronaut untethered from the mothercraft. I especially like the adjective "ectoplasmic" in Birkerts' dismissal of hypertext fictions, because it unwittingly underscores Birkerts' central trope, that hypertext writing is synchronic and self-unreflective, while good old-fashioned paper-based writing is diachronic, haunted, and embodied. (Birkerts picks out several other of the features of writing on paper, its "fixity," "indelibility," and "lack of provisionality" (p. 157), which Heim [1987] summarized under the term "element.") Birkerts speculates that the fluid, provisional gesture of letters written on the computer are, at their "molecular" level, somehow different. A change in writing process effects a change in written product, he claims. Well, why not. But that change in process, says Birkerts, results in a reading experience ultimately dissatisfying because of its weightlessness, its disappointing drifting, its lack of suck and tug. Again, I would suggest to Birkerts that he examine the ways in which these familiar processes of reading and writing are themselves imbricated in dominant culture. He might ask how late print culture is related to late century capitalism before he vents his spleen.

Ultimately, Sven Birkerts and other Luddites like him find hypertext fictions just plain unsatisfying. But dissatisfying to whom? To those of us trained to read the lockstep sequences of pages? To those of us who pace ourselves according to the plodding prose and weighty flip of a page in a codex book? Another quibble Birkerts brings to his experience of reading hypertext is that it is "ungainly." He expands: "[I was] made so fidgety by the knowledge that I was positioned in a designed environment, with the freedom to rocket from one place to another with a keystroke, that I could scarcely hold still..." (1995, p. 161) Although Birkerts's lively prose shifts the vehicle of his metaphor for the limits of hypertext from water to ghosts to rockets during the course of his essay, in each case the metaphor sets up an opposition between the familiar and the new, between the superior, graspable texts of yesterday and the transient, intangible texts of tomorrow. Birkerts's colorful metaphors are essentially nostalgic ones, and, like the questions of the cognitivists and the cultural critics, they draw our attention away from the content of the tale to the materials and apparatus that deliver the tale. I agree with Birkerts that many hypertext fictions sometimes offer a dissatisfying reading experience to those who attempt it, but I think he is mistaken in finding the origins of this dissatisfaction in the story's delivery system.

In Birkerts's most recent book, *Readings* (1999b), he extends his critique of digital fictions and expands his theme of nostalgia into a contemporary version of the "back-to-nature" movement, arguing that hypertext and other computer-mediated communication harm us by removing us away from "the brute realities of nature":

> Our technologies, and our technologically driven employments, have created a secondary world that we inhabit in lieu of the first world that our immediate ancestors, and all of their ancestors before them, inhabited. This original world was determined in many essential ways by the brute realities of nature—by weather, by terrain, by the time required for various processes, and the intervals of long distance communication. The new reality is significantly cut off from nature, largely unaffected by weather, global in reference, and premised on instantaneous communication. For the real we are substituting the virtual. (1999a, pp. 27–28)

Like Richard Lanham's (1990) remarks that a computer forces stories to be shaped according to the norms of certain "genre fictions," Birkerts ultimately mistakes the quality of the delivery system for the quality of the tale. In the remarks that conclude his essay on *Victory Garden*, Birkerts says:

I stare at the textual field on my friend's screen and I am unpersuaded. Indeed, this glimpse of the future—if it is the future—has me clinging all the more tightly to my books, the very idea of them. If I ever took them for granted, I do no longer. I now see each one as a portable enclosure, a place I can repair to release the private, unsocialized, dreaming self. A books is solitude, privacy; it is a way of holding the self apart from the crush of the outer world. Hypertext—at least the spirit of hypertext, which I see as the spirit of the times—promises to deliver me from this, to free me from the "liberating domination" of the author. It promises to spring me from the univocal linearity which is precisely the constraint that fills me with a sense of possibility as I read my way across fixed acres of print.

The ways in which textual constraints yield possibility to readers like Birkerts may well depend on their reader's social position, education, and first world context. However, to some extent, of course, Birkerts is exactly right. The hypertext fiction is not offering the kind of book or story he is accustomed to reading. Michael Joyce and other hypertext writers, though, are quite clear about attempting something altogether different. As Joyce explains in *Of Two Minds* (1995):

We are always painting. The electronic is not at all the touch of the uncertain, the transsubstantiated smear that, like Silly Putty, gives way to liquid or, like a painter's acrylics, forms into still encapsulated light. We are always painting. The electronic is not at all the touch of the uncertain reader, who—like a child poking at a line of ants or lining up raisins—runs a finger along each cast line of print. Rather, it is a certain touch, like holding moths..." (pp. 186–187)

However, Birkerts ignores the hypertext author's intentions, and finishes by explaining the depth and breadth of his disappointment in hypertext, seeing neither possibility nor promise in the genre of stories like *Victory Garden* (Moulthrop, 1991) (and judging the entire genre, at least at first, through the lens of a single example). His attitude is quite different from *Victory Garden*'s reviewer in *The Utne Reader*, Harry Goldstein, who says, "Moulthrop has used hyperfiction...allowing the reader to do what the media and the government made impossible: to explore the story of the war, and of ourselves, for ourselves."

It seems to me that Birkerts (1999a) is making two important mistakes in his appraisal of hypertext fictions like *Victory Garden*. First, he mistakes the tale for the materials lying under storytelling. Second, he meets hypertext fictions with eyes trained on reading books, and he is not prepared to change his reading habits as hypertext demands. Yes, the experience of reading hypertext fiction to date is radically opposed to reading, say, deconstructionism, in that these fictions' degree of seriousness, purpose, and weight, ultimately, that is, their content, is not of the quality of most contemporary fiction being published today. But the problem, emphatically, is not the apparatus upon which they are written, nor is it in their failure to support old ways of reading. To be fair to hypertext fictions and their authors, we

need to be undistracted by their delivery system and to remain open to their innovations in sequence, complexity, and style.

George Landow eloquently underscores a similar point in his recent book
Hypertext Theory:

> [M]any people confronting electronic textuality confuse the experience of reading it
> with the particular technology on which it is read. Given the computer-monitor tech-
> nology most humanists have encountered, [their] reactions make perfect sense: read-
> ing a text on a personal computer or mainframe terminal both constrains one (by
> forcing one to read at a particular location) and, like most cheap paperback books, also
> removes a good deal of the physical pleasure associated with what many academics
> purport to hold as their ideal of the book—the luxuriously leather-bound object....
> [T]his entirely understandable reaction misses the central point about electronic tex-
> tuality—its fundamental distinction from the object on which it is read. (1994, p. 4)

However, according to Landow, too, hypertext fiction seems occasionally light-
weight, puzzling, and unable to achieve a wide readership, but not because of its
delivery system—but because of the preoccupations, language, and nonlinearity of
its form. Landow is correct to direct our attention away from the story delivery system, but he errs in believing that by studying the stories written to date in hypertext,
we will see their true worth and genius. Hypertext fictions are often dissatisfying,
indeed, but not because of their delivery system nor necessarily their language.
They are dissatisfying to some readers because of their content and style, their pacing and plotting, their multilinear and occasionally random sequences, their occasional clumsiness in prose and multiple points of view. They are dissatisfying to
readers like Sven Birkerts because they substitute the virtual for the real, and, furthermore, they allow readings digressive, transgressive, multiple, fast, and furtive—
and ultimately transgressive of dominant convention and culture. He explains,

> Life is changing rapidly and imponderably. Things feel different than they used to; the
> contours of events, of public circumstances, are no longer defined as they once were.
> Too much, we hear on every front. Too many channels, too much data. We hurry,
> double up; we break the beam of attention into its component rays... (1999a, p. 36)

Interestingly, it is the new possibilities of language and form that hypertext writers
like Guyer, Petry, and Coverley find so appealing; and it is the realization of this possibility that leads readers like Birkerts to abhor the product.

The relationship between a story and the materials through which that story is
delivered was discussed at length in Chapter 3. Ultimately, in that chapter we found
that categorizing fictions according to whether they were composed on computer or
paper is as silly as claiming that terra cotta tablets found south of Babylon are all
the same genre because they were inscribed into similar clay. Although there probably are relations between particular media and the stories they best support, it is
more important for us to extend Seymour Chatman's (1978) distinction between

story and discourse to distinctions between materials and the delivery system of story, and to explore more carefully how contexts and processes of the act of reading create meaning and valuation. While it is likely that differences in the scenes and apparatus of reading contribute to different reading experiences, as Heim notes below, it is the language *and* form of hypertext fictions that distinguish them most from other stories, and it is in their innovations, in their ways of telling a story, that makes them most reprehensible, damaging, or radical to readers like Birkerts.

Michael Heim reflects on how hypertexts change a reader's experience in his essay "Hypertext Heaven," reprinted in *The Metaphysics of Virtual Reality* (1993):

> [U]sers [of hypertext] float on the illusion that this hypertext style of reading surpasses without undoing all the earlier styles of reading. Hypertext users feel their minds reveling in intuitive, associational thinking. The more the routine sequences and chores belong to the computer program, the more the human psyche can give reign to immediate insights and creative angles. This trend is in keeping with our general tendency to prefer fast images to the more intricate patterns of internal thought. (p. 39)

No empirical evidence that I am aware of supports Heim's (1993) claim that hypertext allows readers more insight or intuition than they experience reading books, but I am willing to yield that hypertexts seem to insist on a faster rate of reading. All texts have embedded in them, like an unposted speed limit, textual features that speed or slow the rate of reading, a rate that depends also on the reader's experience. Long sentences and paragraphs, high density of propositions, abstract reasoning, specialized vocabularies, and polysyllabic words will slow down even the most experienced reader. One need not read Michael Joyce against Henry James to see the latter's greater syntactic density; one could read Joyce, Moulthrop, or Guyer against Samuel Delaney for a clear example of differences between voice, style, and syntactic density in storytelling. However, the psychological relationships between stories and their readers deserve more attention than Heim's speculation that our hypertext readings draw us away from "the intricate patterns of internal thought" or Birkerts's speculations on how reading speed affects our very substance: "More things [today] are registered, attended to, but the impression any one of them makes is slighter. One result of this is that we feel ourselves as somehow less substantial in the present" (1999a, p. 36). In Birkerts's method of always looking back to measure today's stories and the culture within which they live, he misses all the promise of hypertext fiction, all the innovations that necessarily are erased when viewed through the lens of nostalgia.

Hypertext fictions are interactive stories that invite readers to do the tango, not the waltz; they are stories that require readers to respond on-the-fly to their fluid, paratactic, yes, even ectoplasmic, narrative structures. Hypertext fiction authors Stuart Moulthrop, Carolyn Guyer, and Michael Joyce generously granted me e-mail interviews with them during the course of my writing this chapter, and I include selections from their views in my discussion below. Because I do not ultimately see the same promise in hypertext fiction as these three authors do, and in an attempt to subvert my own tenuous authorial authority in this chapter, I have included remarks and comments of these three well-known hypertext fiction authors in the following discussions of history, meaning, and form in these stories. However, while I do not always see the same promise in the evolving genre, I do recognize the power of these stories to challenge existing codes, and I am a fan of those words of hypertext fiction (such as those discussed below) that do not reify the conventional, but explicitly challenge dominant cultural narratives.

HISTORIES AND DEFINITIONS OF HYPERTEXT FICTIONS

Hypertext fictions—whether read on a diskette or at a computer terminal, whether written in "HTML" on the World Wide Web or in a program called "Storyspace" (by Eastgate Systems)—are computer-based stories that share a particular form, a particular software base (Storyspace or HyperCard, for example) and, for the most part so far, a content that is founded on predominantly first world preoccupations. In form, they are stories that are built out of linked blocks of text, which the reader is "invited" to read in a variety of sequences. Some hypertexts are "exploratory," in which readers simply explore a fictional microworld, while others are characterized by their authors as "constructive" hypertexts, which are intended to be explored and changed by their readers (Bolter, Joyce, Smith, & Bernstein, 1992, p. 22). In these latter hypertexts, readers may add their own responses, scenes, or notes to the existing lexia. In almost all cases, reading hypertext fiction is a solo enterprise, involving one reader and a machine. In content, most hypertext fictions are set in the 20th century, and most feature heterosexual love stories, contemporary problems, or simple human dramas. (One notable exception is Deena Larsen's *Marble Springs* [1993], a hypertextual collection of poems about women in a Colorado ghost town that was once a mining town in the 19th century.) If any claim might be safely made about the evolving genre of hypertext fictions, it would be to note the genre's ironic attention to histories, personal and cultural, and the ways place and person are plotted in ways layered or diachronic, so that iterative readings or deep readings lead one to discover progressively whatever happened before. One important hypertext writer, Michael Joyce, builds on an insight by Jane Yellowlees Douglas when he writes,

> At each crossing a world of possibility can be spewed out in whole or in kernel, like the cosmogonic dragon's teeth of myth. Each iteration "breathes life into a narrative of possibilities," as Jane Yellowlees Douglas says of hypertext fiction, so that, in the 'third or fourth encounter with the same place, the immediate encounter remains the same as the first, [but] what changes is [our] understanding.' The text becomes a present tense palimpsest where what shines through are not past versions but potential, alternate views. (1995, p. 3)

Of all computer fictions, hypertext fictions are those most closely related to the book-based Choose Your Own Adventure stories or Pick-a-Plot books in their discontinuous form, paratactic narrative structure, and vague sense of an ending. Whether we read Stuart Moulthrop's *Hegirascope* (1995) on the Web, a brightly-colored presentation of hypertext in which the reader need not even turn the pages (they evaporate themselves every 12 seconds or so), or sample Carolyn Guyer's *Quibbling* (1993) on a diskette, watching the waves come in and "wash over the edges of things, teaching us lastingness and lace" (Joyce, 1995, p. 89), we are confronted with a presentation of story that is multidimensional, fluid, and occasionally unsatisfying to readers seeking some other kind of narrative experience. Readers of hypertext fictions in general must cope with the abrupt jumps, associative logic, and multilinear paths characteristic of these stories, and their mental models of the evolution of character and event must be rehearsed also in new ways. Moulthrop's title of one recent composition, *Hegirascope 2* (1997), might be the best metaphor for this kind of multiple reading; the reader of that tale is implicitly invited to view ("scope") the diaspora ("hegira"). Or, in other words, to trace multiple journeys themselves guided by larger cultural narratives, in this case the religious narrative of pilgrimage contextualized by our material (consumer-based, visual, and violent) culture.

George Landow's book *Hypertext: The Convergence of Contemporary Critical Theory and Technology* (1992a) explores the resemblance between hypertext fictions and the many questions about textuality and intertextuality raised by post-structuralists. Landow bemoans "the rigidity and difficulty of access" (p. 14) of the codex book and celebrates, not blindly, the networks of stories called hypertexts. (Landow credits Roland Barthes with providing the term "lexia" for these blocks of text and the electronic links that join them.) However, despite the promises of its critics and writers, promises that hypertext fiction levels the playing field between readers and writers, that it democratizes the textual exchange, that it even somehow allows a feminist narrative, and that it allows a new narrative consciousness and understanding of fiction, existing hypertext narratives succeed most often in shaking up the habits of readers more accustomed to a horizontal, page-based presentation of story. While hypertext fictions do, as their writers claim, challenge the stability and fixity of the paper-based narrative, in my opinion they have yet to offer any substantive work that will shake up anyone's canon of the great texts of the Western world. But unlike Birkerts, I can read my own cultural biases and contexts into my rash claim. And again, contrary to Birkerts, I find hypertext fictions valuable both in what they teach us about the flexibility of narrative form, and in what they make visible about the reading and writing process. Finally, I recognize that within my own conflicted view of hypertext fictions lies the unresolved question of how much innovation in textual form can change conventional notions of our place in the world, our status as individuals, and our beliefs in the efficacy of existing cultural institutions.

Hypertext fictions by and large are a genre more limber or flexible than the codex book; they allow writers a new set of tools with which to build narrative structures, and they offer their readers a new kind of navigability, a means of steering oneself through an elusive narrative that has been called topographic, nomadic, rhizomic, or digressive by a range of critics. This new trait, navigability, is probably the one most unfamiliar to readers who have cut their milkteeth on codex books, whose scene of reading is always book, lamp, and chair; and it is in the new ways these hypertexts accommodate and direct readers, mapping their readings, and leading them through the author's links, guard fields, and lexia of a hypertextual web, which gives hypertext fiction its most obvious distinction from stories presented on paper.

Hypertext fictions composed using Eastgate's Storyspace, Macintosh's HyperCard, or, most recently, the World Wide Web's authoring language HTML, have garnered humanist attentions probably because of their relative ease of composition and their relative familiarity as textual artifact. Hypertext fictions have been rhetorically analyzed (Slatin, 1990), defended vehemently as literary (Guyer, 1992), and positioned as a new genre (Coover, 1993), without being sufficiently defined or explored. We need to place hypertext fictions in their historical and theoretical contexts, and to question radically 1) whether we should define any genre boundaries according to computer platforms; 2) whether any fiction using HyperCard, Storyspace, or any other platform has achieved the quality and status of highly valued paper-based fictions; 3) in what ways are hypertext fictions valuable for sharpening contemporary models of how readers and writers compose stories; and 4) what are the invisible links of these stories to larger cultural norms? In Burkean (1955) terms, hypertext fictions shift our attention from strict analyses of story content to the more general questions of production, agency, and the scene of writing story. Also, to use Burkean terms again, hypertext fictions force our attention to how the structures of a story actually motivate readings, and, by extension, readers.

The concept of "hypertext" is usually credited to Vannevar Bush (former president of the Carnegie Institution of Washington and author of the widely used textbook *Principles of Electrical Engineering*), who published a short article in the *Atlantic Monthly* in July 1945 under the title, "As We May Think." Bush conceived of a tool called the "Memex," which would be "a device in which an individual stores his books, records, and communications, and which is mechanized so that it may be consulted with exceeding speed and flexibility" (qtd. in Landow, 1992a,p. 15). Bush imagined being able to write into his "Memex" and take notes, make marginal comments, and even include photographs. Theodor Nelson coined the actual term "hypertext" in the early 1960s as a description of "nonsequential writing, text that branches and allows choices to the reader, best read at an interactive screen" (Nelson, 1987a). In an interview in April 1988, Nelson says:

> I define hypertext as nonsequential writing with free user movement. It has nothing to do with computers logically; it has to do with computers pragmatically, just the way large numbers and large bookkeeping schemes have nothing to do with computers logically but, rather, pragmatically. (cited in Heim, 1993, p. 33)

The idea of hypertext, then, was not originally and need not now be dependent on the computer for its presentation. A hypertextual fiction, and a multilinear narrative strategy, can, of course, exist independent of the computer.

Michael Joyce (1995) directs our attention to other computer-based ancestors of hypermedial systems, including the work of "hypertext pioneer" Andries Van Dam, who developed the Hypertext Editing System (HES) and the File Retrieval and Editing System (FRESS) between 1968 and 1969. Van Dam's research team (Norm Meyrowitz, Nicole Yankelovich, and Paul Kahn, among others) joined Brown University faculty members (including George Landow) to develop Intermedia, a hypertext system that linked together bodies of knowledge in several disciplines, including English and biology. Finally, even a history of hypertext as brief as this one needs to mention the work at Xerox PARC (Palo Alto Research Center) by Frank Halasz, Thomas Moran, Randall Trigg, and others, in creating the dominant metaphor for hypertext authoring—cards with buttons.

In 1987, Apple Computer started shipping its Macintosh computers bundled with a free copy of HyperCard 1.0, the first widely available hypertextual program that allowed a writer to create "stacks" of cards. HyperCard 2.0, a more flexible iteration, extended the abilities of Macintosh users to experiment with reading and writing hypertext fictions. As Michael Heim explains,

> In 1987, Apple Computer brought out the first hypertext commercially available on computers. HyperCard on the Macintosh holds files ("stacks") that resemble electronic index cards. Unlike index cards, however, the stacks are relational, or cross-referenced with one another. Because the stacks are electronically linked, they allow instant cross-referencing. Stacks link everything in a text or in a whole group of texts. Texts then become a hypertext in which everything in the text relates to everything else in the text. In other words, hypertext is a dynamic referencing system in which all texts are interrelated. Hypertext is no less than electronic intertextuality, the text of all texts, a supertext. (1993, p. 30)

The 1990s saw the development of two very popular hypertext browsers for the Internet, Mosaic, and the subsequent and vastly more popular World Wide Web. Millions of sites accessed through uniform resource locators (URLs) provide hyperlinked information, maps, poems, plays, stories, artwork, directories, databanks, search engines, and so on. Web-based soap operas like *The Spot* and avatar-based themed chat rooms like *The Palace* have sprung up in the last couple of years on the Web, offering new sites for analysis of the intersections of technology, story, and culture.

In 1987, Michael Joyce wrote and Eastgate Systems published his first hypertext fiction, an intriguing, multilinear narrative called *Afternoon, A Story*. According to the packaging material that comes with *Afternoon*, Robert Coover (1993) calls it "the granddaddy of hypertext fictions...a legend." *Afternoon* is a story that opens with these words:

begin
I try to recall winter. < As if it were yesterday > she says, but I do not signify one way or another.

By five the sun sets and the afternoon melt freezes again across the blacktop into crystal octopi and palms of ice—rivers and continents beset by fear, and we walk out to the car, the snow moaning beneath our boots and the oaks exploding in series along the fenceline on the horizon, the shrapnel settling like relics, the echoing thundering off far ice. This was the essence of wood, these fragments say. And this darkness is air.
<Poetry> she says, without emotion, one way or another.
Do you want to hear about it?

I want to say
I want to say I may have seen my son die this morning.

The mystery of the opening frames is never resolved, although through many readings and rereadings, we get the sense that the narrator has seen a car accident this morning, in which a woman in a white dress has been injured, perhaps fatally, and lies near another smaller, sprawled body beyond. The narrator thinks that this second accident victim may have been his son. In the course of the story, the narrator explores his relationships with women and his son, contemporary American culture, and the rituals and meaning of work. After following various links, a reader might finally end up with a block of text entitled "yes" and read "There is an end to everything, to any mystery." And the last words of this reading of *Afternoon* are, "I wish I were the Sun King." The next frame shows the opening graphic again, and if the reader perseveres, she will be reminded with a new frame that "Closure is, as in any fiction, a suspect quality, although here it is made manifest..." and with another click of her Return key, will be returned to the opening frames. In Joyce's *Afternoon*, we can hear oblique references to that other Joyce in the echo of Molly Bloom's final "yes" and in the return to the beginning, as in the circling narrative of *Finnegan's Wake* (1958).

The process of reading *Afternoon* is one in which the story is "advanced" by pressing the Return key on the keyboard, by clicking on different icons on a "Toolbar," or by double-clicking on words in the text to follow various lines of the story. Certain words will "yield," bringing readers to a new storyline. In Joyce's reflections about hypertext, included in the pamphlet that comes with Eastgate's version of *Afternoon*, he remarks that he sees the genre moving toward a "post-alphabetic" aesthetic, one in which "[t]he image impinges on the word so much as to imperil its hegemony and maybe its meaningfulness. Storyspace will become more visual even as it insists upon the sensuality and visual qualities of the word" (1987, p. 12). Joyce's remarks echo the early vision of virtual reality pioneer Jaron Lanier (1986), where he predicted that people will be able to "speak and breathe programs just like they talk now." Thirteen years ago, Lanier suggested,

Imagine we're cave people, and someone comes along and somehow communicates to us that there's this thing called language that we can speak. And you ask him, 'What's that for?' We're in a similar situation today. Now we use symbols, called words, that when spoken invoke meanings in our minds. But what is more interesting to me is that you can actually build full models of concepts instead of just giving them names ... I think this capacity to *make* models, as opposed to just giving concepts names, will be the most worthwhile contribution computers will make for humanity... (p. 288)

Lanier's imagining of "a post-symbolic universe," one in which humans hurl graphics and models to one another, may be the most extreme version of the ascendancy of image over word in computer-based worlds; Storyspace is the glimmer, and virtual reality the quick sketch, of what may be to come.

Michael Joyce traces his own work in hypertext fiction to a lineage that includes some of the early computer literary experiments of the type described in Chapter 2, specifically, James Meehan's Tale-Spin and Natalie Dehn's AUTHOR. As Joyce explains in a footnote to his provocative *Of Two Minds: Hypertext, Pedagogy, and Poetics* (1995):

Natalie Dehn's (1981, 1989) AUTHOR was an attempt to generate a story based upon the intentions of the computer "author." Dehn's work on STARSHIP, as yet unpublished, moved even closer to genuine interaction, creating a science fiction world in which stories changed according to the program's perception of the reader's comprehension of the story as it developed, based upon comprehension questions generated by the program. Much of my thought on interaction and multiple fiction is indebted to Dr. Dehn... (p. 262)

Since the publication of Joyce's story, dozens of hypertext fictions, electronic books, hypertext e-zines, and nonfiction webs have been published by Eastgate Systems and others. Today, Eastgate Systems (eastgate.com) features subscription information for a disk-based journal, *Eastgate Quarterly Review of Hypertext*, a nonfiction program called Perseus, and advertises many fascinating new hypertext fictions, including *Samplers* (1997, 1998), "a sampler quilt of hypertext" by Deena Larsen, a "multi-level contemporary nightmare" by Edward Falco called *A Dream With Demons* (1997), and Judy Malloy and Cathy Marshall's efforts to "weave threads of electronic mail" in *Forward Anywhere* (1998). Today, we can also read electronic versions of books like William Gibson's *Neuromancer* (1984) and *Mona Lisa Overdrive* (1988), published by Voyager Expanded Books; we can browse hypertexts with complicated graphics and startling sound effects like Eastgate Systems's *Ambulance* or The Computer Lab's *Beyond Cyberpunk*. We can even purchase CD-ROMS of magnificent, searchable renderings of the first editions of very rare books, such as first editions by Milton, Shakespeare, and Copernicus.

Uncomplicated by the multiple authorship of interactive fictions like those written by the Oz Project, nor blurred by the synchronous coreadings of the crowds of people who engage in MUDs, hypertext fictions offer theorists a new site from which to consider how the process of composing stories changes on computers, and how these new stories change us.

PROBLEMS WITH HYPERTEXT FICTIONS

In 1927, during a lecture series reprinted as *Aspects of the Novel*, E.M. Forster drew a distinction between the terms "story" and "plot," a distinction that is of some relevance to those of us who study and write fiction composed and read in the new rhetorical spaces such as Storyspace. Forster said that a story is "a narrative of events arranged in their time-sequence." According to Forster, on the other hand, a plot is "a narrative of events," with "the emphasis falling on causality" (p. 86). Hypertext fictions like Carolyn Guyer's *Quibbling* (1993), Stuart Moulthrop's *Victory Garden* (1991), and Michael Joyce's *Afternoon* (1987), are marvelous at avoiding monocausality. But they are not always apt at providing a good reading experience, in part, I believe, because they do not observe the conventions of narration and plotting to which print has accustomed us.

Forster's distinction between story and plot is illustrated by him in two sentences. The first, "The king died and then the queen died," is a story. On the other hand, the second, "The king died, and then the queen died of grief," is a plot. As we explore the potential of digital narratives, such as virtual realities, the Web, and hypertext fictions, we need to balance our enthusiasm for their potential with a clear understanding of what makes a story good—and how to distinguish between simple stories and compelling plots. E.M. Forster's (1927) classic text helps us remember what, in its most basic bones, makes conventional fiction successful: conflict and resolution, problem and solution, or cause and effect, presented in some dramatic fashion. Forster does not go far enough, however, in identifying the ways in which a story acts on its readers, in its choice of narrator, content, and conflict, in the ways in which its structure and preoccupations relate to the cultural context within which it is presented and read.

When we study hypertext fictions, we must remember to pay attention to the reader's encounter with the *fiction* itself—if our goal is to evaluate the quality of the story and its plot, characters, setting, discourse, or any part of the rhetoric of fiction. As we saw in the last chapter, when we analyze the old Infocom games like *Deadline* (1991), *Plundered Hearts* (1991), or *A Mind Forever Voyaging* (1991), it matters less that they are read on a disk and matters more what the quality of reader engagement is. The equipment used to present the story to the reader is not an adequate site for a rhetorical analysis of how stories act on their readers. We need not examine the helmet or the dataglove to understand the evolving story.

In *Aspects of the Novel* (1927), E.M. Forster continues by defining a novel as "a fiction in prose of a certain extent," an extent which he arbitrarily defines as not less than 50,000 words. Most hypertext fictions published by Eastgate Systems and written by authors such as Michael Joyce, Stuart Moulthrop, Carolyn Guyer, John MacDaid, George Landow, and others, loosely fit Forster's definition of a novel. Michael Joyce's *Afternoon* (1987), for example, a "classic" hypertext fiction, is comprised of *many* tens of thousands of words if we allow for the iterative readings it supports. But every hypertext fiction I have read is very different from almost all paper-based fictions—all except for such literary experiments and postmodern stories such as *Mulligan Stew* (1979) by Gilbert Sorrentino, "The Babysitter" (1969) by Robert Coover, *Locos* (1936) by Felipe Alfau, *Hopscotch* (1975) by Julio Cortázar, practically anything by Paul Auster or Robbe-Grillet, or *If on a winter's night a traveler* (1981) by Italo Calvino—and I am not sure that difference is always good.

Michael Joyce himself, in an unpublished interview with Francesca Pasquali, aligns himself with various postmodern and cyborgian theories of composing, and other members of the TINAC electronic arts collective (founded by Michael Joyce, Nancy Kaplan, John McDaid, and Stuart Moulthrop) likewise see their texts as realizing the best in contemporary, post-structuralist, narrative theories. However, in my view, despite the promise that hypertext fiction realizes—the promise of malleability, bifurcated plots, and reader-driven selection of events—texts like *Afternoon* and *Victory Garden* lack the dramatic tension, the purposes and causes, the trajectories between concatenating events, which Forster identifies as central to good plots—and that we are accustomed to at this point in history. Imagine sitting at a computer screen and pointing and clicking between around 600 frames, or *lexias*, and through almost as many links between those frames. Narrative progression, if it exists in any way in this form, is, indeed, postmodern.

No hypertext fiction I have read, in my opinion, is of the quality of any great novel written in this century. Again, I don't mean here to blame the pencil for the author's mistakes. I have thought a lot about my own dissatisfaction with a medium that promises so much, and I have come to believe that the thin narrative power of hypertext fictions in particular springs from its failure to recommend sequence, to require chronology, and to dictate an evolving series of events; in other words, to manage the plot. However, I also suspect that my tastes for those conventions are themselves culturally embedded.

Any successful story, Forster (1927) reminds us, is based on an evolving series of events arranged in a meaningful sequence. As readers, we are riveted by the desire to learn what will happen next. Even in the novels of Sir Walter Scott (which Forster doesn't think much of because he finds them curiously passionless), the reader will find a compelling narrative, a rigorous ordering of events that demands she continue reading to find out what happens next. In Forster's words, when a reader reads Sir Walter Scott, he gets "so docile under the succession of episodes that he just gapes, like a primitive cave-man" (p. 36). Forster accuses Scott of "dumping down" (p. 37) events one after another "without bothering to elucidate them." But the reader of Sir Walter Scott is compelled to keep reading in a way a hypertext fiction reader is not—because of her desire to find out what happens, and because the book itself demands a particular sequence pretty rigorously. On the other hand, writers of hypertext fiction are writers like Michael Joyce, who hope that the time will come when "we will come to see books for their multiplicity rather than their authority" (personal communication, May 21, 1996), that fictions written in Storyspace, still the most common hypertext authoring system, will acknowledge and represent the unselected, unevaluated, unorganized, and unordered reality we commonly experience outside of books.

The problem, I think, with much of contemporary digital fiction is that it knows story but not plot, or conceives of story as nomadic rather than mapped, to use similes more appropriate to the spatial metaphor implicit in most hypertext fictions. When we write stories such as hypertext fictions or Web-based fictions, or participate in MUDs, while we must do more than pay attention to the new capacities of the *materials* of storytelling, we must not lose sight of the classical elements of any successful story: what Forster (1927) calls plot and what we might today call narrative progression (Phelan, 1989) or the rhetoric of fiction (Booth, 1983). Disk-based interactive fictions, and mainframe-based interactive fictions currently under development, like the murder mystery being explored at Carnegie Mellon University, suffer too from the double-edged sword of liberating the reader from the dictatorial directions of the traditional author. In some ways, hypertext fictions provide the final resting place for Barthes's (1977) dead author, the latest realization of our century's growing critical envy of the author and her magical ability to tell a story. But in other ways, hypertext fictions raise to the highest level the tensions between reader and author. Listening to the remarks of three hypertext fiction writers below helps resurrect the author and reinstalls the *deus ex machina* as hallowed device. Implicit in these remarks, too, is a rogue and innovative way of understanding story, and, by extension, the cultural hierarchies within which we compose.

MICHAEL JOYCE'S *AFTERNOON*

When Walter Ong (1982) traces the evolution of human consciousness and ties that evolution to advances in print technology and the development of writing, he is speaking (or rather, writing) the same language as Sven Birkerts. Ong connects the rise of individuality, or an increase in our understanding of ourselves as human individuals with specific rights, views, and capacities, to the "highly interiorized stages of consciousness" (p. 178), which are fostered by those who can read and write—and forfeited by those who cannot. Ong writes,

> The evolution of consciousness through human history is marked by growth in articulate attention to the interior of the individual person as distanced—though not necessarily separated—from the communal structures in which each person is necessarily enveloped. Self-consciousness is coextensive with humanity: everyone who can say "I"

has an acute sense of self. But reflectiveness and articulateness about the self takes time to grow. (p. 178)

Ong goes on to develop his thesis that literacy leads to individuality and insight, by citing the work in "a Jungian framework by Erich Neumann (1954) in which stages in consciousness are described as progressing towards becoming a being that has 'a self-conscious, articulate, highly personal, interiority'" (p. 178).

In recent published writings as well as interviews with Michael Joyce, we can hear Joyce taking a very different perspective on the importance of interiority, reflectiveness, and the ways in which stories can help an individual realize these qualities. Rather than bemoaning the short attention span of today's readers, Joyce addresses it in his fiction by creating room for "successive attendings" to the text; rather than searching for words that will deepen a reader's sense of self (and, by extension, substance and soul), Joyce seeks ways for readers' presence to be "distributed," or to achieve greater "amplitude"; and rather than seeking to disconnect readers from "the communal structures" (Ong, 1982) within which they compose, and thus deepen interiority, Joyce seeks a "flow" in his stories, one that allows both story and reader to move outward toward a "great convergence."

Michael Joyce (1995) positions his work within a theoretical framework very different from Jung's preoccupation with archetypes, the collective unconscious, and transcultural structures and shared images of human conflicts and desires. Joyce's theoretical frame is made up of voices like those of Donna Haraway, Hélène Cixous, and Gilles Deleuze and Félix Guattari, all readers and writers whose sense of textuality is a far cry from that of Ong or Birkerts. Again, as I see it, the primary reason for complaints about the pace, plot, and level of engagement of hypertext fictions is that those readers are looking for the ideas and conventions of narrative that evolved coincident to books (and the print-based literacies they supposed), and that don't recognize other ways of reading and being such as those suggested by Haraway and others. Each of these points is developed in more detail below, based on remarks made in recent interviews by author Michael Joyce, conducted over e-mail by me in 1996.

Joyce calls his own work "multiple fictions" or, on occasion, "hypernarratives," work that he sees as responding to a paradigm shift in the way we read. He says,

> If there is a paradigm shift I think it is one toward a rethinking of coherence in terms of the forms things persist in taking and I think it can be found in one I have called elsewhere the shift toward successive attendings, i.e., 'in an age like ours which privileges polyvocality, multiplicity, and constellated knowledge a sustained attention span may be less useful than successive attendings.' Increasingly it is not the substance of what we say but its expression and construction (literally its location and our embodiment in that location) which communicates. (personal communication, May 21, 1996)

In these remarks, Joyce is trumpeting his ties to theoretical positions including the post-structuralist, which look outside the bounds of conventional texts to examine who got to write them and how they got circulated, the *how* as much as the *what* that got said. Joyce implicitly echoes the Foucauldian shift from studying the "author" to studying "authorial function." Joyce ties this important notion of attending to the *processes* of expression and construction to a consideration of democracy, and democratic reading and writing habits. He says that the notion of "successive attendings" demands,

> a necessary recalculation of what we could mean by democracy in such a setting. "Equal distribution of power," itself a radical and never attained view of democracy, i.e., a narrative of governance, is likely to be replaced by something like what rhetoricians call "amplitude," a sense that our presences are sufficiently distributed or, if not that, sufficiently accessible as to be able to be recognized. (personal communication, May 21, 1996)

In other words, Joyce construes the possibilities of readerly presence in a narrative as itself a kind of democratic action, a notion of democracy that is more plausible than were many of early claims for hypertext's potential for "liberating" the reader and "revolutionizing" textual practices. Replacing failed democratic intentions with distributed presence or "amplitude" in a hypertext is exactly the kind of explicit connection between theory and practice that causes readers like Birkerts to bristle.

In remarks that Michael Joyce gave in a panel at Hypertext '96, he expands on his theme and questions how "multiple narratives" and the apparatus that carries them (in this case, the Web) are themselves steeped in cultural conventions, economic systems, and established hierarchies of information and meaning. He offers an example based on the virtual urban sprawl we call Netscape:

> Netscape's decision to evict Yahoo to an offscreen barrio below the scroll in order to sell high-rise screen placement demonstrates how supposedly neutral tools and interface aspects are not merely C++ code, but the other kind of programming that spews from the box of televised light on the wall. The notion that we must filter out the mass of information, of course, implies a hierarchy of information and of human beings, and suggests an immanence of cultural values rather than a culture [that] is constructed by human presence, discussion, and community. (personal communication, May 21, 1996)

Here, Joyce is advocating an admirable position, one that reminds readers that we must attend to the systems that construct our virtual presence—on the Web, in computer games, or in digital fictions—and realize the values, choices, and hierarchies (of information, beauty, volume, style, and economics, to name just a few) inherent therein. By taking this position, Joyce's notion of "successive attendings" takes on a new meaning. Not only do readers attend time and time again to the possibilities of movement and disguise in hypertext fictions, but they must attend to the ways those possibilities are constructed—all the way down to the programming languages in which they were written and all the way up to the metacultural views embedded in the spatial architectures of sites like Netscape. Joyce's "successive attendings" allow a more thorough reading than any proposed by Sven Birkerts and his fetishizing of books, and such a reading strategy also exposes many of the values and norms implicit in Birkert's canon.

Joyce also develops the term "flow" to describe the way information travels on the Internet, and to explain the ways self is diffused, reassembled, disguised, the ways access and distribution are constructed, within hypernarratives and other Web-based fictions. In paying attention to the patterns of flow (trickle and flood) on the Web, for example, Joyce urges us to look at how we might send "credit card info up" and experience the flood of "HotWiredTimeWarnerDisney down." In our interview, Joyce explicitly draws on the important work of Donna Haraway, looking to her theories of partial knowing to anchor us within that flow. He quotes Haraway in his rejection of relativism and advocacy of attention to "flow," reminding us that "the alternative to relativism is partial, locatable, critical knowledges sustaining the possibility of webs of connections called solidarity in politics and shared conversations in epistemology [that is],... a doctrine and practice of objectivity that privileges deconstruction, passionate construction, webbed connections, and hope for transformation of systems of knowledge and ways of seeing" (Haraway, 1991, pp. 191–192). Finally, in some very interesting ways, Michael Joyce connects Haraway's idea of partial knowing to what he described in one interview as "interstitial narrative, the interstitial imagination," an idea that he represented visually in the composition of his book, *Of Two Minds: Hypertext, Pedagogy, and Poetics* (1995).

Within the creative, elegant, and intelligent reflections on art, narrative, and textual production that have been bound between two covers and packaged as Joyce's *Of Two Minds* (1995), we can plainly see the ways in which hypertextual preoccupations with self-reflexivity, successive attendings, and "flow" are translated into a paper form, a print-based database, if you will, that includes previously published work, frequent allusions to writings (and interviews with writers) that were constructed by other hypertext writers, and narratives both personal and public, interleaved. Indirectly reminiscent of Calvino's (1981) *If on a winter's night a traveler* (incipits and numbered chapters shuffled together), Cortázar's *Hopscotch* (1975), or the sometimes perplexingly random results of a Yahoo search, the intertwined, diffused narratives within Joyce's text are marvelously broken, reassembled, and presented in an echo of a hypermedia performance. One aspect of this performance is the occasional interruption of text with an "interstitial," usually a tale of creation, an interview with self or other, and in the broadest terms some kind of reflection on what we do when we write. Perhaps Joyce's interstitials, or interruptions, more fairly represent the mode of contemporary thinking, our patterns of mind.

In one of Joyce's (1995) interstitials, one called "Networks of Woven Water— The Dangers of Transparency," Joyce quotes and connects work by Carolyn Guyer, Martha Petry, Gail Hawisher, Cindy Selfe, Catherine Smith, Patricia Sullivan, and Nancy Kaplan to comment on the extent to which this new medium blurs traditional boundaries of reading, writing, and authorship: He explains reading is no longer confined to the plane of a page, writing grows more obviously collaborative, and authorial attribution and notions of textual property are blown out of the water. Joyce's interstitials finally mirror the possibilities and project of hypertext fiction, trying as best he can to achieve on paper the qualities Catherine Smith ascribes to hypertext networks: that the network "develops in a stream of successive, mutable fields permeated by influences from the organism and its environment" (qtd. in Joyce, 1995, p. 62). For Joyce and other hypertext writers, composition becomes architecture.

Within Joyce's interstitials (1995), we can see a composition related to the pastiche, the bricolage, a rhapsodic stitching-together of other people's words and his own past and present, a composition that fits a pattern that Rebecca Moore Howard (1999) calls "patch-writing" and that echoes the aggregative, associative compilations that Ong (1982) ascribes to oral cultures. I see Joyce's "patch-writing" as also echoing the cultural constraints on writers composing under the shadow of newly imposed copyright laws: the Edinburgh literati, for example, who composed their ideas of good taste not only in light of England's supposedly superior literary models, but in the wake of the newly imposed Statute of Anne, which prescribed a pattern of textual attribution and ownership that was at first imperfectly understood or applied.[26] Joyce's interstitials likewise have evolved from the observations, commonplaces, and shared knowledge of a small community of hypertext authors, a community that is exclusive and homosocial in its own way. None of us composes in a vacuum.

But the print-based "patch-writings" of hypertext authors (George Landow, Michael Joyce, Carolyn Guyer, and Stuart Moulthrop, among others) are different from past collaborations in two important ways. First, they bring a confident, exclusive theoretical grounding to their claims, finding in the writings of post-structuralists, deconstructionists, and feminists an explanation and validation of their hypertext narratives. In one interview with Michael Joyce, for example, he routinely cites the work of other theorists, borrowing terms and ideas that fit his hope for understanding "the textual encrustration of hypertext." He says,

> Deleuze and Guattari [1987] propose nomos against the logos; wandering against the word; being-for against being-in space. Their process of becomingness shifts between the smooth space of for-time (the gappiness of utopia) and the striated space of in-time (though not intimé) much in the way Carolyn Guyer's sensuous narrative forms in *Quibbling* [1993] shift so that character and place (her lovely coves) veer and intermix into an erotic spatialization. Sometimes the interstitial nature of hypertext seems to offer a paradigm of constant becomingness (the "betweenus" of Hélène Cixous [1981]) as a way out of what we are in, a way in where we are put out. (personal communication, May 21, 1996)

Joyce understands and theorizes his own sense of the composing process, and draws on contemporary writers and theorists, to a far greater extent than did the oral cultures described by Ong or the closed community of 18th-century Scottish writers, who had only a foggy sense of the proprieties of textual attribution at best. When we hear claims that electronic textuality is a kind of orality, we need to see their differences, too.

Second, hypertext fictions and their writers and imitators have a strong and visible sense of history, including histories personal, cultural, technological, and economic; the textual representations of these histories that hypertexts allow is a true innovation. As Joyce says in his interview, "most yesterdays fade both from memory and from the physiological landscape with little ado." (Joyce is speaking here about the production of memory, both within a person and within the dynamics of a hypertext.) In the visual representations of memory, and in the postmodern aesthetic that seems best to embody the way memory works, we see crazy concatenations, quick cuts, quirky realignments, and rearrangements of remembered events that exist in some bizarre, imagistic alliteration of mind and the stories it holds. (We can see this postmodern, hypertextual aesthetic operating also in contemporary videos like David Blair's [1991] *WAX or the Discovery of Television among the Bees,* a cult classic shown at virtual reality conferences, a marvelous meditation on personal and cultural histories, narratives of love, accretions of knowledge about technology and its destructive capacities, and reflections on parallel universes, mirrored realities, representation, and consequence.) Joyce and other artists working with a hypertext aesthetic have made memory visible, have transposed the loops, twists, gaps, and reiterations of thought into words and images we can read asequentially on a screen. Joyce comments on the results of this kind of transposition, in his colorful remarks about memory's representation and agency:

> The Buddha recalls the Bo tree, the lover recalls the crimson sugar maple beneath which he fell into the arms of his first love. No matter what I attempt to recall tomorrow—whether redemption, my father's death, a maple tree or a simple yesterday, I have the sense that in recalling it, I am accessing, if not traversing, an actual—and actualized—space. This sense of traversing becomes especially evident if, on some tomorrow, I come to write about what I recall of this particular yesterday. Whatever our critical disputes about the nature of writing, we seem to share a common recognition that, in writing, a mental act becomes a thing, that time, the most primordial of mental acts, yields space, the most primitive of things. (personal communication, May 21, 1996)

Ultimately, though, memory is not story, and mimetic, true representations of consciousness, whether in the frozen compositions of the page or the fluid architectures of the screen, are not often paced, plotted, or rhetorical in a conventional sense. In Joyce's hypertext fictions, story is web rather than line, and the rhetorical models that accommodate it should be three-dimensional rather than two. However, despite the rich metaphors and genuine vision that inform Joyce's remarks, hypertext fictions still attract only a small audience interested in the experiments of literature and mind that the form accommodates so well.

CAROLYN GUYER'S *QUIBBLING*

While Michael Joyce helps us understand the principles of reading he sees arising
from the structures of hypertext (the importance of "successive attendings" in nav-
igating the "flow" of narratives), Carolyn Guyer's interviews and writings give us an
opportunity to concentrate on the processes by which a hypertextual fiction can
innovate form, voice, and sites of reading. In Guyer's interview, published essays,
and the reviews that accompany *Quibbling* (1993), she claims her preoccupation with
what she calls the "buzz-daze" and "...the coalescent, rhythmic ability to create
nothing from anything." Carolyn Guyer's hypertexts and published critical reflections on the process of writing represent even more vividly the mechanics of memory made visible, histories encoded in space, personal and cultural stories made
alive, recurrent. Echoing narratives like Abbe Don's groundbreaking "We Make
Memories"[27] Carolyn Guyer's *Quibbling* is a hypertext fiction that literary critic
Carolyn Guertin says is "[w]oven together of bits of glass, windows and moons, the
curve of necklines and the hint of breasts." Guertin reports that reading *Quibbling*
made her feel as if she were underwater, and as if the story were made of her own
characters, not ones that Guyer invented. In Guyer's interview, she helps us understand the innovations in form and concern for representing women's voices in
hypertext fictions written in Storyspace. Further, she offers a straightforward
account of many of the mundane details accompanying the production of *Quibbling*.

A typical reading of *Quibbling* would proceed as follows. A reader would probably be intrigued by the advertising copy accompanying the story diskette. It says,
"Through motifs of mothering, distance and intimacy, geography and labyrinths,
art and writing, nuns and priests, the moon, and sexuality, *Quibbling* recreates the
experience of writing, of assembling a story from fragments..." This advertising
copy also includes a quotation from Carolyn Guyer, in which she explicitly positions
herself as someone interested in rethinking and repositioning fiction and text, rather
than as a wholly original writer creating stories *sui generis*. Guyer says, "Just as creativity is more about elaboration than fabrication, so hypertext is more a verb than
a noun, more about the flux of making, it is a re-forming rather than a form."
Quibbling is described by Eastgate Systems as a new kind of hypertext fiction:

> Guyer's *Quibbling* returns control of the web to the reader. Using few guard fields,
> *Quibbling* studiously avoids subterfuge. The text is mapped and laid before the reader;
> unlike Joyce and Moulthrop, who use the simpler Page reader, Guyer intends *Quibbling*
> to be read with the Storyspace reader, or in Storyspace itself. *Quibbling* offers free and
> knowing navigation, a hypertext in which the reader is master, and the text follows her
> command. The central image of *Quibbling* is a lake, shifting and glimmering yet always
> the same.

The story of *Quibbling* is the story of several pairs of people, which focuses in
particular on one woman's memories, sexual awakenings, her relationship with a
man named Priam, lesbian imaginings, and work experiences. A reader copies the

diskette onto her hard drive and then opens the story by double-clicking on the appropriate icon. A screen (sometimes called a dialogue box) appears asking the reader to select between "begin a new reading" or "resume a previous reading." The user clicks on either option, and the story "loads," "places," and "links." A "help" screen explains the navigational tools at the bottom of each text and textlink. A reader can "page" through the story automatically by clicking on the double arrows at the bottom of each screen. Multiple readings of the text succeed in reinforcing this reader's sense that *Quibbling* is a Bakhtinian carnival, with free admission for all comers or conversationalists. The text's untouchability is echoed by my feeling unmoored, the text unanchored. That is, there are such abrupt jumps in time and space, unconnected scenes and moments that do not reward my hard work at stitching them together, and no doubt would doubly disappoint a reader like Birkerts, intent upon discovering the single narrative thread that will lead out of the labyrinth and directly into the self. However, viewed as an experiment, *Quibbling* holds promise.

In my e-mail interview with Guyer, she talked about both the processes and the scenes of her writing.[28] To compose *Quibbling*, Guyer used a Mac IIsi with a 14-inch Hitachi color monitor, and a 9600-baud modem. For hypertext software, she used only Storyspace because "being a visual artist as well as a writer, [she found she] really needed the graphical layout provided by Storyspace." According to her own account, she wrote the story in two different locations: Olathe, Kansas, and Manistee, Michigan. Guyer says: "In Kansas I worked in a room with the shades drawn, concentrating on creating the general parameters of the thing I was writing. I didn't set out consciously to proceed in that way, but rather, it seemed to become necessary, in this form without tradition...." After framing the story in Kansas, Guyer moved to a small cottage on Lake Michigan, where she "developed many interactions, events, non-events, fuller characters, deepened layers of complexity in lives, brought in allusional aspects, worked through some of the knottier artistic and hypertextual issues, and finally sent it off to Eastgate." Guyer explains that being alone in this cottage, without a job to go to, and surrounded by waves and beach, affected the rhythms of both her composing process and the final product. She would write for as many as 12 hours a day, looking out the picture window in her cottage on a bluff, hearing and seeing the waves, and gaining the "philosophical space and rhythm" she said she needed to compose *Quibbling*. Guyer explains,

> With the days and nights to myself there in Michigan, I eventually set up a personal rhythm of working late into the night (often 3am), then sleeping till 9 or 10 the next morning, get up, go for a walk on the beach (during deep winter not really possible because of severe weather, though once I did risk my life to walk well out onto the ice formations that accumulated thickly along the shore, simply to have done it), then return to house, cat, and organize the day's [10–12 hours] of writing...

In *Leonardo Magazine*, Guyer also developed the notion of the scene of writing being related to the resulting preoccupations and form of *Quibbling*. She wrote,

> In hindsight, I can see why water and its properties became one of the pervasive, propelling metaphors in the work. A lake with many coves is how I saw it. The coves being where we focus, where individuals exist, where things are at least partly comprehensible; the lake being none of that, but, naturally, more than the sum of the coves, or more than what connects them. As a metaphor, the lake and coves stand not just for the form of this hyperfiction, but hyperfictions generally… (n.p.)

And in her interview with me, Guyer discussed some of the relationships she sees between feminist consciousness or feeling, the literal waves outside her cottage, and the figurative waves in the story of *Quibbling*. In her own synopsis, Guyer refers to *Quibbling* being about "how women and men are together," or, she explains, "…one could say it is the story of someone's life just before the beginning or a little after the end." As she develops the idea of *Quibbling* being a story about "four couples who are variations of complex mixtures," like Joyce, she draws on Deleuze and Guattari, but she deliberately attempts to convert theory into practice, as a close reading of the "process journal" Guyer kept during the composition of *Quibbling* reveals. She wrote,

> As for the general method, I've tried to model what I see as "the quotidian stream." Simply, the stories we tell everyday. The gossip, family discussions, letters, passing fancies and daydreams that we tell ourselves and each other almost all day in order to make sense of things. They are not "whole stories" like literary fiction. They are instead the small bits, intimate and personal, that get us through a day, string together the days, and eventually, seen from a distance, create the patterns of a life. I also see this, inevitably, as a model of how women in particular tell each other their stories.

Interestingly, one of Guyer's own characters in *Quibbling* also is a writer working on a hypertext fiction, one who keeps his own illuminating journal. He echoes many of Guyer's concerns about the tension between textual constraint and freedom, between the voice of one and the collaborations of a few (that Guyer claims are more typical of women's writing), between reality and "the buzz-daze." Her character writes in his journal, "…sometimes writing this stuff is like being in a daze. The shifted, split focus; the overlay and the interchangeability of reality and invention. Altered state? jeez. No wonder they all drink" (Guyer, 1992). Figure becomes ground in Guyer's hypertext fiction; writer becomes she who is read (as well as she who is reading); there is no single path through Guyer's *Quibbling* that yields unequivocal meaning, universal truth, or even an impartial view of situation, no doubt by Guyer's design. The computer simply allows a more visible process of writing to emerge, right before our very eyes. Guyer explains her interest in computers as an attraction to a medium that allows mutable form and reforming. She says,

Specific attractions drew me to the use of computers. The first and easiest, and indeed, the seduction for most people, was mutable text. Just the words themselves become fluid, more on a beam (motes on a beam) with the way language is in me. Word processing is a dry distance of a label for what is, more accurately, writing with light. But once that became possible, once I found I could think better when the words reforming on the screen in front of my eyes began to approach the speed of the ones behind them, I found myself wanting the synchrony to increase.

In other places in our e-mail interview, Guyer talked about her own ambivalence about some hypertext fictions, especially those with visible "hierarchies" and ultra-clear linings as to which "path" to follow through the text. Writers like this are implicitly saying "no straying, no trouble, this way to the castle," according to Guyer. She says that she wants to yelp, "[l]et go of the leash!" to these ham-fisted writers who do not leave enough freedom for their readers to explore. She explains,

Some people have done things with hypertext that cause me to ache. The best have been the worst writers, the ones who have joined collaborative ventures with undeveloped skills and plunked what they felt right in the middle of someone else's sinuous prose. These I am grateful to for revealing to me my own biases, and for showing me the perspectival quickstep.

When I asked Guyer about her own conception of an ideal reader, she said:

Never had an ideal reader ... I can think of things that would make me happy if they were true of a reader, but I never had the expectation of anything but widely varying individual responses. I suppose in some sense one always looks for someone like herself. Or better still, someone who would find things in the work that I didn't realize were there.

Guyer goes on to note that while many readers have cared about *Quibbling*, she has not been terribly surprised at how most have not. When I asked her what responses to *Quibbling* she wished for, she said: "Truly, what anyone wants to make of it is fine. I deliberately constructed *Quibbling* to encourage readers *to invent reading it*, and also to make changes in it if they wanted to."

Clearly, Guyer is concerned with her reader's experiences, even as she gives that reader the freedom to discover her own "path" and direction. That is, Guyer has had to create a body of work that counters the heavy-handed guides and links in some of the worst hypertext fictions to date. But clearly also, the formal constraints of blocks of text and links, and the author's part in choosing and defining them, are concerns that weigh heavily on Guyer. Her choice to include as many links as she plausibly can in *Quibbling* is a choice she ultimately sees as wrong. As she said in her interview:

The business of links, here at the end when I'm trying to mash/mesh them all in, is changing form even as I attempt to form. I've always felt dense linkage meant more options for the reader, and so greater likelihood of her taking the thing for her own.

But this idea now seems wrong to me. Excessive linkage can actually be seen as something of an insult, and certainly more directive. When I make a link, I'm only expressing my sense of the story (or one of my senses). This is the same for any reader. How dare I, just because I have first go at it, try to make connections for everyone else, too? Is the reader left only with following me around in the thing?

For Guyer, finally, the number and quality of links and endings are closely related to her working answers to questions about identity, feminine selves, freedom, and even metaphysics. As she debates number and quality of links, she is also negotiating degrees of readerly freedom and constraint. In a 1994 book review, Guyer speculates about the artist's voice, singular and plural, and looks to the history of women experimental writers to frame both her own work and the questions intractably embedded there. She says, "[H]owever much of a cultural equation we might make of women and "co" words, collaboration, cooperation, community, and connection, we also need to pay attention to the clearly distinct voices" (p. 13). Carolyn Guyer's *Quibbling* is one example of such a distinct voice.

STUART MOULTHROP'S *HEGIRASCOPE* AND *VICTORY GARDEN*

While Michael Joyce's remarks on composing *Afternoon* (1987) reveal a preoccupation with new techniques of reading, new possibilities for the diffusion of identity, and the importance of allowing "flow," and while Carolyn Guyer's discussions of how *Quibbling* (1993) allowed her to set water and its waves, currents, and questions as the form for her hypertext narrative in a new feminist voice, Stuart Moulthrop's comments during the course of an e-mail interview with me presents a broader view of hypertext fictions and an intriguing braid of personal and cultural histories. When I asked Moulthrop about the promise of hypertext fictions, he directed my attention to larger concerns of economics, culture, and millennial possibility and panic. His Web-based fiction, *Hegirascope* (1995), is an intriguing meditation on these same concerns, one in which a reader chooses from among several options on an opening "alternative home page" to explore transient contemporary worlds. In *Hegirascope*, the reader is met by a series of screens flickering one into another, first black, then yellow, all marked by short sentences reflecting on contemporary life, for example, the Internet, diaspora, hegira, hypertext, excess, ballast, eating oysters with a spoon, not mutually exclusive categories. The first familiar looking bit of narrative begins like this:

They got into the car in Dallas at the crack of dawn
Friday, directly after Bent picked up the keys from the
mission people. It was a big silver Ford like a state car.
The mileage was just over 32,000, which Gina doubted.
The guy who owned it must have liked drugstore

cologne, but you didn't notice after a while. It would
get them where they were going.

Bent would take the first shift, from here to Little
Rock. They drove up I-30 into the summer sunrise. It
wasn't really hot yet, so they tried rolling the windows
down, only the windshield got fogged. Bent sat up
straight with his hands at ten and two just like in
driver's ed. Gina started to laugh. It was so much like
when they were kids starting off on vacation with the
folks.

Hegirascope continues by describing the journey of Gina and Bent, driving toward
Memphis and breakfast, or rather, toward "the dream of breakfast," shifting
between second- and third-person address, between settings, between styles of narration and diction, between allusions to Wallace Stevens ("Sunday Morning") and
to the "mayhem" on the street below the window, between Bosnia and Oklahoma
City. The references feel interior, personal, associative, yet the narrative intrigues.

I talked to Stuart Moulthrop about *Victory Garden* (1991) and *Hegirascope* (1995).[29]
Our exchange went like this:

SJS: What is the promise of computer-based fictions from your perspective as
a writer of them? What are their dangers, if there are any?

SM: I have to quibble…. Your question puts too much importance on the fictions (or by extension the games, the MUDs, the other sorts of cybertext).
These things are less significant in themselves than as signs of a disturbance
propagating through the culture. Something may be changing at long last, or
getting ready to present itself. Where's that W.B. Yeats when you need him?
Dangers? Fiction is always dangerous; that's why we have Hollywood.

Moulthrop continues in the interview to speculate on the ways computer platforms "enable, define, and thus constrain" content and movement (and, I would
add, reading and writing in general). Moulthrop says he sees hypertext fictions such
as his own *Hegirascope 2.0* as "more *place* than text." In discussing his decision to
name one of his first stories *Victory Garden* (see Birkerts discussion at the beginning
of this chapter), he mentions at first that titles don't really matter, then changes his
mind when he remembers the importance of names on maps:

SM: I'm tempted to say that titles only matter when (and for whom) they matter; though I suppose electronic texts ask more from their particular acts of
naming than do print texts. Probably it's because they are more *place* than
text. Places seem not to exist, in our occidental scheme at least, until we've got
something to put on the signpost.

Furthermore, in his discussion of platforms in constraining and defining form and meaning, Moulthrop mentions that, "[p]eople who still seem to regard print as the One True and Angelic Medium (e.g., Sven Birkerts) seem eager to forget [that all platforms enable, define, and thus constrain]." He offers as an example the popular hypertext fiction composing program Storyspace, which he says mattered "enormously" to his own composing process:

> *SM:* Storyspace alone among affordable hypertext systems provides a graphical map of structure and textual relations. This map is in fact the workspace. So it was possible to achieve a much more successful degree of coordinated convolution than I had ever managed before, notably in my earlier experiments with HyperCard (my older piece "Chaos" is not accidentally a fragment). Though "Hegirascope" probably looks on first presentation like narrative confetti, it is in fact obsessively (and linearly) structured, which clever readers could have figured out for themselves if I hadn't spoiled the joke. "Hegirascope," by the way, was also built with HyperCard but recently I've used HyperCard mainly as a scripting environment, not a presentation tool.

Finally, in his explicit acknowledgment of the ways books construct linear reading experiences, and in his implicit acknowledgments of the potential of hypertext fiction to allow a wider range of reading experiences (and qualities of human consciousness), Moulthrop is clearly seeking his own metaphor to describe the possibilities. In the comments below, Moulthrop is musing among the fragments, throwing a handful of "narrative confetti" up in the air to see where it flies. Moulthrop mentions,

> *SM:* I've just been editing a story for *Postmodern Culture* that has a certain stylistic similarity to "Hegirascope" (i.e., it's a series of discontinuous fragments—much more elegant than my stuff) —and I quite like this piece. But I assume that I'm meant to see it as a single trace, a reduction from some more complex and kinetic ur-state—just as multiple fictions seem pale shadows of the *really* turbulent, chaotic, polyvocal cyberforms (MUDs, MOOs, jam spaces).

But a few minutes later, in response to a question about the trajectories of his development as a storyteller who uses paper, Storyspace, and the WWW, Moulthrop changes the metaphor to one more vegetal than mechanistic. He responds in the following way to my question about his development as a storyteller:

> *SJS:* How are the trajectories of your development as a storyteller and your choosing the media of paper, Storyspace, and Web parallel, if they are? That

is, how has the range of your storytelling abilities developed in tandem with or against your experiments with writing in different media?

SM: There's no linear, teleological unfolding here. Or if so, it's more of a vegetable teleology—the way a plant germinates, comes up, blooms (and all the rest)—not the kind that goes with big, intentional structures. I feel more like a craftsman than an artist in the old-fashioned sense. Here are some tools, look what you can do with them. Something unfolds and it's important to examine it very closely as it happens, to bear responsibility for the happening. But this doesn't mean I know what I'm up to even some of the time.

So, in Moulthrop's reflections on his own processes of reading and writing hypertext fiction, he freely admits the influences of chaos, chance, or organic evolution in nearly every phase: in the writer's failure to know what he is up to "even some of the time"; the text's own "polyvocal cyberforms" that Storyspace allows; and the reader's parade through the spaces, literal and figurative, shaped by the random flutter of this "narrative confetti."

All three writers interviewed here have shown us a great deal about the ways in which their composing processes ultimately contribute to open-ended (not to mention open-middled) hypertext fictions.

PROCESSES AS CRITICAL CATEGORY

They've got computers
that draw conclusions
from minor details & faded clues.
When is your birthday?
Who paid your phone bill?
What were you wearing
the last time I saw you?

—Lyrics from "Find Me Too" (Tjardes, 1998)

Again, hypertext fictions demonstrate visibly, on a screen right before our eyes, a dynamic that is the virtual incarnation of several post-structuralist notions: the ideas that subject and identity are always fractured and multiple, that the univocal author is irrevocably dead, and that there is no such creature as an "objective" text. Digital fictions in general make visible the competing, dissonant contexts of reading and writing acts. The fluid exchanges, we might even say contests, between a computer fiction reader (as she constructs a story) and an author (as his intent is conveyed in a mercurial text and its underlying layers of programmed instructions) are particularly vivid enactments of post-structuralist—and feminist—theories. But that is not all they are. George Landow's *Hypertext: The Convergence of Contemporary Critical Theory and Technology* (1992a) explores how post-structuralist ideas embedded in the literary theories of Roland Barthes, Michel Foucault, Mikhail Bakhtin, and Jacques Derrida, among other critics, are realized in the text-blocks, links, and webs of hypertext fiction. If we are to understand how hypertexts convey the intentions of their authors and support the expectations and needs of their readers, we need to understand better all the dimensions of this new contract between reader and writer.

The failed contest (discussed in Chapter 3) between the reader-detective of *Deadline* (1991) and its resistant text, which will not yield crucial clues when addressed in the "wrong" syntax, for example, demonstrates visibly the dissonant contexts—and competing wishes—of readers and authors. The entry points permitted by *Quibbling* (1993) in its circled words and phrases (reminiscent of ancient Egyptian cartouches) themselves destabilize the fixed text and any controlled revelation of narrative strategy, plot, or character. Hypertext fictions indeed visibly demonstrate a feminist predisposition to question the roles of readers and authors, as they respond to texts, and enact a postmodern multilinearity, pacing, and shattering of the narrative flow. More importantly, though, for our purposes, these fictions also explicitly perform the post-structuralist critical enterprise of redefining (and ultimately shattering) the rhetorical triangle.

The models of reading and writing that most completely encompass the dynamics of reading and writing hypertext fictions, based on Eastgate Systems's Storyspace, are probably those generated by researchers in the field of cognitive science. Using language may seem uncontroversial, seem a simple and transparent act of translating world into words, but as I have argued several times already, using language, writing or speaking about any parts of our shared world, is never so straightforward as the cognitivists would have us believe. The central metaphor of a realist, or cognitivist, model of the reading–writing relationship is the *code*: Writing is the process of using symbols to compose a text that is a portable, durable, and a coded string of symbols that directly correlates in every particular to a knowable and describable world; reading is the process of coding and decoding the singular meaning of that text. Although most rhetorical theorists draw a strong distinction between cognitivist and expressivist views of writing, I find the cognitivist metaphor of the code surprisingly close to the Platonic ideas usually read as expressivist.

For example, in Plato's dialogue *Cratylus* (trans. 1998), Socrates expounds on his understanding of language as a metaphoric representation of something real in the world in a speech that could have come out of the mouth of a contemporary rhetorician who holds to a cognitivist view of language:

> [B]ut then you know that the original names have been long ago buried and disguised by people sticking on and stripping off letters for the sake of euphony and twisting and bedizening them in all sorts of ways: and time too may have had a share in the change. Take, for example, the word [κατοπτρον]; why is the letter "p" inserted? This must surely be the addition of some one who cares nothing about the truth…" (p. 100)

Like Socrates in this dialogue, in general cognitivist models of reading and writing consider these two activities as goal-directed processes of coding and decoding objective descriptions of a knowable world. A text exists in a synecdochal relationship to the world, and the primary task of readers and writers is to reveal the terms and workings of that synecdoche, to position a magnifying glass over microcosms, to detail the metonym. Misunderstandings or misreadings of texts are understood as flaws in the processes of coding and decoding. Such models and understandings of reading and writing do not permit easy discussion of the influences of cultural knowledge, any contextual knowledge, or other social constructs, on text processing.

Stories in general are a version of human expression that is sometimes formulaic, sometimes didactic, sometimes instructive or moralistic, or sometimes purely entertaining or informative, but as Wayne Booth (1983), Kenneth Burke (1957), Seymour Chatman (1978), and, more recently, J. Hillis Miller have argued, stories are always rhetorical. Work by feminist narrative theorists such as Rachel Blau DuPlessis (1985), Louise Rosenblatt (1995), and Teresa De Lauretis (1984) demonstrates how larger cultural myths and dominant values are embedded in the content of published fictions—and in the reading practices we bring to these fictions. These critics generally acknowledge that stories act on their audiences in a variety of ways, employing diverse narrative techniques that vary according to historical period, cultural milieu, authorial intent, audience disposition, and publishing apparatus or delivery system. A question I think that writers of hypertext fictions have not adequately answered is this: When a story is delivered on a hypertext platform, and built into that story is the capacity for substantial reader intervention, how are the rhetorical resources of story altered? And how can writers working in these new digital, topographical (Bolter, 1991b) writing spaces create narratives that engage their readers as much as any best-selling author today?

In a rhetorical move that I hope would please Birkerts, I propose looking again at the important ideas of E.M. Forster's *Aspects of the Novel* (1927) to move us toward a comprehensive understanding of the potential and pitfalls (not to mention pratfalls) of hypertext fictions. E.M. Forster very intelligently traces the relations between plot and character in his discussions of Jane Austen's novels, among others. He talks about the strength of her *interdependent* characters, about the differences between flat and round characters; he tells us that sometimes characters overpower the best intentions of the author and the evolving plot. Forster says, "[T]he plot, instead of finding human beings more or less cut to its requirements, as they are in the drama, finds them enormous, shadowy and intractable, and three-quarters hidden like an iceberg. In vain it points out to these unwieldy creatures the advantages of the triple process of complication, crisis, and solution so persuasively expounded by Aristotle" (p. 85).

As we explore ways of making characters rounder on-line, as we explore ways to develop characters in a multilinear unfolding of narrative, we need to develop the strategies for connecting the reader to her virtual self represented in the text—as I think the Oz Project is trying to do, and as some MUDs try to do, and as I think hypertext fictions need more to explore. As I have discussed elsewhere (Sloane, 1994), why can't our narrative bodies be completely different, why couldn't we encounter a story as a body of water or a kind of flame, sputtering and guttering our way through a narrative? What will happen when online gaming worlds like *The Palace* support three-dimensional avatars like those forecast by Neal Stephenson's *Snow Crash* (1992)? (And how will gamers feel when their avatars die in gameplay, becoming cadavatars?) We need to explore these new capacities for reader-character engagement in virtual realities. Instead of kings and queens dying of grief, we need novel protagonists and antagonists that react in their own tailored, plotted, fascinating ways.

Digital fictions in general provide us a new site to ask questions also about how the self is represented in writing. When we explore the electronic masks the computer allows us to assume, and when we explore those masks as dynamic, layered artifacts that are in some ways gendered and otherwise "situated," we may ultimately learn more about the ways we define ourselves in this fluid world at the turn of the century. And if we can come up with ways to connect the round characters of traditional fiction with compelling plots in digital fiction, we will have a winning recipe.

The most obvious difference between books and hypertext fictions may be their delivery system as Birkerts and others have pointed out, but the most obvious is not necessarily the most important. When we consider the flexibility, fragmentation, and occasional fun of hypertext fiction, and if we measure those qualities against what a more conventional reader might be seeking from a story, we can see the origins of the complaint of Birkerts and others like him. However, hypertext fictions are ultimately important, I believe, because of their capacity to give people interested in how reading and writing processes evolve—over a course of a text as well as over the course of a life—a window into what readers and writers do when they compose stories. The sometimes clumsy apparatus and operation of reading a hypertext fiction like Michael Joyce's *Afternoon* (1987) repays its readers, I believe, in the differences it highlights between reading on paper and reading on the screen. Hypertext authoring systems like Storyspace give writers a new range of forms in which to script narratives; readers likewise find more choices in the narrative progression they assemble themselves. While many hypertext fictions I have read are haphazard or unstrategic because of their language and content, they are valuable because they expand the range of storytelling methods, the forms or packages in which their stories are wrapped, and the way they highlight our processes of reading—as they change at the end of a century.

I want to end with another echo of E.M. Forster (1927), with his words that speculate on the appeal of novels to the general reader. Forster says of the power of novels:

> We cannot understand each other, except in a rough and ready way; we cannot reveal ourselves, even when we want to; what we call intimacy is only a makeshift; perfect

knowledge is an illusion. But in the novel we can know people perfectly, and, apart from the general pleasure of reading, we can find here a compensation for their dimness in life. (p. 63)

I hope that by listening to Forster and by reflecting on our own experiences with writing and reading hypertext fictions and other stories, that we will eventually write the powerful stories our culture desperately needs to be fully alive today.

5

Muddy Rivers, Malestreams,[30] and Splitting the Atom of "I": Locating the Reader in Digital Fiction

ARRIVING SOMEWHERE I DIDN'T WANT TO GO

My ferry arrives under a long-perplexed sky
a rain crackling into the unsteady Sound
the sky slate and toneless all the way down
to the sodden pilings dripping below
a heron hunched and wet
the solid heft of her feathers
living proof that birds have a different sense of
    time.

What I see:
The narrow beach punctuated by boulders.
A snarl of old netting.
Driftwood trunks from the old sawmill
closed down thirty years ago.
A plastic bag, several green tails of kelp,
four broken brown bottles,
and the longhand script of salt-
edged writing tracing the bones of waves

across the long sand beach.
I see where the tide has gone down.

What I hear:
An untidy creaking of boat pressing against pier.
Sullen gulls. Car engines coughing.
Foot passengers preparing to disembark,
each metal step striking the ear
like an offkey bell. The diagonal wake
of the ferry tangling in the waves breaking
on the beach. I hear the seams of rain
changing on the roof.

Diesel fumes rise
the trucks chug by
and I shift my knapsack across my shoulders
and I walk off the boat sadly sure
I no longer remember your face.

LOCATIONS IN READING

[R]eading, by definition, is rebellious and vagabond.

—Roger Chartier (1994)

the book i'm not reading's on the internet
the book i'm not reading is a brand new movie
the book i'm not reading isn't out yet
and it's all new to me...

—Patty Larkin (1997)

There will obviously still be books, in such a [future] world, and people studying literature—the
question is whether such activities will be any more pertinent to the main business of education
then, than the study of calligraphy (a remnant of a still earlier literacy technology) is today.

—Myron C. Tuman (1992b)

I liked the idea of reading; in fact I really wanted to be a reader, not a writer.

—Richard Howard, qtd. in Ellis, Seebohm, and Sykes (1995)

Nobody is going to sit down and read a novel on a twitchy little screen. Ever.

—E. Annie Proulx, qtd. in Nunberg (1996)

How will text-based interactive systems for writing and interaction like the World Wide Web and
MOO's affect the development and evolution of textual norms? Will the book as a material object
still maintain some of its symbolic value, or it will [sic] disappear into the realm of merely virtu-
al entities? Will new technologies enable us to look at ancient texts in a new way, discovering hid-
den structures?

—Patricia Violi, qtd. in Nunberg (1996)

All texts act on their readers. All fictive texts act on their readers by using a variety of rhetorical strategies to entertain, to persuade, to motivate. In the previous chapter, we saw how readers' dissatisfaction with hypertext fictions derives from the vast difference between what readers expected and what those stories deliver. For some readers, there is a disturbing dissonance between the ways they are accustomed to construing a print story's event, sequence, and meaning, and the ways hypertext fiction forces them to pattern *lexias*, pursue *links*, and construct narrative progression. Another part of the picture, though, is that the way the *locations* of readers and writers, construed in their widest senses, contribute rhetorically to the emotional, intellectual, and ethical experiences of readers interacting with writers. By looking at the ways digital fictions ask to be read, and by noting the dissonance between that asking and the answers their readers make (as their fingers tap the keyboard), we will find another source of the disenchantment that many readers of digital fictions report. The concept of *location* is central to understanding the reception of works of fiction; it is a term of particular importance for those of us theorizing about the rhetoric of digital fictions—and the metaphors of text-as-space implicitly operating in them. By connecting the theories about looking and knowing offered by critical thinkers from Horace to Haraway, and exploring the ways reception theories (including those proposed by Benjamin, Burke, and Bakhtin) must adjust to accommodate digital fictions, we are prepared to explore how readers and digital fictions inhere, or how "the splintered ray of reader's attention" (Birkerts, 1999b) meets the formulae of MUDs and develops its unique, interactive rituals of reading.

The important critical work of Donna Haraway (1991, 1997) has examined the general concept of *location* in terms socialist (1985), feminist (1991), and implicitly semiotic (1997). Her work-to-date has always acknowledged that knowing is partial, that the situations of knowing always color what is known; and she has argued persuasively for the informed critical position of "perspectival objectivism" and "situated knowledge" in her work, which ranges from studying primate behavior to indicting computer chip manufacturing practices. In her most recent published work, *Modest_Witness* (1997), Haraway argues again for a critical position that acknowledges the roots of "knowing" in culture. She writes,

> Strong objectivity insists that both the objects and the subjects of knowledge-making practices must be located. Location is not a listing of adjectives or assigning of labels such as race, sex, and class. Location is not the concrete to the abstract of decontextualization. Location is the always partial, always finite, always fraught play of foreground and background, text and context, that constitutes critical inquiry. Above all, location is not self-evident or transparent. Location is also partial in the sense of being *for* some worlds and not others. (p. 37)

Haraway's definition of *location* (and her vision of the ways in which knowledge is constructed and reified within cultural context) is complicated when we look at the ways digital fictions compose alternate realities and invite readers to enter them. Location becomes an extremely complex term that must be unfolded carefully.

Critic Wolfgang Iser also helps us understand the operation of location (through the dissolution of the reader into a real self and "an alien me") in the dynamics of reading in general. Iser (1978) claims that "every text we read draws a different boundary within our personality" and that the relationship between "the alien me" with its "alien thoughts" and the real reader is what allows "the unfamiliar to be understood" (pp. 293–294). He explains:

> If reading removes the subject-object division that constitutes all perception, it follows that the reader will be "occupied" by the thoughts of the author, and these in their turn will cause the drawing of new "boundaries." Text and reader no longer confront each other as object and subject, but instead the "division" takes place within the reader himself. In thinking the thoughts of another, his own individuality temporarily recedes into the background, since it is supplanted by these alien thoughts, which now become the theme on which his attention is focused. As we read, there occurs an artificial division of our personality, because we take as a theme for ourselves something that we are not. (pp. 293–294)

Iser's (1978) idea of the text "artificially dividing" the reader as she reads, and Haraway's (1997) sense of an emerging partiality as people construct themselves and their place in the world, helps us understand the reading cultures of digital fictions. When we consider *location* within the context of reading experiences engendered by digital fictions, we can extend Haraway and Iser's notion of a blurred subject–object relationship. In fact, we might usefully consider *six* kinds of locations operating in the digital fiction–reader relationship, and it is in the distances or gaps between these locations that allows the reader to incorporate "alien" ideas, suspend disbelief, or identify with particular characters. Figure 5.1 attempts to delineate these six qualities of location, and the properties and potential of each.

Haraway's important consideration of *location,* then, and Iser's notion of the dissolution of subject and object, can be extended by us to explore the relationship between implicit and explicit sets of locations in the virtual world and the reader's

**The
Digital
Fiction
On-Screen**

1. The Real Reading Scene

2. The Reader's Cultural Locations

**3. The Reader's Sense of Her Location
in the Digital World**

4. The Story Setting

**5. The Reader's Place in
the Narrative Progression**

**6. The Virtual Presence (or
puppet, avatar, interactant)
of the Reader in the Digital
World**

FIGURE 5.1.   Six locations in the experience of reading digital fiction that contribute to the Iserian sense of "artificially dividing" the reader.

world. Speaking rhetorically, within the dissonances between the two worlds, the text conjures its call to action, its request that readers listen, think, and act.

Digital fictions throw into relief the peculiar energies of a reader measuring herself against a text, and locating herself within and against the people, places, and conflicts of the story or virtual world. Because digital fictions demand a new quality of interaction, the places where a reader's construction of herself and her world conflicts with her location in the virtual world and ongoing narrative grow both more numerable and more visible. The following discussion defines some of the locations of story and reader that may exist in all reading experiences, but whose possibility for dissonance or disruption grows more potent within the materials of digital fictions, materials that lead to a different quality of reading.

First, we must consider the ways the scenes of our reading, *les espaces lisibles* (Chartier, 1997), operate on our processes of understanding, synthesizing, or "actualizing" (Booth, 1983; Burke, 1957; Iser, 1978) the digital fiction under scrutiny. Today, most readings of digital fictions take place in a home office or a shared space, such as a networked campus computer lab or an Internet café. These latter shared spaces have an implicit set of rules of reading behavior far different from the hushed and reverent behaviors that are the convention in most libraries, prompted in the past by their weighty, chained books and today by the quiet scoldings proffered by inveighlators in British research libraries, such as The National Library of Scotland. The reading space of computer-based literacy practices in general demands an altogether different protocol. Think of the last time you entered a student computing lab, and contrast that experience to the public scene of reading described in Tolstoy's *Anna Karenina* (trans. 1965) as he describes Anna preparing to read on a long train journey. In the progress of this passage, we can see Anna moving psychologically from responding to the shared public space of reading to a gradual immersion into the private space of actualizing a story:

> Anna took pleasure in arranging herself for the journey with great care. With her deft little hands she opened and shut her little red bag, took out a cushion, laid it on her knees, and, carefully wrapping up her feet, settled herself comfortably. An invalid lady had already lain down to sleep. Two other ladies began talking to Anna...Anna answered a few words, but not foreseeing any entertainment from the conversation, she asked Annushka to get her lamp, hooked it onto the arm of her seat, and took from her bag a paperknife and an English novel. At first her reading made no progress. The fuss and bustle were disturbing.... Further on, it was continually the same again and again: the same shaking and rattling, the same snow on the window, the same rapid transitions from steaming heat to cold, and back again to heat, the same passing glimpses of the same figures in the twilight, and the same voices, and Anna began to read and to understand what she read. (p. 106)

Consider the myriad scenes of reading. When Anna Karenina opens her book to pass the time on a long train journey, the accouterments of reading are far different from the highlighters, keyboards, monitors, desks, dictionaries, cans of soda, and flickering fluorescent lights we might see in computer labs today: Anna reads with a paperknife, oil lamp, and a small cushion on her lap. Italo Calvino playfully sketches the circumstances of the modern reader embarked on the same psychological journey from engagement in the real space of reading to sinking into the imagined worlds *actualized* by reading in the opening chapter of *If on a Winter's Night a Traveler* (1981): He reminds us we must ignore the sound of the television in the next room; we must cope with the impertinences of a sloppy printer, misbound volumes, uncollated pages; and we may either sit or stand (or read in a saddle on a horse), but we must attend to the printed page in the middle of a hundred distractions. Readers in computer labs must do the same, reading in a shared space, interrupted by friends, printers' noise, classes arriving and leaving, a café manager reminding one how much time at the machine one has reserved. Finally, Sven Birkerts and Walter Benjamin understand the scenes and conditions of contemporary reading in their respective essays, writings that identify the important ways the character of a reader must change in response to the digital fiction.

Walter Benjamin's essay, "The Work of Art in the Age of Mechanical Reproduction" (1955/1988), helps us develop a sense of the disjunction between the scene of reading and the reader's evolving understanding of a particular text. He discusses some dimensions of the differences between painting and photography, of the rate of change in cultural "substructures and superstructures" when they are forced to accommodate machines of reproduction like printing presses, the characteristics of film, and the relations between politics and art. One of his most interesting observations in terms of the scenes of reading, however, is his idea that mechanically reproduced art destroys the links between its "presence" in time and space, and the traces of its unique history, as it were; he explains that reproducing any work of art erases all traces of its "aura." He links a work of art's uniqueness to its permanence, and its reproduction to its transitoriness. Benjamin claims that "to pry an object from its shell, to destroy its aura" (p. 225) is the primary result of reproducing art. Reproducible art, he claims, has no historical trace, is not imbedded "in the fabric of tradition," and instead of being based in ritual or history, "begins to be based on another practice—politics" (p. 226). Of course, we can hear echoes of Plato's complaints about writing's power to decontextualize the spoken word, a writer's words gaining a visibility and a portability so that they are no longer tied directly to whoever said them first, so that they might be distorted or misconstrued by yesterday's Sophist or today's spin doctor. Benjamin's criticism of contemporary scenes of reading connects, too, with Birkerts's (1995) idea of the ungainliness of the equipment and the contemporary loss of subjectivity, discussed in Chapter 4.

When the reader's physical locations of reading (the reading space) and the reader's cultural locations overlap and diverge, as they always do, we can see some interesting results. In Sven Birkerts's (1995) lively complaints about Moulthrop's *Victory Garden* (1991), for example, we see Birkerts responding negatively to any contemporary scene of reading that includes computers; the origins of his response must be found in his own cultural locations. Attached as he is to what he considers the masterworks of the Western tradition, he sees his resistance to digital fictions as participating in the debates of the ancients and moderns, and between the philosophers and the rhetoricians. He is invested in maintaining the hierarchies of the existing canon; he implicitly subscribes to an Aristotelian conception of drama; and he remains attached to present valuations of aesthetics, taste, and the sublime. If we refer back to Figure 5.1, we can see how Birkerts's own cultural location biases the way in which he interprets or "reads" his own physical location of reading.

The reader's cultural location also, of course, affects the way in which she senses, assimilates, or incorporates the stories themselves into her own worldview. In all stories, she will sense occasional dissonances with the visible traces of the reader's place in the narrative progression or in the ways the text represents the timing of her participation in the chronology of events. But small incongruities between the general reader's idea of the story and what is written on the page can turn into gross distortions and troubling dislocations when they are writ on the small screen. For example, readers of some digital fictions are offered a set of tools they can use to leave traces of themselves in a story, showing where they have already read. Michael Joyce reminds us of "[Mark] Bernstein's 'breadcrumbs' (Hansel and Gretel-like markers for hypertext trails), compasses, and link apprentices ('swift, friendly, but dumb' search programs),...examples of what Patricia Wright (1991) has termed 'cognitive prostheses' against temporary overload—or being 'lost in hyperspace'" (1995, p. 27). Builders of virtual worlds talk about constructing a virtual text as a palimpsest, one that will show faint inscriptive traces where the "reader" has already gone. The first time I put on the helmet and glove and "visited" a virtual world at the University of Washington's Human Interface Technology Laboratory (HIT-Lab), I flew too fast over a virtual Seattle and straight into the blue, beckoning sky. As I flew upward into the thinning atmosphere, unable to stop myself, a voice outside the virtual world informed me I was lost in the void (Sloane, 1994). Today, virtual worlds, like those under construction at the HIT-Lab, explicitly show a reader/user her progress by letting that world retain traces of her progress. In the absence of customary textual boundaries, one is freer to impose her own cultural locations and knowledge to get oriented in a virtual world. The problem becomes how to model these virtual locations in real-time and real-space, as well as how to leave evidence (memories? markers?) of where the participant has already been. When a reader/user walks through the HIT-Lab's SpiderWorld, for example, she knows where she has been by the placement and number of spiders (Sloane, 1999b).

Another potential area of glaring disparity between locations in virtual and real worlds is in the lack of congruence between all three of the reader's locations in the virtual world and the way she herself is imagining that location. For example, a reader in Tucson, Arizona, playing an MUD in a student computing lab writes of a memorable evening in the evolution of Western–Arab relations. Implicit in the following account is this reader's bewildered sense of dislocation when a reader's world and digital world cohere only in the most superficial ways:

One rainy monsoon night in Tucson, Arizona, in 1993 I ended up at the lab again to check into the Mud I was playing. Being the average American, I didn't really know what was going on in the world, except what the most popular songs were, who was winning the latest sports, and so on. I didn't know the specifics of what had happened in Kuwait, or just how serious things were...

Anyway, I stepped into a lab full of mudders all trapped here by the rain. More than half the people in the lab I had come to know well. We all hung out together, mudded together, went to the nearest convenience store for sodas and snacks together, and so on. We even went to class together sometimes.

We had all heard stories of the distant war that may take place. We even wondered if the draft would come into effect again. Regardless of this fact, I got onto the Mud and started on an experience rampage. I was destroying the Drow area, when someone said on the gossip channel that SCUDs were exploding near his town. I recalled and asked him where he was. "Tel Aviv," he responded; apparently Iraq was missiling his country at the moment... (Shah & Romine, 1995, p. 135)

In this MUDder's remarks we can see a number of dislocations, or moments of disorientation, as imagined world meets a real world (what many MUDders call "RW"). The Mudder in Tucson and the MUDder in Tel Aviv are literally miles apart, their cultural locations (one walking to the nearest convenience store, the other listening for SCUD missiles; one dimly aware of a Gulf War and the other acutely aware) radically dissimilar, yet their shared space within the MUD presumably is quite well (and mutually) understood.

Sherry Turkle's excellent book, *Life on the Screen* (1997) is a wonderful introduction to some of the ways the electronic mask of the computer allows us to disguise self, genders, and emotions, and all the problems such disguises inevitably incur. In the following passage within her book, Turkle is speculating on the links between the real self and representation of that self (and its emotions) as it appears or is located within an MUD:

If I type "emote feels a complicated mixture of desire and expectation," all screens will flash "ST feels a complicated mixture of desire and expectation." But what exactly do I feel? Or, what exactly do I feel? When we get our MUD persona to "emote" something and observe the effect, do we gain a better understanding of our real emotions, which can't be switched on and off so easily, and which we may not even be able to describe? Or is the emote command and all that it stands for a reflection of what Frederic Jameson called the flattening of affect in post-modern life? (p. 254)

So that we might better understand the kinds of readings (and misreadings) that can occur in the clashes between locations, real and perceived; and so that we might better construe what happens when one is "in" or "of" a digital text in these new ways, I wish to explore here in more detail the variety of kinds and qualities, the *movements* of reading and their consequences, as they are evolving between readers and digital fictions.

KINDS OF READINGS

There's no there, there. They taught that to children, explaining cyberspace. She remembered a smiling tutor's lecture in the archeology's executive crèche, images shifting on a screen: pilots in enormous helmets and clumsy-looking gloves, the neuroelectronically primitive "virtual world" technology linking them more effectively with their planes, pairs of miniature video terminals pumping them a computer-generated flood of combat data, the vibrotactile feedback gloves providing a touch-world of studs and triggers…. As the technology evolved, the helmets shrank, the video terminals atrophied…. (Gibson, 1988, p. 88)

Digital fictions complicate those locations that we feminists routinely recognize today in our narrative theories, especially reader-response theories, including the complex locations of gender, race, ethnicity, sexuality, class, region, age, politics, cultural location, abilities, and historical period. While these categories are of immense importance in understanding the dynamics of who gets to write, what gets written, and who gets to read it, the locations of who we are when we write and read need to be understood differently when we analyze digital fictions; the locations of reading need to be considered as dynamic rather than static. By complementing our feminist analyses of readerly location by exploring also how different readers *move* through texts, we can sketch an approximate understanding of readers reading in a digital medium. In particular, we can explore those locations that are appropriate not only to different tasks, but to different genres and materials of presentation, and we can assemble a fuller, moving portrait of readers to complement our notion of readerly stances. Finally, by applying these theoretical terms to digital fictions, we can begin to describe the terms of "reader-function" as a counterpoint to Foucault's notion of the "author-function"—and thus move toward understanding how notions of readers and reading operate in virtual worlds. Ultimately, we will need to consider the conjunctions between mental space and digital fiction space, in which, as William Gibson (1988) reminds us, *There's no there, there* (p. 88).

Lunsford and Ede's *Singular Texts / Plural Authors* (1990) explores the ways in which the traditional definitions, theories, and conventions of authorship are destabilized, diffused, and realigned by the post-structuralist critique of agency proposed by French theorists (including Foucault, Barthes, Lyotard, Irigaray, Derrida, Cixous, and Baudrillard) and the material practices of authors engaged in writing together. Lunsford and Ede note that "contemporary challenges to the concept of authorship reflect material changes in writing practices and in the ways in which written products are 'counted' as intellectual property" (p. 95). Parts of what Lunsford and Ede claimed in their book have evolved today into worrisome questions about corporate appropriation of textual property, in the wake of our 1980s concerns with ossified Romantic authorial attributions and questions about the construct of individual authorship and originality. Lunsford's compelling essay "Rhetoric, Feminism, and Textual Ownership" (1999) examines how the feminist and post-structuralist critique of the construct of the singular author, the "electronic revolution," and collaborative writing practices of workplace writers have today converged into a set of questionable corporate practices regarding intellectual property. She writes that during the 1980s, she and Lisa Ede "sensed a moment where change might be possible, change that would give voice to many women and members of other underrepresented groups, as well as to many means of cultural production not valued by modernist epistemologies or economies. It felt like a 'postmodern moment'" (p. 530). Lunsford ends wearily, though, by saying that "in retrospect, Lisa and I should have been more wary..." (p. 531). Today, we can see the fruits of this corporate appropriation of intellectual property in the design of the boxes and other packaging that accompany digital fiction, as in Activision's reissue of all of Infocom's text adventures without any authorial attribution on the box or packaging.

As Lunsford revisits some of the ideas proposed by her and Ede in their earlier work, *Singular Authors/Plural Texts* (1990), she does not touch on those parts of the dynamics of collaborative authorship that they got exactly right. One important point that they got right was understanding the ways in which "writing" itself may be construed as a number of different intellectual and rhetorical activities, an insight that might be useful in developing a taxonomy of *readers'* intellectual and rhetorical activities. In their (1990) discussion of collaborative authorship, Lunsford and Ede call our attention to a resource used by librarians to cope with the difficulties of cataloguing jointly authored texts in their collections: Michael Carpenter's *Corporate Authorship: Its Role in Library Cataloging* (1981). Carpenter's work acknowledges the perplexing ambiguities of who owns what in debates about intellectual property, explores the dynamics and rankings in citations of those writers who have composed together, and "deconstructs the word *writing* into the following categories: 'writing down,' 'writing up,' 'writing out,' 'writing in,' and 'writing over'" (p. 126). It is this latter deconstruction of kinds of writing that remains so useful to those of us interested in how reading might be considered rhetorically, as an activity transacted between a reader and a digital story. Here, I parallel Carpenter's deconstruction of the kinds of writing by exploring five categories in the acts of *reading*, hoping to problematize practices and theories of reading in ways that acknowledge the material changes in digitally-based narratives and the strategies through which we encounter them.

Lunsford and Ede's summary of Carpenter's work distinguishes among four kinds of writing. "Writing down" refers to "the kind of writing requiring the least intellectual involvement on the part of the writer" (Carpenter, 1981, pp. 126–127) and appears to be the kind of informational transcription involved in copying an address, a telephone number, a teacher's words, instructions from a doctor or an insurance company, or, as in Carpenter's example, of transcribing criminal proceedings. On the other hand, Lunsford and Ede call Carpenter's "writing up" the kind of writing that is most closely related to traditional notions of authorship: "'Writing up' challenges writers to produce both form and content," and demands "the creation of the semantic content of a precise text" (1990, p. 94). Examples offered by Carpenter to describe "writing up" include Yeats's work of transcribing poems from prose drafts or a researcher's practice of detailing the results of an experiment done collaboratively in a laboratory (pp. 127–129). In contrast, "writing out," in Carpenter's taxonomy, occurs "when the formulation of the ideas into language takes place just prior to or simultaneously with their expression in written form (p. 131). Conversely, "[w]riting in" entails a writer filling in the blanks of contracts, invoices, will forms, titles, or, as Lunsford and Ede point out, writers who draw upon "boilerplate materials" to write multiple grant proposals or to recycle textual materials to fulfill several functions. Finally, "writing over" refers to "revising, compiling, redacting, abridging, and expanding, not to mention updating materials" (Lunsford & Ede, 1990, p. 95). All these categories painstakingly developed by Carpenter are designed to distinguish among the types and qualities of corporate and collaborative authorship. In particular, they are designed to help librarians decide to whom to ascribe textual ownership when they are cataloging books for their collections.

The work of Carpenter and Lunsford and Ede frames my notion that the word *reading* might also be usefully distinguished as occurring in five distinct motions. Each of the following motions of reading discussed connects also with a particular kind of theorizing, an ideological position, and a critical stance on what we do when we are reading. Each of these categories acknowledges the body and the ways in which a material human body encounters figurative stories, whether that story is written on paper, vellum, codex, scroll, or screen. Mark Johnson's (1987) work on the body's influence on language and metaphors is invaluable in understanding this somatic/semantic relationship, and the secondary corporeality that results from inserting ourselves in digital fictions. Johnson writes, "the epistemic senses are intimately connected with their root senses and ... the basis for this connection is that we understand the mental in terms of the physical, the mind in terms of bodily experience" (p. 53). (Johnson goes on to explicate the metaphorical interpretation of *force* and *barrier,* ultimately claiming that we understand "mental processes of reasoning as involving forces and barriers analogous to physical and social forces and obstacles" [p. 53]). In the case of the following motions of reading, the literal body is entwined in these metaphors in its ideological stance and direction of vision. I can feel the pull of gravity as I read up on a subject; I resist the pull of centrifugal force as I read across and away in the World Wide Web. Interestingly, one of the motions *not* discussed below, *reading away,* remarks the disappearance of the literal body, the wading out into the oceans of imagination, leaving *soma* behind as words breathe life into the characters and places that live in the mind—or that we see in the mind's eye, as people used to say.

Reading Up

We write down, but we read up. "Reading down" isn't an expression native speakers of English would ordinarily use. To the contrary, "reading up" appears to be the category that most closely approximates the reader's activity in "writing down," as in "reading up" on a subject to learn more of the basic facts about it. Reading up is preparatory, it is the hunter-gatherer's approach to text (not to mention the poacher's), and it usually happens before writing down. One kind of intensive "reading up" on a topic is the practice students bring to learning materials for content-based exams, what Americans might call "cramming" and the British "swotting up" on a subject. This kind of "reading up" might be used to prepare for a citizenship exam, to prepare for a trip to another country, or to gather information with which to prepare for a conversation with a doctor about courses of treatment, a lawyer about divorce proceedings, or even a professor about the contents of an end-of-term academic essay.

The metaphor of "reading up" demonstrates an ideological stance, too, a metaphor that indicates the power relations between writers and readers, teachers and students, authorities and dissidents, authors and really just about any of those who read and absorb their ideas. Those of us who "read up" are ready to take a stance of lesser knowledge or power, a stance often taken by those of us who grew up or live outside dominant cultural narratives, including working-class people, people of color, gays, lesbians, transgendered people, transsexuals, or bisexuals, immigrants, emigrants, and rural and inner-city residents.[31] Once we have read up on a subject, we are ready to have our mettle tested and we often prepare to climb the rungs of whatever occupational ladder we might find ourselves hanging from. As we professors watch our students "reading up" on a subject, we should remember Donna Haraway's warning to avoid "the scholarly temptation to forget one's own complicity in apparatuses of exclusion that are constitutive of what may count as knowledge" (1997, p. 39).

Reading up is not an activity that is apt nor particularly useful when we encounter stories on/through a screen. "Reading up" is the activity undertaken by apprentices, graduate students, amateurs, acolytes, and is connected most often with making plans or proving knowledge to those who wish to judge or test one's readings. As discussed in the first chapters of this book (you'll want to read back, if you haven't been there already), the undifferentiated, paratactic logics of words on the Web(s) invite nonlinear, multilinear, atemporal, synchronous, and asynchronous exchanges, which are not easily ordered and evaluated, at least not yet. Reading up is a relationship between reader and text that does not usually occur in digital fictions, probably because these stories are considered acanonical, ahistorical, or worse, as Birkerts reminded us in the last chapter.

Reading Out and Reading Back

Reading out and reading back are likewise terms best used to describe readings done from a stance less powerful, less active or dynamic, more audible but less transformative, than those readings done between or across texts. "Reading out" is a literate activity that requires speakers to consider the complex questions of addressing and invoking their audiences. In an echo of the debates between proponents of reception theory, discussed below, rhetoricians often fall into two camps as they consider the role of audience in framing delivery. As Park (1982) states:

> The meanings of "audience" ... tend to diverge in two general directions: one toward actual people external to a text, the audience whom the writer [and the speaker] must accommodate; the other toward the text itself and the audience implied there, a set of suggested or evoked attitudes, interests, reactions, conditions of knowledge. (p. 249)

To "read out," as most veterans of a public school education will remember, is an elision of the phrase "to read out loud," or to speak aloud a text already written down. It is a way of making the past present again, of taking the facts and visible marks of silent space and enlivening them with voice, the audible, a way of calling out past experience into the present space, often a classroom. On the other hand, "reading back" is the activity of a parrot. That is, to read back means simply to read aloud what was just written down. Reading back is an activity that takes place in settings similar to those that require writing down. For example, in a typical telephone conversation between a secretary and a caller, the caller might say her telephone number, and the secretary will "write down" that number and then "read back" the number. A similar pattern of speech and repetition might occur in an accountant's recollecting figures, an administrative assistant's shorthand, or any communicative scene where speaker and listener do not share the same literal space, as in CB radio exchanges, telephone calls, or the marine maritime mobile net. It is an activity of check and double-check, a reflexive repetition, an unimaginative carbon copy writ in sound on air.

"Reading out" and "reading back" are categories that likewise do not generally apply well to our analyses of digital fictions. While computer game designer Brian Moriarty (1998) may dream of an "all-sound" interactive fiction or computer game, none currently exists. Bruce Damar describes the intriguing cyberworld of *OnLive! Traveler* in his recent book, *Avatars* (1998), a world in which users choose "a giant head, or a costume party mask" and speak in their own voices to others in the room, which Damer says is like using ham radio (p. 193). Recent developments in feminist theory are also expanding the notion of "voice" beyond the expressivist ideas of authenticity and sincerity to reclaim the echoes, chimes, rhymes, pitch, and timing that words acquire when they ring the tongue, lungs, bones, and sinews of body, when they gain the sonority of the house of bones we ultimately are.

For example, Ruth Salvaggio's intriguing book, *The Sounds of Feminist Theory* (1998), suggests that feminist theorists listen to the ways in which words change things, in which "our language inevitably means more than it says" (p. 2). In a body of work that echoes the somatic/semiotic relation posed by French feminists, including Monique Wittig, Salvaggio reclaims the dimension of sound in our readings of printed text. Salvaggio calls this theoretical project "hearing the O" (p. 2), in which readers study "the actual effects of sounding, wavering language in critical and theoretical writing—a distinctive turn toward the oral within the panorama of contemporary thought" (p. 2). In a fascinating twist on the notion of *reading out,* Salvaggio's project demands that we readers exercise our imaginations in resurrecting the audible voice in the texts we read. As Patrocinio Schweickart reviews this interesting theoretical project, she sees Salvaggio is moving beyond the familiar feminist position of celebrating voice as it is opposed to silence, of celebrating speech as "a trope for agency, creativity, and empowerment" (back cover of book). Instead, Salvaggio offers us the possibilities of orality—the potential of sonority, rhythm, pacing, meter, bodily resonance—as underlying much persuasive written prose.

Reading Into or Reading Between the Lines

Many narrative theorists attempting to encompass stories written in a digital medium have turned to Wolfgang Iser's (1978) notion of an implied reader as an important and useful starting point for understanding how readers "read [and write] between the lines" of digital fictions. Anthony Niesz and Norman Holland's (1984) essay on the "literariness" of interactive fiction is the first essay to connect Iser with the dynamics of computer fictions, and several writers since have drawn the same seemingly logical conclusion: Iser's category of the implied reader—and his notion that texts have implicit gaps that are the mechanism by which that reader is implied and that wait to be activated—seems beautifully designed to encompass the visible gaps offered in many computer fictions. At first glance, Iser seems a likely choice for a theory of textual reception that might be usefully applied to digital fictions. Iser's acknowledgment of a text's implicit openness or "gaps," its accessibility to a plurality of meanings, and its ability to move readers to reconsider their own codes of understanding, seems custom-built for theorists trying to describe the dynamics of digital fictions. However, as discussed earlier, closer readings of Iser show that his usefulness to understanding digital fictions is limited, and that the correspondence between Iser's implicit textual gaps and a digital story's explicit textual gaps is to some extent illusory. In fact, Iser's notion of textual gaps may be at its most useful when we recognize the dissonance between a reader's representation of story and the computer's model of story. Iser's notion of a reader being "implied" by the implicit gaps in different textual arrangements and tales relies on aesthetic considerations to an extent not useful for analyses of MUDs or other digital fictions. My critique of Iser follows in part Terry Eagleton's (1996) insight that Iser's "liberal humanism" is concerned more with aesthetic dimensions of the text than with the social responses of an individual reader, and also develops the independent notion that Iser does not adequately account for the range of readers nor their reading contexts when he develops his notion of "the implied reader."

For Iser, reading is a dynamic, interactive process that involves a receptive reader trying on the alien ideas of a convincing storyteller, and then being transformed by those ideas. In his important work, *The Implied Reader,* Iser explains:

> [C]onsciousness forms the point at which author and reader converge, and at the same time it would result in the cessation of the temporary self-alienation that

occurs to the reader when his consciousness brings to life the ideas formulated by the author. (1978, p. 292)

By examining the dynamics of reading literary texts from John Bunyan's *Pilgrim's Progress* through James Joyce's *Ulysses*, Iser develops his central claim that all "valuable" works of fiction demand responses from their readers that make those readers question, transgress, or reform their notions of self and world. In Iser's introductory remarks to *The Implied Reader*, he explains:

> This term ["implied reader"] incorporates both the prestructuring of the potential meaning by the text, and the reader's actualization of this potential through the reading process. It refers to the active nature of this process—which will vary historically from one age to another—and not to a typology of possible readers. (p. xii)

It is precisely Iser's focus on the text rather than on the reader that makes his particular flavor of reception theory so inadequate for our purposes. By concentrating on the aesthetic rather than the social, by examining only the strategies of individual texts and not the quirks of their readers, Iser's narrative theory misses the most important feature of the reading–writing relationship as it is reconfigured in digital fictions. Iser offers a theory of reading that presumes an ideal reader and that does not actually fit in the diverse experiences and cultures of readers.

Reception theories typically claim that a reader brings to a text a variety of life experiences and locations that affect his or her reading. As Terry Eagleton (1996) summarizes the way reading is understood by reception theory, readers are always partial, and readings are complex and dynamic interactions with a text:

> The process of reading, for reception theory, is always a dynamic one, a complex movement and unfolding through time. The literary work itself exists merely as what the Polish theorist Roman Ingarden calls a set of "schemata" or general directions, which the reader must actualize. To do this, the reader will bring to the work certain "pre-understandings," a dim context of beliefs and expectations within which the work's various features will be assessed. As the reading process proceeds, however, these expectations will themselves be modified by what we learn and the hermeneutical circle—moving from part to whole and back to part—will begin to revolve. (p. 67)

Terry Eagleton goes on to note Iser's attachment to the Constance school of reception aesthetics and that school's predisposition to identify and assess the strategies embedded within a text and the "repertoire" of experiences that inform any reading. Eagleton ultimately criticizes Iser for being closed to experiences that lie outside his own ideological stance. Eagleton claims,

> Iser's liberal humanism, like most such doctrines, is less liberal than it looks at first sight. He writes that a reader with strong ideological commitments is likely to be an inadequate one, since he or she is less likely to be open to the transformative power of

literary works. What this implies is that in order to undergo transformation at the hands of the text, we must hold our beliefs fairly provisionally in the first place. The only good reader would *already* have to be a liberal: the act of reading produces a kind of human subject which it also presupposes… (p. 69)

In Wallace Martin's (1986) neat summary of Iser's work, he explains that the role provided for by the writer's text in Iser's conception

is not one to which we can commit ourselves without qualification. The meaning we infer from the text emerges from a productive tension between "the role offered by the text and the real reader's own disposition."… Furthermore … the implied reader is not the "addressee" of a fictional narrative, as the communication model suggests, but simply one of several standpoints that provide perspectives on its meaning. (p. 161)

Iser (1978) decries those literary critics who concentrate only on the text and not on the reader's expectations or the way the reader's imagination is changed through reading. However, I read Iser's early versions of "the implied reader" as focused almost exclusively on the text's roles, strategies, and dynamics in engaging a reader, and judge that he actually says very little about how different readers might be accommodated by a "valuable literary text" or how, precisely, they might be said to "discover" meanings. And while his more recent work brings up the interesting notions of memory and forgetting in the ways a reader reads fiction, the central focus of his work remains on the aesthetics of the text itself.

Iser has developed his ideas over a long and productive career examining the dynamics of interpreting narrative, and some of his latter essays offer a bit more help in our attempts to understand the behavior of readers. In 1991, in concluding remarks reprinted in *New Literary History,* Iser mused that "[t]radition, belief, and the intricate relationship of forgetting and rememberings" are among the most powerful agents to govern interpretation (p. 233). For our purposes, it is Iser's discussion of forgetting and remembering that best extends his categories of textual "gaps" and the ways those gaps imply a particular reader. Iser says in these same concluding remarks that "forgetting may be regarded as a lacuna in interpretation which now makes the gap appear in a different guise and also testifies to the gap's capacity for either undoing or enabling something. Forgetting … allows for a constant refashioning of what we remember…" (p. 233). Iser continues with a question:

In what way does this interrelationship between forgetting and remembering have an effect on interpretation? As the act of recognizing what had been previously forgotten, it is a strategy of discovery, while as memory it is the capacity to fashion not only the items to be interpreted in an act of interpretation, but also the very beliefs that determine how the constituent items are arranged. (p. 235)

Iser (1991) concludes this section of his remarks with the comment, "Realism, then, is not so much a representation of how we observe the external world, but a representation of memory, since we tend to believe in the reality of whatever memory has fashioned" (p. 235). So, here, Iser brings in an interesting human dimension into his theory of interpretation, admitting that individual sets of memories, and the ways that texts "refashion" those recollections, might affect our readings. He implicitly acknowledges a *range* of interior experiences of texts. Nonetheless, Iser's thinking about reading and readers is insufficient for the task of encompassing the digital fictions under discussion in this volume. Iser ultimately offers us an account of processes of discovery, a way of reading into texts, that grants us an implicit reader that may or may not match us flesh-and-blood readers. Interesting, insightful, maybe even brilliant, but not a point that is finally relevant to the widely distributed, idiosyncratic, culturally-based audiences who read digital fictions.

It takes Donna Haraway and Alluquere Roseanne Stone to extend Iser's sensitive questions about forgetting and remembering into meditations about what these gerunds might mean when strung out on digitally-based Webs, situated in partial knowings, and constructed of the mixed material presences of the cyborg, the transsexual, even the chimera, of these post-postmodern days. In the opening pages of *Modest Witness* (1997), Haraway instructs us as to what she means by the term "modest witness":

> [T]hink of a small set of objects into which lives and worlds are built—chip, gene, seed, fetus, database, bomb, race, brain, ecosystem. This mantralike list is made up of imploded atoms or dense nodes that explode into entire worlds of practice. The chip, seed, or gene is simultaneously literal and figurative. we [sic] inhabit and are inhabited by such figures that map universes of knowledge, practice and power. To read such maps with mixed and differential literacies and without the totality, appropriations, apocalyptic disasters, comedic resolutions, and salvation histories of secularized Christian realism is the task of the mutated modest witness. (p. 11)

Haraway is not suggesting a stripped, decontextualized knowledge here; she is asking that we readers substitute one set of contexts for another. That we don't yield to the booming voices of the right or left, nor heed the fundamentalist critiques of contemporary life that we hear from politicians of all political stripes when we consider how we might contribute to the narratives we read. She suggests we read with a different tradition breathing down our backs. We build from the detritus, the margins, the voices on the edge, and not in the malestream, in the colorful words of Lorraine Code (1993). Donna Haraway's essays and books proffer an implicit invitation to read across, up and down, to understand the hybrid, the cyborgean, the chimerical discourses of digital fictions. Donna Haraway's essays invite us into the disintegrated PoMo perspective of readers reading across materials and genres of digital fiction, discussed next.

Reading Across

Yo soy la DESINTEGRACIÓN.

—Frida Kahlo (1995)

The center does not hold.

—W. B. Yeats (1951)

Read with the Minotaur in the center of your palm.

—S. J. Sloane

Frida Kahlo's (1995) vibrant, living journal for the period 1944–1954 is a rich and beautiful diary comprised of equal parts drawing, colloquy, bestiary, medical musings (she had surgery at least 22 times in her life), political announcements, paint recipes and painting tips, complaints and rhapsodies, and art, art, art. The quotation above, *yo soy la desintegración*, is Kahlo's caption to a two-page journal entry (Plates 40–41), a glorious and complicated pen-and-ink drawing that I would like to appropriate as an emblem for the kinds of *reading across* demanded by stories composed in a digital medium. In both content and form, Frida Kahlo's drawing represents well the shift from modernist readings *between* the lines to the postmodernist readings *across* lines, pages, genres, and media. Frida Kahlo's journal entry is one map to understanding the metageographies and the new literacies required by digital stories.

Kahlo's (1995) journal entry is comprised of three figures of women painted across the two pages. At the center of the drawing is a woman's naked body wearing a bull's head, the Minotaur personified. Superimposed on this huge-headed, horned creature, are two profiles, two opposing faces like Janus's, one dark and grim profile looking left toward a noble self-portrait of Kahlo, and the other a lighter, speckled, grimacing profile looking right to a broken woman falling off a pedestal. As the commentator, Sarah M. Lowe, explains:

> Kahlo's reference to Janus is not incidental. Janus, god of the new year, is usually pictured looking backward and forward. What s/he sees in the past, on the left-hand page, is a strong, imposing profile of a woman—Kahlo as figurehead on a Roman coin. But when Janus (and Kahlo) gaze to the right, into the future, they foresee disaster. The figure of Kahlo, looking like a marionette with disjointed limbs, teeters atop a classical column. Parts of her fall away—an eye and a hand—both used to make art. Above the precariously balanced figure Kahlo writes: "I am disintegration." (p. 224)

Lowe does not mention the Minotaur in any detail, but it is worth noting that this hybrid creature (half-bull and half-human) is at the center of the portrait, provoking the disintegration of the image of Kahlo. In addition to watching the falling eye and hand mentioned by Lowe above, in the sketch we can see a head falling, an apron splotched with green paint, one leg dangling and the other one missing, a dim pink smudge that might be an isolated foot fading away in the distance. If Kahlo's sketch of disintegration is the emblem of the disintegrated stories, "the narrative confetti" (Moulthrop, 1996) of digital fictions, then the Minotaur is the totem. That is, the disruptive, disjointed, hybrid energies of the Minotaur symbolizes the computer's fractured agency, the ways stories break into pieces and can only be made whole again by reading across. The pieces do not cohere; the center does not hold; remembering works its way back to forgetting, like some Buster Keaton comedy run in reverse through the projector.

As Kahlo's drawing clearly shows, the Minotaur is a woman's body with a bull's head, a satisfying gender-blending figure of potency and mystery, *mythos* and *ethos*. Robert Graves helps us understand the Minotaur as symbol by telling us its history. In *The Greek Myths* (1988), Graves offers several versions of the origins, life, and capture of the Minotaur. According to Graves's summaries, the Minotaur was born out of the unnatural lust of Pasiphaë, daughter of Helius and the nymph Crete. He explains that the god Poseidon made Pasiphaë fall in love with a white bull, one that had been improperly held back from sacrifice by Minos. Almost mad with lust, Pasiphaë sought the help of the famous Athenian craftsman Daedalus (who was living in exile at Cnossus, occupied by carving "animated wooden dolls" for Minos and his family). (One wonders about those animated wooden dolls.) Daedalus rose to the occasion and built Pasiphaë a sort of Trojan cow that sounds more like a device of torture than an aid to lust:

> Daedalus promised to help her, and built a hollow wooden cow, which he upholstered with a cow's hide, set on wheels concealed in its hooves, and pushed into the meadow near Gortys, where Poseidon's bull was grazing under the oaks among Minos' cows.... Soon the white bull ambled up and mounted the cow, so that Pasiphae had all her desire, and later gave birth to the Minotaur, a monster with a bull's head and a human body. (Graves, 1988, pp. 293–294)

Graves (1988) goes on to explain that "[a]fterwards, the bull grew savage and devastated the whole of Crete, until Heracles captured and brought it to Greece where it was eventually killed by Theseus" (p. 294). Of course, as readers of Mary Renault will remember vividly, Theseus had to penetrate Minos's kingdom and an inextricable maze called the Labyrinth to kill the Minotaur and rescue Pasiphaë, concealed at the heart of the maze of Cnossus. The Minotaur is a good choice of emblem or totem of digital fictions because of its power to destroy conventional alignments of people, places, and power structures, and the labyrinths he builds to trap the unwary or foolhardy are remarkably like many early digital fictions. Further, as agent of other people's destruction, and born of an unholy alliance, a creature that reminds one of Yeats's rough beast slouching toward Bethlehem, the Minotaur is a mythic reminder of the associative logic of reading across, the hybrid and aggregative knowledge of narrative that accrues when we read digital fictions.

There are many echoes (or much intertextuality, to use another register) of the Minotaur and its labyrinths in the caves described in many digital fictions, from the original *Dungeons and Dragons* to the mainframe-based *Adventure*, the interactive fiction *ZORK*, and contemporary MUDs. Even before digital fictions were available, writers, especially fantasy writers (see, for example, Tolkien, 1984) and experimental fiction writers (see, for example, Borges, 1972) seized on the imagery of caves and labyrinths as the setting for their tales (Graves, 1988).[32] Caves have always had appeal as image or symbol of hidden knowledge, the unconscious, or whatever lies buried below the ground of world, self, and other. In the late 1950s and early 1960s, in this country, for example, seekers, hippies, yippies, and Beats sought the lost or obscure knowledge in a mystical New Age, living with Chinese hermits in the mountains, hanging out with rock musicians in the limestone caves of southern Spain, or joining Druid circles at Stonehenge or Glastonbury in Great Britain. The metaphor of knowledge occluded, hidden, concealed, or buried was transformed into action by those who explored Mammoth Cave in Kentucky, as the figurative became literal and the spelunkers went looking under the ground for whatever treasures they might find, an experience mapped, rewritten, and then atomized or digitized in Crowther and Woods's *Adventure*.

Reading across is the primary movement of readers encountering digital fictions like the MUDs discussed below, and that movement is prompted by the nexus of cultural location, physical setting, and imaginary world presented in digital fictions. Consider, for example, the words in the opening screens of one mythic MUD:

> High upon the rock, you stand before the open valley; the musk of scented oils waft up from below mingling the vertigo that you feel from your prominent position with another more alien smell. The dark valley opens in all directions guarded only by a large mountain range in the distance. You can see the fires of war and devastation poxing the innards of the valley; and beyond, you can smell the searing heat of the River of Flame.
> Karilian and Merin are here with you.
> Hades Minotaur arrives.
> The black form of the minotaur reeks of putrid flesh.
> The strength in its undead muscles causes your mind to scream out. Steam evaporates from its nostrils, as it snorts at your puny form. This corpse of a Minotaur has been brought back to life for one reason alone: to guard the entrance to the valley.
> Karilian says, "Hah! no problemo Señor. I'll be done with this one before you can say 'Call me Ishmael'"
> Karilian hits Hades Minotaur.
> Karilian smashes Hades Minotaur's left arm to a pulp.
> Karilian says, "See? nufin to it"
> Hades Minotaur massacres Karilian to a million fragments with its gigantic battle axe.
> Karilian dies in a fit of agony.
> Merin cringes in terror!!!
> Merin screams, "Craaaaaaapppppp!!!! Run!"
> Merin casts a spell and disappears in a puff of smoke.
> The Minotaur bellows out in rage and turns to face you. (Shah & Romine, 1995, p. v)

There are a number of features that this MUD's lurid passage illustrates, both literally and figuratively, about the instrument and agency of the Minotaur. The literal Minotaur in this passage defies a character (Karillian) and breaks him into a million pieces before he has even set foot inside the Minotaur's labyrinth. The Bakhtinian carnival of language, cross-cultural and cross-textual remarks like "no problemo Señor" and "call me Ishmael" are evidence of a digital aesthetic that should be familiar by now, a rhapsody of clichés and common allusions. Like Kahlo's Minotaur, this Minotaur, too, is an agent of disintegration, rehearsing its destructive powers before "you" the reader tries to break down its guard. In reading across the Minotaur's world as it exists in this passage, we can see how a reader would be drawn across the plane of the screen and into the alien world, or, in the terms Bakhtin would use (discussed below), linking horizon and event.

Readers of digital fictions often read across the texts available—interactive fictions, hypertext fictions, MUDs and MOOs—searching for the one story they can read into with pleasure and engagement—for some readers the literal caves of MUDs based on *Dungeons and Dragons*. When we grow more expert at reading across digital fictions, we may see that our patterns of reading across themselves are organic, that evolve. Maybe we'll find ourselves reading across MUDs' spirals, imposing a narrative thread across the lines of a shell, in the way that Daedalus did in Graves's (1988) recounting of the myth. Minos was so angry at Daedalus for escaping his labyrinth (and no doubt, for providing the means for Pasiphae to mount the white bull) that he raised a fleet and pursued Daedalus around the world. Everywhere Minos went, he brought a Triton shell, and he promised to reward anyone who could pass a linen thread through the whole shell. (Crafty Minos knew that only Daedalus would be able to solve the problem.) Sure enough, at the port of Camicus, a man mastered the riddle of the Triton shell and threaded it. Here is how Daedalus accomplished this:

> Fastening a gossamer thread to an ant, he bored a hole at the point of the shell and lured the ant up the spirals by smearing honey on the edges of the hole. Then he tied the linen thread to the other end of the gossamer and drew that through as well (Graves, 1988, pp. 312–313)

Our path through MUDs echoes the torturous winding of thread through shells, whether the literal shells of the beach or the shells of software. And we can hear echoes of Minos' vengeful quest and Daedalus's transcendent art in numerous digital fictions, especially the genre of MUDs and MOOs, which explicitly rely on classical myths.

In an attempt to understand better the ways in which *reading across* is a narrative activity that best captures the mood and direction of reading digital fictions, to better explain the incoherencies and disjunctions of current digital fictions for which the Minotaur is an apt emblem, and to expand the range of digital fictions under discussion, we turn our attention now to MUDs.

THE HISTORY OF MUDS

The history of MUDs is well-known and has been recounted by numerous researchers (Turkle; Reid; Aarseth), programmers (Crowther; Woods; Scott Adams; Rick Adams), and players (Shah and Romine), in print and on the Web. In general, these accounts agree that an MUD is understood to be an acronym that stands for "multiuser dungeon" or "multiuser dimension" and is the name given to multi-player text adventures played by many people at a time. Unlike the single-user text adventures marketed by Infocom in the 1980s, and dissimilar to the hypertext fictions marketed by Eastgate Systems in the 1980s and 1990s, MUDs are synchronous, expandable, interactive spaces encountered by many users through a text interface most usually on the Web. Today, MUDs are often distinguished by their habitués as either "social" or "adventure-oriented," and the worlds programmed as MUDs can be "chat-oriented," "fight-oriented," and designed for audiences with different needs: players, academic researchers, or readers interested in different historical or fantasy settings. MUDs have also been developed into MOOs (MUD, object-oriented) and MUSHes (multiuser shared hallucinations). Again, we will confine our attention primarily to text-based MUDs.

The account most comprehensive to date is that offered by Elizabeth Reid in a 1994 thesis submitted to fulfill degree requirements for an MA in the Cultural Studies Program, Department of English, at the University of Melbourne (available on the Internet at ftp://ftp.lambda.moo.mud.org/pub/MOO/papers/CulturalFormations.txt). Reid details the origins of MUDs in the text adventures written in the late 1970s in the United Kingdom and the United States. She explains:

> The name "MUD" first appeared in 1978 when Roy Trubshaw, then a student at the University of Essex, England, wrote what he called a Multi-User Dungeon. The name itself was a tribute to an earlier single-user Adventure-style game named DUNGEN.

Reid's account notes the importance of Roy Trubshaw joining Richard Bartle to build a "networked multi-user game which allowed users to communicate with one another, to cooperate on adventures together, or to fight against each other." According to Lauren P. Burka (1995), Bartle and Trubshaw completed the first version of an MUD written in MACRO-10 for a PDP-10. In addition, Burka summarizes remarks by Bartle (1995):

> The D in MUD doesn't mean a dark, dank, clanking dungeon. It means DUNGEON (or, pedantically, DUNGEN), the name of a Fortran version of ZORK that was doing the rounds on DEC PDP-10s when Roy was programming MUD. Having played ADVENT, Roy wanted to try other games along similar lines. We had access via EPSS [Experimental Packet-Switching System] to the ARPAnet (one of only a handful of UK universities to do so, and probably the only one to let students on-line). We found there were two other games available apart from ADVENT, namely HACK and

DUNGEN. HACK was weird and basically shallow, whereas DUNGEN/ZORK was very, very good. At this time, there was no generic name for the genre, but Roy wanted to name his game so people would get a sense of what it might be like, and be encouraged to play. Assuming that since DUNGEN was by far and away the best of the 3 games available, we thought the genre would come to be known as "Dungeon games," so he called his program "Multi-User Dungeon." They subsequently became known as "Adventure games" after ADVENT, however, so this didn't really work out as planned! If DUNGEN had gone under its real name of ZORK, we'd maybe all be playing MUZzes now..!

The writers of this first MUD, Trubshaw and Bartle, went on to form their own company, MUSE Limited, and to market a version of their game, which ran on CompuServ as "British Legends." Over the last 15 years, MUDs based on a variety of computer platforms have evolved.[33] In the early 1990s, the online roleplaying games popularly called MUDs, MOOs, TinyMUDs, DikuMUDs, LPmuds, DUMs, AberMuds, and MUSHes became widely popular. Most conventional accounts of the gradual development of MUDs note that the games attracted an ever-growing global participation and that the sophistication of worlds, universes, characters, voices (parsers), and speed of response all increased dramatically during the last two decades.

Few accounts of the development of MUDs explore the important parallels between them and the social milieus within which they were developed. The origins of these digital stories' content can be found in the social groups of graduate students and professors at large research institutions, as these new programmers took the knowledge they had gained in "real world" fantasy roleplaying (including sessions of *Dungeons and Dragons*, and meetings of science fiction and fantasy clubs) and applied it first to the primitive computer games and then to the more sophisticated MUDs that they built. Members of a model railroad club at MIT in 1961 are given credit for writing the first computer game, Space Wars. The social contexts of these first computer scientists have affected the content as much as the delivery systems of these games. Like interactive fictions and hypertext fictions, MUDs' online roleplaying games are characterized by content that is often fantastical, including characters that are often trolls, dwarves, elves, humans, mutants, or aliens, settings that range from spaceships to dungeons but that are almost always unrealistic, and narrative content related to science fiction and fantasy. Like interactive fictions and hyperfictions, too, these stories muddy traditional notions of author, privilege play, and often valorize the most hackneyed cultural scripts of courtship and war.

According to Michael Marriott's (1998) recent article published by *The New York Times*, multi-player games are one of the fastest rising categories of uses of the Internet. Players like Daniel Chiffon, "a lanky 25-year-old" profiled in the article, spend hours each day playing games like Myth: The Fallen Lords, "wielding a computer joystick with the alacrity of Wayne Gretzky on the ice and pounding his keyboard with speed and accuracy that might make boxing champ Evander Holyfield wince" (page D1). Some of the statistics in the article are startling: More than a million users of Microsoft's online Internet Gaming Zone have registered to play Spades, one of the Zone's most popular games; 3.4 million users logged onto America Online's popular Games Channel in August 1998 alone; and "[a]t any given time, millions are bustling from Web site to Web site, looking for someone to play." Designers, trend watchers, and development specialists are quoted in the course of the article as predicting a continuing "sonic boom" as the 76 percent of computer game companies who have multi-player games under development will hit the market this year. As Marriott notes,

> The early Internet games took shape in a text-defined computer world of MUD's— Multi User Dungeons, relatively primitive multiplayer games—and Unix operating systems. Since then, games have progressed to the point of evoking convincing 3-D environments that offer movie-quality sound effects. But oddly enough, with all the technology, what is most important is that they deliver real people as opponents. (p. D7)

Within these multi-player games, the element of chance we saw earlier in Oulipian literary experiments, the fracturing of stories we saw in the "narrative confetti" of hypertext fictions, and the genre fictions (science fiction, myth, and fantasy) of text-based MUDs is inflected by game theory. Like all digital fictions, these new games exploit patterns of identification and desire engendered by readers reading across them and comparing the locations of self and virtual self, real world and imagined world, comparisons made possible by the growing computer networks, increasing speed, and widening access to the Internet.

The *New York Times* article also draws distinctions between games that are free or charge by the hour or the month, that arrange charges according to the level of the game (America Online's Virtual Pool versus Air Warrior II, for example), and those that provide a "persistent universe" or "massively multiplayer gaming." Marriott (1998) explains the notion of *persistent universe* as follows:

> In a persistent universe, the computer-generated world is changed continuously as players enter, affect it in various ways and exit. Such environments—like the mysterious medieval land of dragons and sorcerers of Ultima Online, a pay-for-play game— exist, almost organically, whether 5,000 people are playing or no one is playing. (p. D6)

Programmers (and some players) of "persistent universes" no doubt believe the virtual worlds of these universes exist independent of their players, and current worlds like *AlphaWorld* or *The Palace* tend to reinforce that impression. However, such a position ignores the readings that leap across the proscenium separating player from audience, and discounts the player's part in actualizing a fictive text in all its colorful variety. In particular, such a view ignores the idiosyncratic or rogue readings of individual players and misses the individual patterns of identification and desire that the players' social and cultural locations urge them to bring to the heroes and minor characters of any digital fiction. In other words, not only do we have to consider the *espaces lisibles*, but we must explore those features of digital fictions that govern their circumstances of actualization, what Roger Chartier (1992) calls *effectuation*.

For example, take the opening remarks of two popular shared online worlds, *Eternal Struggle* (1998–2000), which appears to be a straightforward fantasy action game, and *Atlantis* (1995), a shared chat space (or "talker") that has a few rooms and a 'bot called Ghost with whom users interact. Notes to beginners open the former:

> *Eternal Struggle* is what's known as a MUD, or Multi-user Dungeon. It's a text-based game, played over the internet, in which players from all over the world may battle beasts, save maidens, get married or become mayors. *Eternal Struggle* is easy to learn, filled with both remarkable features and remarkable experiences. It's an integrated fantasy world without equal, and costs nothing to play.

Atlantis (1995) relies on participants called "Super Users" to help players around the world. A study deserves to be done of the discourse communities forming in these MUDs, especially insofar as the opening screens attempt to guide or limit particular kinds of speech. The opening screens of *Atlantis* read, for example,

> This place is Atlantis-][, one of the best talkers on the net today. Atlantis has achieved this through the belief that our users make the talker what it is. Our Staff is always ready to assist you in any way they can. Over 1000 people daily come to chat there...
> Atlantis has been up since January 1, 1995, and has grown to have a faithful following of over 5000 users. More than 500,000 thousand different people have logged into Atlantis. Why don't you?
> [Who is on?] - [Gossip Page] - [User Profiles] - [Ftp Site]
>
> ———————————- Guidelines for using this talker ——————————-
> Welcome New User!
>
> There are a few rules here that we request you keep otherwise you will not be welcome. They are as follows:
>
> 1) Bad language is out!
> 2) Violence is frowned upon. Playing (such as a bop or a pillow fight)
> is acceptable, but things such as kicking, punching, etc is not allowed.
> 3) English is the language of choice in the Main room (main_room)
> If you want to speak another language, take it to another room.
> 4) Multiple Characters are NOT allowed.
>
> Please remember that others, as well as yourself, are here to have FUN! So respect their rights and privileges as you wish them to respect yours and everyone will have a good time and enjoy themselves.

The more we rhetoricians analyze the relations between readers, writers, and digital fictions, the more clearly we can see the need for new vocabularies, taxonomies, critical terms, and shifts in our entire epistemological framework. Because these MUDs and MUSHes so obviously rely on spatial metaphors (in the textual descriptions of their worlds), and visible characteristics (in the design of player's individual traits), literary theorists whose methods see text (and the fictional worlds evoked by text) as spatial, visible, malleable, pictorial, and curiously plastic, are those theorists of most use to us. Mikhail Bakhtin's general place as a Russian Formalist, and particular methods in "The Spatial Form of a Character" (1993), then, are of great use to understanding more about how a reader "effectuates" or actualizes the persistent universes of MUDs and MOOs. Bakhtin's analysis of what "verbal art" has to do with "the spatial form of the hero and his world" in fiction grants theorists a vocabulary with which to delineate how verbal language constructs fictional characters. In this provocative essay, Bakhtin asserts two important distinctions of use to us today. The first distinction is that which separates a work of fiction's aesthetic form from its material form. The second distinction is a more abstract one that is critical to our understandings of how the dimensionality of characters (including agents, 'bots, and other players or avatars), and even their illusion of palpability, is extended by their virtual presence in digital fictions. Like E.M. Forster's important distinction between round and flat characters, according to Bakhtin, characters (including, we may presume, fictive personae in digital media), can evoke or deny patterns of identification and desire among their readers.

Bakhtin (1993) uses the terms "horizon" and "environment" to delineate and explore two of the questions raised and answered in the essay: "How are objects of the outside world [here meaning the fictive or virtual world] imaged [sic] with relation to the hero in works of verbal creation?" And even more interesting, "What place do [fictional characters like heroes] occupy in verbal creation?" (p. 41). Bakhtin is asserting two kinds of writing about fictional characters here. He claims that there are two ways of combining the outside world with the character of a human being: from within (his or her horizon), and from outside (the environment). Readers actualizing a fictional text need to be able to infer a character from both these locations, from descriptions implicit and explicit. Readers, says Bakhtin, are best able to see and understand the spatial, "plastic-pictorial" in fiction, and are hobbled in their attempts to intuit the inner, the emotion, value, and significance of a hero's inner world. That we can know horizon only through environment seems to be one useful inference we might draw, and the thin narratives of many digital fictions may occur because we know all about environment and very little about horizon; our perspective sees objects, not dreams, desires, or forgettings.

Bakhtin's (1993) essay disregards the dynamics of point-of-view, instead developing horizon and environment as the two terms that best describe the relationship between the world created by a writer and a hero created for and in that world. He explains that the verbal arts of fiction (and lyrical poetry) most obviously deal with a hero's exterior traits and that the reader can infer a character's meaning or worth only intuitively, or, I would add, based on her own set of experiences, terministic screens, or locations brought to the act of interpretation. Bakhtin writes,

> In narrative literature, [a] degree of visual actualization is higher; the description of the hero's exterior in the novel, for example, must necessarily be recreated visually, even if the image produced on the basis of verbal material will be visually subjective with different readers. (p. 39)

In other words, different readers will imagine a particular character in a novel quite differently, a point relevant to our developing understanding of *location*. Bakhtin argues that understanding "the plastic-pictorial moment" in verbal creations is crucial to our understanding of how stories act on their readers. Bakhtin's essay also assumes that the fiction writer's point of view is always external to the heroes that she creates, an assumption that is peculiarly suited to the externally guided, object-oriented linguistic descriptions of characters and agents in MUDs. Bakhtin chides his readers and asks them to remember that "the author must assume a firm stand outside the hero and his world and utilize all the transgredient features of the hero's exterior" (p. 40). But paralleling Bakhtin's demand for an authorial distance from her creations is his curious insistence on distance between a hero and his world, or between a character's "horizon" and his "environment." Bakhtin writes,

> [a] verbal landscape, a description of surroundings, a representation of every day communal life, that is, nature, city, communal lifestyle, etc.—all these are not constituent features within the horizon of a human being's active, act-performing consciousness... (p. 41)

In fact, according to Bakhtin (1993), these are features of an impervious environment, the ground against which the figure of the hero acts. So, while Bakhtin offers us a vocabulary by which to know the spatial, plastic-pictorial dimension of verbal art, separating hero from ground and horizon from environment, he ultimately gives us less help in this essay in understanding how a hero's thoughts or feelings are verbally embedded in "the spatial world within which the event of [the hero's] life unfolds," not to mention actualized and verbally embedded within a reader's evolving sense of hero and narrative. For help with such rhetorical questions, we must turn to the always interesting writing of master rhetorician Kenneth Burke.

And we must consider again the perplexing question of how the interior experience of the reader coheres with or against the representations of interiority in fiction, whether that fiction is written online or offline. For it is largely in these representations that the rhetorical resources of fiction lie.

DOING THE LOCOMOTION WITH KENNETH BURKE

Every question selects a field of battle, and in this selection forms the nature of the answers.
—Kenneth Burke (1957)

We began this chapter with the provocative assertion that all texts act on their readers. Pursuing this claim by first delineating the locations of readers and texts, and then exploring the dissonances and consonances between those locations when "read across," we have found only incomplete theoretical accounts of what happens when a fictive text is actualized. Furthermore, when the Minotaur (in its various incarnations as postmodernism, technological innovation, or digital aesthetic) interrupts traditional contracts between readers and writers, and proposes something altogether new, we are at a loss as to how to understand how that something new might be absorbed by readers. Kenneth Burke's early work, *The Philosophy of Literary Form* (1957), explicitly addresses the questions of how texts are actualized by their readers, and how different allusions, tropes, and forms "call" or "compel" their readers. In regard to the problem raised by Bakhtin—analyzing how character and his world relates to reader and her world—Burke sees the problem as one of *motivation*, of realizing how a reader transforms "scenic materials" into "psychic materials" and is thus compelled to act. Burke writes,

> Hence, one will watch, above all, every reference that bears upon expectancy and foreshadowing, in particular every overt reference to any kind of "calling" or "compulsion" (i.e., active or passive concept of motive). And one will note particularly the situational or scenic material (the "properties") in which such references are contexts; for in this way he will find the astrological relationships prevailing between the plot and the background, hence being able to treat scenic material as representative of psychic material (for instance, if he has distinguished between a motivation in the sign of day and a motivation in the sign of night, as explicitly derivable by citation from the book itself, and if he now sees night falling, he recognizes that the quality of motivation may be changing, with a new kind of act being announced by the change of scene). (p. 229)

In Burke's critical lexicon, then, the scenic material of the text (encompassing both horizon and environment, to use Bakhtin's terms) is actualized by the reader's interpretive strategy, which appears to be one that both identifies motives (of character and scene) and synthesizes psychic content.

Burke's (1957) metaphor of "astrological relationships" and the example he offers in the previous passage are roughly akin to "the pathetic fallacy," derided by some critics of Romantic poetry. In his essays, Burke explores the idea that "sensory imagery" including natural objects (like rocks, trees, and birds) and natural events (like rain, windstorms, or mudslides) might be understood as "replicas" of corresponding mental states. Burke explores this dimension of the rhetoric of fiction: "Thus, no matter how concrete and realistic the details of a book, they may be found, when taken in the lump, to 'symbolize' some over-all quality of experience, as growth, decay, drought, fixity, ice, desiccation, stability, etc...." (p. 31). In short, the story acts on the reader and Burke begins to identify *how* in the course of his analysis of literary structures and the ways they motivate certain readerly acts.

According to Kenneth Burke's *The Philosophy of Literary Form* (1957), when we analyze a work of poetry (which he takes to stand for all work "of a critical or imaginative cast" [p. 3]), one of the levels of symbolic action we might choose to analyze in that work is "the body or biological level" and then we can examine how those descriptions of bodily function might be incorporated into our imaginings. Burke details the traces of body that might be found in a work of creative writing, in a category he calls "the body or biological level [of a creative work]," which I would be tempted to call "secondary corporeality" (see Chapter 1). Burke offers as examples of this biological level

> kinaesthetic imagery. Symbolic acts of gripping, repelling, eating, excreting, sleeping, waking (insomnia), even and uneven rhythms (pace and puzzle, as tentative thought corresponds somewhat to the arrhythmic movements of an experimenter's animal in an unfamiliar maze, while assertive thought corresponds to the thoroughly coordinated movements of an animal that has learned the workings of the maze, and proceeds to freedom without hesitancy). (p. 31)

According to Burke, then, the whole body might become engaged in a reading, doing the locomotion (as Carole King used to sing), and swaying in sync with the suggestions of a rhetorical text.

However, Burke's (1957) analogy draws out another feature in the labyrinthine experiences that implicitly or explicitly underlie contemporary fictions from *Ficciones* (1999) by Jorge Luis Borges to *Afternoon* (1987) by Michael Joyce to many MUDs like *Atlantis* or *Eternal Struggle*. That is, one aspect of the labyrinthine mind is the seeking, the practice of looking for freedom. If freedom is understood to be the world that lies outside the bounds of the story or maze, if that direction is left vague and undefined as we whack through the forest or lunge through the maze as the thumb-sized humans did in the short-lived 1970s television series *Land of the Giants*, then that which is sought can easily be discovered or "actualized" by whatever an individual reader wants. And in those chance actualizations, whether it is the reader wanting to rescue the prisoner in *Riven* (1997) or the one who wishes to find the treasures in the maze of twisty paths in *Adventure*, the ways in which a story motivates our imaginings and actions, is an important part of the story.

As Burke explains, "[t]he symbolic act is the dancing of an attitude.... In this attitudinizing [of a creative work], the whole body may finally become involved" (p. 9). Presumably, bodies of both writers and readers become involved in these textual transactions. Burke recounts some remarks by Hazlitt about Coleridge and Wordsworth, in which Hazlitt reads into Coleridge's shifting gait an "instability of purpose or involuntary change of principle," which he contrasts with

Wordsworth's manner, one more "equable, sustained, and internal." Hazlitt believes Coleridge's habit of composing while "walking over uneven ground, or breaking through the straggling branches of a copse-wood" reveals character, while Wordsworth's custom of writing while "walking up and down a straight gravel-walk" allowed the continuity of his verse, his very lyricism as a poet (Burke, 1957, pp. 9–10). It seems to me that Burke is here directing our attention to both the connection between the writer's body and his style, and the reader's body and her interpretations. In addition, he prompts us to take a critical stance that allows us to interpret the characters in digital fictions as acting, directly or indirectly, on our own bodies. Consider, for example, video games like Packy and Marlon or Bronky the Bronchiasaurus, which help its child reader-players to take positive steps to control their own diabetes or asthma.[34]

Again, all texts act on their readers, or, as Kenneth Burke (1957) would assert, all texts have a hortatory aspect; all texts are essentially suasive. In addition, I believe that all texts ask something of their readers. And "that something" asked by digital fictions is a powerful request, one that attempts through its layered material gestures to draw in the reader into a veritable undertow of perspectives, practices, and meanings, sometimes with radical consequences. Let's take Kenneth Burke's rhetorical perspective to heart and ask: In what regard are digital fictions suasive; to what extent do their tropes, gestures, and semiotics act on their readers? What is a digital fiction's *functionality*? What are the mechanics of its desire for readers, and how does the desirous reader herself respond? How do audiences, social context, and the texts that surround the readers and the writers of digital fictions affect what gets said, who gets to say it, how it gets said, and how it gets read? Ultimately, how does *form* complement *content*, and *structure* foment *motive*, in a digital fiction?

Consider, for example, the following passage from Kenneth Burke's *The Philosophy of Literary Form* (1957):

> You come late. When you arrive, others have long preceded you, and they are engaged in a heated discussion, a discussion too heated for them to pause and tell you exactly what it is about. In fact, the discussion had already begun long before any of them got there, so that no one present is qualified to retrace for you all the steps that had gone before. You listen for a while, until you decide that you have caught the tenor of the argument; then you put in your oar. Someone answers; you answer him; another comes to your defense; another aligns himself against you, to either the embarrassment or gratification of your opponent, depending upon the quality of your ally's assistance. However, the discussion is interminable. The hour grows late, you must depart. And you do depart, with the discussion still vigorously in progress. (pp. 95–96)

Kenneth Burke uses this much-quoted analogy, between joining a conversation and entering a scholarly discourse community, to illuminate his central contention here that all verbal assertions necessarily take place within a situation, and that that situation itself is largely constructed of past conversations. Further, from a rhetorical standpoint, that context is typically *agonistic*. To paraphrase the quotation above, *context matters* to the act of persuasion. As Burke says, "[i]t is from this 'unending conversation'...that the materials of your drama arise" (p. 96). Drawing on the important work of Malinowski and Mead, Burke claims that among these "contexts of situation" are those factors and material interests "that you symbolically defend or symbolically appropriate or symbolically align yourself with in the course of making your own assertions" (p. 96). These factors do not cause you to speak nor cause you to speak only about a particular subject, according to Burke. Instead, the contexts within which you speak "greatly affect the *idiom* in which you speak, and so the idiom by which you think" (p. 96). We can presume, then, that the contents of the stories we read themselves become part of our contexts, and the ways in which we answer them, speak of them, or assimilate them, are a response to both content and context.

Rhetorical studies in general help us see what texts ask of their readers and how those texts function as persuasive documents. In particular, Burke's rhetorical standpoint permits the postmodern borrowings, the cross-textual perspective that talks about computer multimedia, print, television, theater, and film in the same breath. In his own rich set of literary examples, extending from oral poetry to essays on taste, from popular fiction to semiotic analyses (although he does not use this term himself) of football games, Burke makes clear that the heart of his theoretical strategy is to discover what in the text itself persuades, what literal cues or watersheds, what moments, does a text offer that shifts our attention from reading to acting, or at the very least, to imagining action. He wants to discover, as he says in various places, what "sort of *eventfulness* [a] poem contains" (1957, p. 62), and what is the motivation of any creative work. That motivation is the hortatory status of any work, and it is that carefully structured motivation that I see missing in our digital fictions so far composed, although in the total shape of digital fictions, in the radical reconfigurations of the author–reader relationship, we can hear a broad cry for change.

Burke reminds us of many notions that we already instinctively know: that language is always social, that it is "most public [and] most collective in its substance" (1957, p. 38). That creative writing itself, to use an American term, when it is working well is offering its readers "equipment for living ... a ritualistic way of arming us to confront perplexities and risks" (p. 51). And that stories themselves are meant to raise questions, to foment change, to signal distress, to heal, to comfort, to make uncomfortable, to assert some moral imperative. Stories are hortatory, Burke would claim, and in their exhortations they invariably ask readers to change. It is precisely the explicit details of emotional and spiritual compulsion that is the hortatory dimension of story that is missing from digital fiction. We can see all the ways digital fictions hesitate to persuade in the failed connections between the way the reader is located in the real world, and how her virtual presence and movement in these nonlinear, fractured fictions is a horizon that does not yield internal event, or connect smoothly with the external environment.

As one more example of how digital fictions fall short, compare Burke's turning his eye to "critical points" in fiction and our own faltering attempts to find their corollary in digital fictions. Burke exhorts his own readers to attend to these "critical points" within a creative work, noting such points exist in addition to traditional places of emphasis, such as the beginning and ending of any written work. These "critical points" in traditional fictions, says Burke,

> are often "watershed moments," changes of slope, where some new quality enters. Sometimes these are obvious, even so obvious as to threaten the integrity of the work. There is such a moment in *Murder in the Cathedral*, where the medium shifts from verse to prose (with critics divided as to whether the change is successful or a fault). In Louis Aragon's *Bells of Basel*, such a break occurs where Clara Zetkin enters—and here the change of personality is so great. (p. 66)

To contrast these "critical points," compare the critical opportunities made available by the opening screens of EliteMUD. In MUDs in general, it would seem that "critical points" are best fomented by an active reader, when she changes location or discovers a coveted prize, for example, or when she encounters another player and performs an action (a conversation, a spell, a diabolical murder) that lets her move on. These are not much like Burke's "critical moments" or those that inspire, that offer "equipment for living."

(1) Adventure in the Realm of EliteMud.

Welcome to the land of EliteMUD! Stay awhile…. Stay FOREVER!

The temple of Midgaard
You are in the southern end of the temple hall in the Temple of Midgaard.
The temple has been constructed from giant marble blocks, eternal in appearance, and most of the walls are covered by ancient wall paintings picturing Gods, Giants, and peasants. Large steps lead down through the grand temple gate, descending the huge mound upon which the temple is built and ends on the temple square below. To the west, you see the Reading Room. The donation room is in a small alcove to your east.
A large, sociable bulletin board is mounted on a wall here.
An automatic teller machine has been installed in the wall here.
Firebird The Vulcan's Fire Sword is standing here.
Mistress Nymph will do anything if you WORSHIP her! is standing here.
Trentreznor the Lizard Magic-apprentice is standing here.
Funnyguy the Minotaur Master-Blade/Patriarch is sleeping here (Zzzzzzz).
Lioness the Half-elven Novice/Spell-delvress is resting here.
Gelon the Drow Swordpupil/Believer/Magic-apprentice is standing here.
Raster the Half-elven Knight/Patriarch/Minor Elemental is sleeping here (Zzzzzzz).
Toyota the Minotaur Rogue/Minister (linkless) is sleeping here (Zzzzzzz).
+A horse is standing here.
+The Priest is standing here, offering his services.
[Exits: neswd] (Buscy, 1995, pp. 65–66)

There is little in this textual encounter that exhorts or compels, not because the MUD is fantastical, not because it is reheated Tolkien, and not because of the unlikely names of the characters, or the mixed PoMo quality of the space. This MUD fails to engage its readers on the level that Burke describes because it lacks critical points of entry; and because its motivations are muddy. The combination of symbolic geographies, which attach to nothing of significance, either rhetorical or literal, and the flat characters with which this reader, at any rate (and one who enjoys fantasies by J.R.R. Tolkien, I might add) can neither identify with nor respond to on any emotional level, coalesce into a portrait of a failed virtual world, a digital fiction that fails to engage its readers because the text's hortatory aspect is simply not there. Only the bizarre inclusion of an automatic teller machine approximates Burke's (1957) "critical point of entry" as it poses an interruption in the fantasy world—and suggests our own cultural preoccupations with money, commerce, power, and access.

Ultimately, MUDs and MOOs deserve the kinds of extended observation and ethnographies undertaken by Sherry Turkle (a sociologist studying MUDs as "emergent identity workshops"), Amy Bruckman (a cultural critic and computer scientist studying MediaMOO), and John Suler (a psychologist studying *The Palace*, whose papers are available at this writing on the Internet at http://www1.rider.edu/~suler/psycyber/palacestudy.html), as well as general longitudinal and descriptive studies. Among other topics, the hierarchies of players (sometimes distinguished according to their abilities, strength, race, place of origin, degree of experience, personality) and writers (including self-described magicians, wizards, gods, and immortals) should be analyzed for implicit and explicit knowledge/power arrangements. In contrast, the purpose of my remarks about MUDs here is to introduce a theoretical framework that will help rhetoricians and narrative theorists identify some of the primary differences of this form, and to explore the primary action of reading across characters, hierarchies, and worlds in these digital fictions. Of all the digital fictions I have discussed in this book so far, MUDs in all their variety would probably most reward future study. In particular, more study of the masks of gender, the injunctions against multiple characters, and the general disguises of players swimming in and against the malestream, seem to me worth investigating in the future.

MATERIALS, PROCESSES, AND LOCATIONS REVISITED

"If," Jane Greenfield says, "you have termites in your bookshelves, or if you are stacking books from suspect areas, like barns, cellars, and attics, you should freeze the collection before placing it in your library." She reports that a simple at-home method was developed by Yale University biology professor Charles Remington: Make sure the books are completely dry, thereby preventing the formation of ice crystals. Seal books or wrap them well in plastic bags, preferably made of polyethylene, and freeze them at 6° F. in a domestic freezer. (At Yale, books are frozen at -20° F. for seventy-two hours.) This will kill all beetles and insects at all stages of development. (Ellis, Seebohm, & Sykes, 1995, p. 201)

As we have seen, the materials of digital fictions are certainly different from those of printed books, and the processes for preserving the narratives encoded in chip or book, much less the rituals for remembering route or lesson, are very different in their particulars. Books and programs are ideally both kept free of bugs, stored at certain temperatures, and made up of a complex symbolic logic, but each technology has its own patterns of portability and durability, circulation and reception, exhortation and response. Our locations, the ways in which we inhabit the reading space, are changing, as well as the processes by which we read and interpret literature. Henri-Jean Martin's colorful book, *The History and Power of Writing* (1994), reminds us that Petrarch always kissed his copy of Virgil, and Erasmus his copy of Cicero, before they read; Machiavelli dressed in his very best clothes to read his favorite authors. And Montaigne, "[l]ike many of his contemporaries...considered reading a fatiguing exercise that made the mind work while it 'tied down' and 'saddened' the body. He tells us that he liked to walk about as he read, supervising his household through the three windows that brought light into the room..." (p. 363). Today's acts of reading computer-mediated texts occasionally require a helmet, but in most cases the reader and her computer are stationary, only eyes and fingers moving. The new rhetorical situation of reader encountering the bright lights and sounds of a networked, multimedial performance of story has not yet developed the rituals and rhetorical devices that will engross traditional readers used to more conventional symbols frozen on a page.

Ut pictura poesis

The phrase "ut pictura poesis" is one that originates in Horace's *Ars Poetica* (trans. 1992), a treatise Horace wrote nearly 2,000 years ago. Horace's study of some of the mimetic features common to art and poetry is one of the first instances of a coherent aesthetic theory that would encompass both visual and verbal art. Horace's Latin phrase means approximately "as painting is, so is poetry," and Horace intends by such a phrase to assert that painting and creative writing are "sister arts" engaged in parallel acts of *imitation,* especially imitation of the natural world. Horace's cross-textual understanding of mimesis prepares the ground for contemporary critical assertions like my own designed to encompass digital fictions. Today, semioticians, feminists, post-structuralists, reader-response critics, and contemporary rhetoricians claim that our students need training in how to interpret a wide range of visual media, from illuminated medieval manuscripts to digital multimedia, from Italian *fumetti* (named after the speech that emerges like puffs of smoke from character's mouths) to film.[35] Horace's understanding that poetry and painting share practices and precepts in their representations of the real world helps prepare contemporary literary theorists for our contention that critical theory can easily encompass both verbal and visual phenomena, and especially those hyper-media performances that offer a saturated instance of multimodal and multisensu-al art. However, any critical work into the aesthetics of digital fiction should be combined with a respect for and interest in their hortatory aspect. The theory toward which these essays intend is one that combines elements of theories narra-tive, aesthetic, feminist, and rhetorical.

Narrative theorists like Seymour Chatman (1978) undertake cross-medial analy-ses of narrative, exploring how story is presented in print and film and identifying strengths and weaknesses of each medium; feminist theorists like Peggy Phelan (1993) and Teresa De Lauretis (1984) can explore the images of film by relying on the previous work of art historians like Gombrich and Berger, looking within the properties of cinema for traces of cultural preoccupations with sex, death, courtship, and love (not necessarily in that order). Reader-response critics like Jane Tompkins (1992) can consider the ways westerns and romances act on their read-ers; media critics like Neil Postman (1992) can study the rhetoric and patterns of television's mostly dull representations; and postmodernists like Mark Poster (1990) or Jean-Francois Lyotard (1984) and cultural critics like W.J.T. Mitchell (1986) can read and interpret everything from perfume advertisements to the wrapping of aspirin bottles. Digital fictions are just the latest in a long series of verbal/visual phe-nomena that demand an aesthetic and social understanding to encompass them.

The latest reiteration of *ut pictora poesis* may be heard in the cries of curricular critics, who see a glaring need for a return to rhetorical studies so that curricula might encompass both visual and verbal phenomena. Those rhetorical studies, according to writers like Richard Lanham (1993), Robert Scholes (1998), and Terry Eagleton (1996), will invigorate (and widen the scope of) textual criticism and return literary studies to its roots in rhetoric. I think there is no doubt that studies of digi-tal fictions and analyses of the ways in which they reflect and are inflected by their surrounding communities of theorists, speakers, writers, and visual and audio artists absolutely require that our students understand something of both aesthetic theo-ries and reception theories. Most important of all, I agree that critical studies (and humanities students) of the twenty-first century need to be grounded in studies of rhetoric, not least so they can more objectively observe and resist the barrages of media and messages corporations increasingly are directing at consumers.

Eagleton (1996) calls rhetoric "probably the oldest form of 'literary criticism' in the world" and suggests a return to rhetorical studies in the academy as one of the best ways for students and faculty to come to terms with the range of texts, or in his term "discourses," that enliven contemporary communication. He says:

> Rhetoric, which was the received form of critical analysis all the way from ancient society to the eighteenth century, examined the way discourses are constructed in order to achieve certain effects. It was not worried about whether its objects of enquiry were speaking or writing, poetry or philosophy, fiction or historiography: its

horizon was nothing less than the field of discursive practices in society as a whole, and its particular interest lay in grasping such practices as forms of power and performance. (p. 179)

Eagleton (1996) continues by explaining that the original purview of rhetoric was neither solely humanistic nor formalistic; that the natural interdisciplinarity of its subject must have been complemented by a methodological breadth that would see discourse as action:

> Rhetoric in its major phase was neither a "humanism," concerned in some intuitive way with people's experience of language, nor a "formalism," preoccupied simply with analysing linguistic devices. It looked at such devices in terms of concrete performance—they were means of pleading, persuading, inciting and so on—and at people's responses to discourse in terms of linguistic structures and the material situations in which they functioned. It saw speaking and writing not merely as textual objects, to be aesthetically contemplated or endlessly deconstructed, but as forms of *activity* inseparable from the wider social relations between writers and readers, orators and audiences, and as largely unintelligible outside the social purposes and conditions in which they were embedded. (p. 179)

Eagleton's (1996) characterization of early rhetorical study has implications for those of us interested in understanding how digital fictions motivate their readers, and how fictions in general function with these "wider social relations." In sum, rhetoric's natural interdisciplinarity, in connection with a social perspective that sees all discourse as action, particularly persuasive action, makes a study of its theories and stances very useful to understanding all computer-mediated communications, including digital fictions.

Rhetoric and the Liberal Arts Tradition

A number of prominent literary critics like those already mentioned, including Richard Lanham (1993) and Robert Scholes (1998), have sounded the trumpets and proclaimed that the general liberal arts curriculum (sometimes referred to as a "core curriculum") must return to its roots in the rhetorical tradition. Richard Lanham, in particular, believes such a change is prompted by the convergence of media and sensual imagery that digital media allows. Lanham claims that current social pressures in tandem with the new postmodern digital aesthetic demands a return to the rhetorical *paideia*:

> This revival of our traditional paideia [would include] those parts of contemporary literary criticism and cultural studies which have rediscovered that all arguments are constructed with a purpose, to serve an interest—a rediscovery symbolized for me by that wonderful moment at the end of Terry Eagleton's [1983] theory book when, after having surveyed the whole brave new world of literary theory, he pauses and reflects that, "Gosh, folks, maybe we might just as well call it 'Rhetoric.'" It departs, as does

much current thinking, knowingly or not, from Kenneth Burke's revival of the *Theatrum Mundi* metaphor for study of the arts and letters. (p. 46)

(Lanham and Burke, discussed above, are both extremely useful in analyzing how books work on their readers, as well as how plays prompt their audiences and films galvanize their viewers.) Lanham goes on to develop the notion of an essential instability in the educational enterprise, which can best be met only by grounding general education in rhetorical study. By returning to studies in rhetoric, and noting the ways in which rhetoricians from Aristotle to Henri-Jean Martin have developed rhetorical notions of character, theater, and mind, students and teachers alike will more readily understand and interpret the ways digital media, and all visual media including cinema and television, *act* on their readers, viewers, and users.

More recently, Robert Scholes's *The Rise and Fall of English* (1998) encourages contemporary students and teachers to turn their attention to rhetorical study.[36] Scholes outlines a general educational curriculum, one that he claims is "radical" because it proposes going back to the roots of a traditional liberal arts education. Scholes's core curriculum is based on a contemporary trivium:

> I propose to go back to the roots of our liberal arts tradition and reinstate grammar, dialectic, and rhetoric at the core of college education.... To envision such a thing, we need only rethink what grammar, dialectic, and rhetoric might mean in modern terms. My own rethinking of these terms has taken the form of seeing all three of the trivial arts as matters of textuality, with the English language at the center of them, but noting their extension into media that are only partly linguistic. (p. 120)

Scholes develops a core curriculum based on "a canon of concepts, precepts, and practices" (p. 120), a modernized trivium that would end in studies of rhetoric and that would take as its texts media that might be print, digital, or cinematic. After reading Aristotle's *Rhetoric* and *Poetics,* students would move on to Nietzsche's *Birth of Tragedy* and Brecht on "Epic Theatre." Finally, students would move

> from the rhetoric of theater to the rhetoric of film and visual spectatorship in general, in which the gendering of subjects and objects of viewing could be considered (as in Laura Mulvey, Teresa de Lauretis, and John Berger, for instance), along with other ideological analyses of the rhetoric of the mass media in both direct (overt) and indirect (covert) manipulation of viewers. Plays, films, and television texts would be the objects of rhetorical analysis in such a course, along with such more overtly persuasive texts as political speeches and advertisements. (p. 126)

Like Lanham, Scholes (1998) interprets contemporary textuality as encompassing theater, television, cinema, and digital media, and he suggests a return to rhetorical study as central to a curriculum that appropriately acknowledges these new textual forms—and activities. In contrast to Lanham, Scholes does not explicitly acknowledge Kenneth Burke in his discussion, but Burke's precepts and methods clearly underlie the contemporary rhetorical tradition he suggests.

Scholes and Lanham are right to see a glaring need to ground contemporary general education in rhetorical studies. That need is propelled by the proliferation of digital texts, including stories, and the expert visual and verbal literacies required to read them, to understand how they, too, are hortatory, and to interpret their often mixed exhortations. Digital fictions constitute a set of texts that does not easily yield to the interpretive apparatus of the aesthetician or the methods of the traditional literary theorist alone; they are not wholly encompassed by composition theories cognitivist or social constructionist; and digital fictions require rhetorical analysis for them to reveal their full meanings and range of possibilities and disappointments. Ultimately, digital fictions are strong evidence for the necessity of grounding the liberal arts tradition afresh in studies of rhetoric, and they are but simple versions of the far more powerful and persuasive images, words, and technologies that we will see in the next century. Rhetoric is essential to understanding the messages soon to appear on high-definition televisions, wide bandwidth cables, and whatever collaborations of high-definition televisions, phone lines, computers, and micro- and radio-waves are yet to come.

Digital fictions, from the interactive fictions, hypertext fictions, and MUDs mentioned in this book, to the visual and aural jewels that comprise sophisticated interactive stories like Red Orb's *Myst* and *Riven,* are stories that tantalize us with their complex processes, materials, and locations of participants in the new reading-writing contract. And while the function of these digitally-based stories remains the same as the function of all good tales—to entertain, to exhort, or to win over an audience—the functionality of digital fictions is different. Rhetorical analysis, in concert with reader-response theory, semiotics, and feminist perspectives, illuminates better than any other method the ways in which digital fictions engage us, bewilder us, and intrigue us.

6

Afterword: Foxes in Space

THE INSIDE OF NIGHT IS LINED WITH VIOLETS

How many faces can peel in the rain?
They were silk, I think, and not stained by bogwater.
Their octaves glistened like bankruptcy.
I hear the voices of sickles and they are small tickles
in the damp moonlight. In the university of fire
the sky furls down and quenches all the wanting limbs.
In fact, the spring arrives on the margins
of every green idea sleeping furiously, the smell
of wet sails drying in the stars' heat gleams
and you running to meet me
hands full of Pythagorean melodies and violets.

The fox froze in the angle of light made by my car's high beams, and as I braked hard, I looked right into the metaphysical glow lit in the interior of her eyes. Both life and fear lodged in that glow, and her native intensity was barely contained by her stock-still body, her rusty fur, her tail more aura than being. In the shadows thrown by my headlights and in the overhead blue glare of a street lamp, she looked more gray than red, but gray with a potent hint of fire. We stared at each other in the middle of the night, she on her way back from scavenging at Snake Lake, I driving too fast down an empty midnight road. I was racing from the copy center to turn in my tenure file, no other creature abroad, when I saw the fox. I took the sight of her as a sign of something good, but what precisely I was not sure.

Our eyes locked. The fox was smaller than you'd expect, scrawny, maybe even mangy, with less of a long jaw and more of a crouch to her limbs than I had first seen. As we stared at each other for a good few seconds, it felt like she had sketched a tight circle around herself, that she could strike out in any direction from her crouch, cutting an arc through the light and the night as she disappeared. Of course it was her eye that was most brilliant, an ancient, animate stone placed in the body of a scavenger, the scarred body of a survivor. I recognized something of myself in that eye. The wide brush of her tail flicked once more, and in a heartbeat she sped from my roadside to her fields, her tread so light it was both weightless and sound-less, gone before I even recognized she was leaving. And after a moment longer on that deserted road, now lit just for me alone at that late hour, I shifted back into gear and continued down the course I had set for myself long ago, a course that had led me through three graduate programs and a job as an assistant professor in a small liberal arts school, that finds me now tenured and wondering near the same place.

I figured that fox had to be an omen of something, of luck, good or bad, or strat-egy, successful or failed, or even my own sorry heart thrusting a reflection of its small, earnest self into the night air. Of course, the fox had barely disappeared before I set to the task of interpretation, asking my grad school buddies, my partner, and my assistant-professor cohorts at neighboring schools to help me in figuring what such an omen might portend. Schooled by deconstructionists and semioticians, not to mention having had our heads spun *Exorcist*-style by feminists, post-structuralists, and cultural critics at our various graduate programs, we were predisposed to see the whole world as a text, and that fox as a moving symbol (of something). We were no less superstitious than the ancient Greeks who scried the sky for signs of the gods' pleasure. My friends bent to the task of interpretation with alacrity and no small abil-ity. One friend made copies of pages describing each person's 13 totem animals and suggested my fox was an omen of my own totemic links. Another friend quizzed me about other animal sightings in my life, dredging up buried memories of the baby raccoons I regularly rescued from a dumpster behind my apartment in Amherst (where they fell in at least once a week one whole spring); the box turtles I played with in the woods behind Sean McCarthy's house as a child (the patterns on their backs the color of cedar shingles etched by fine lines); the cats and dog that live with me now. The vast majority of my friends preferred the analytic method of beer and con-versation, but we had not arrived at any firm conclusions by the time my department met in early October to discuss my bid for promotion and tenure, nor by December when the president of the college decided I was worthy to retain. Eventually, though, we came to decide the fox was an emblem of craft and cunning, and that like her, I had survived in sometimes hostile terrain. One of my grandmother's textbooks describes the fox in a way that I recognize:

> Many are the wiles of the fox to mislead dogs following his track: he often retraces his
> own steps for a few yards and then makes a long sidewise jump; the dogs go on, up to
> the end of the trail pocket, and try in vain to get the scent from that point. Sometimes

he walks along the top rails of fences or takes the high and dry ridges where the scent will not remain; he often follows roads and beaten paths and also goes around and around in the midst of a herd of cattle or sheep so that his scent is hidden; he crosses streams on logs and invents various other devices too numerous and intricate to describe. When chased by dogs, he naturally runs in a circle, probably so as not to be too far from home... (Comstock, 1941, pp. 252–253)

I suppose you may not believe me when I tell you that I saw a second fox six weeks later, on the evening following my department's vote to grant me tenure, but it's true. And this second time I saw a fox, under a cool October moon in a suburban backyard not far from where I live, I had witnesses with me to prove it. Still, the hair on the back of my neck rises to remember it. It was a different fox, in a different neighborhood, but conveying the same reminder, I am sure. It reminded me of what had already happened; it reminded me of where I was going; it reminded me of who I am.

Now I am ever vigilant, looking out for the fox in the world and in myself, the silent tune of its running away a color in my mind, like smoke or the space where a friendship used to be. My mind is full of empty outlines, lines like the chalk outlines of dead bodies drawn by the police on a damp city road in front of a busy restaurant ... perhaps I have been reading too much Calvino. Everyone has a story, and all of us experience charged recollections. But Memory is all that is left after Story has packed up the top hat and the rabbit, putting the wand and the cards back in their boxes; and then we are left with the empty stage, the spaces inside no longer lit by imagination, waiting for the storyteller to return.

There is so much I could say about these fox visitations, using the story as trope or icon, offering it up as symbol or lie. But the fact of it is, I just wanted to tell you this story. Because it's true, because it happened to me, and because thinking about the story of the fox makes me wonder about all sorts of larger connections, such as those between seeing and being, technology and nature, academic writing and the world, education of the mind and experiential education, the rhetorics of the real. And I do think the fox and the exact moment of its appearances offered a kind of syzygy between the realm of my imagination, the realm of our passing bodies, and the realm of our larger worlds. And I am glad that I was awake both those nights in time to see those foxes.

As we have already discussed, many literary critics—from Sven Birkerts to Richard Lanham, from Robert Scholes to Stuart Moulthrop—have explored the question of what reading stories on computers will do to our mind and spirits, to our notion of ourselves. Probably each of the critics I have cited in these pages would read my experience with foxes in a different way, Haraway teasing out the relations between coyotes and foxes as emblems of discourse, DuPlessis questioning the *narrative telos* of both fox journey and this book, Kenneth Burke exploring fox-speak as metonym, and Lunsford and Ede, perhaps, enjoying the collaborative acts of interpretation underlying this very text. But ultimately, I want to claim, the meaning of texts, like the fox, resides in ourselves, and whether we read about foxes within the context of a computer or on these paper pages, its message and music will alter little.

My best guess is that adding computers to the storytelling relationship will ultimately matter little in the long run. My best guess is that a good story will always be a good story, regardless of its medium or mode of presentation. My best guess is that while current digital fictions (and their writers and readers) have not yet learned the best ways to exploit the rhetorical resources of the computer, in time they will, and in time we will see computer-based stories as just another kind of fiction, another kind of interesting text that accommodates multiple interpretations. Furthermore, my guess is that much of the fuss about these stories and much of the flurry that attends each new iteration of digital storytelling derives simply from their novelty. Once we have established narrative conventions and genres, once we have improved the sense of seamlessness between reader and fictive world, our critical theories will do a better job of responding to the structures of fiction and the motivations lodged there. And we will again turn to the important tasks of evaluating fictive texts for what they tell us about ourselves and our worlds.

Just for the sake of argument, imagine that the book was invented after the computer. What questions would we be bringing to *its* novelty? What if critics raised as screen-readers were suddenly confronted with the medium of the book? No doubt we would see the initial prints of familiar stories as an interesting innovation, clumsy yet exciting. No doubt our attention would focus on the quality of the sewing of signatures, the rag content of the pages, the implications of size, durability, and portability. Instead of the plaintive cry we hear today about not being able to read a computer in the tub, we might hear the complaints about the *book* constraining where we might read: if we forget a copy of a popular mystery when we travel to France, we're not likely to find a new copy there; we might celebrate the book's new malleability, the way we can excerpt single pages and tape them to the walls like Dadaist *papillons;* or the ways we can disassemble their pieces and build new structures, like Irnerio in Calvino's *If on a winter's night a traveler* (1981):

> "I was looking for a book," Irnerio says.
>
> "I thought you never read," you reply.
>
> "It's not for reading. It's for making. I make things with books. I make objects. Yes, artworks: statues, pictures, whatever you want to call them. I even had a show. I fix the books with mastic, and they stay as they were. Shut, or open, or else I give them forms, I carve them, I make holes in them. A book is a good material to work with; you can make all sorts of things with it." (pp. 148–149)

If we looked at books afresh we would also see that translations from paper to paper are so cumbersome, and that the printed material that makes up their pages is so frustrating because the text doesn't *move* when you write into it. After computers, the frozen rigidity of a book may well feel intolerable.

In my view, although the technologies of fiction may change, and the mechanics of representation shift, the fact of stories and the acts of storytellers are timeless. Returning to Kenneth Burke's insight cited at the beginning of this book, a human being is a storytelling animal. And the actual subject of stories is always the human in conflict—with herself or with the world—even when the characters are invented as other-than-human. (The hobbits of Tolkien's worlds, the aliens of *A Voyage to Arcturus,* and the Raven of Native American cosmology come to mind.) The characters may change, materials may alter, gender roles grow more flexible, particular ideologies advance or recede, the basis of the conflict grow more technological or urbane, but nonetheless, the basic shapes and truths of stories are never going to change. Let the programmers remember and the programs encapsulate this central truth: the story is primary, the medium secondary. The narrative may borrow its subject, material, and structures, even its mode of narrating from computers—but ultimately the story itself will never be overpowered by the powder and flash of a new presentational medium. The story (*roman*) in time may well subsume its presentation (*fabula*), narrative and rhetoric may well weave together more tightly, and the fabric of the material world may well change the settings, conflicts, and goals of our imagined ones. But every successful story will continue to be one that offers a conflict implicitly or explicitly human, interesting characters who work on resolving that conflict, and ultimately, a discourse that confronts its listeners with a narrative about themselves, their families, their tribes and cultures, their choices, their values, their lives. Stories are an essential part of becoming human.

And one more time: Stories also have their hortatory aspect, as Burke would call it. Stories exhort their listeners and cajole their readers. When we read, then, we are engaged in an activity of judgment. We judge the story, ourselves, and our relationship to the world based on our encounter with story. Stories are more than chronological, predictable, and patterned events; they are interpretable and meaningful; they are rhetorical. They tell us who we are, and whether and how we should act. They reflect the values of ourselves and our contexts, and invite their readers to reflect on the same. Stories educate through symbol or example or counterexample. All narratives by nature are oxymoronic, in the sense that reader who is real is always meeting an "alien" other. They are an exercise in reconciliation, whether a successful reconciliation, a failed one, or everything in between. They are meaningful, they can be cathartic, they educate, and they carp and coax. When we read, we read to measure ourselves, to weigh our own souls, to compare ourselves and our choices with those of other people and creatures. We read to confirm ourselves, to needle or assuage our consciences, to confirm or deny some larger system of cultural values. And we read to be entertained or to escape the restlessness of our own thought. Stories allow readers to project themselves into their worlds and to emerge reconstructed, reformed, galvanized, horrified, or somehow changed.

Can a story exist without readers (or listeners or viewers)? No. You might as well write the story in invisible ink. Can a story exist without writers (or tellers, composers, assemblers)? No. Without stories, we would not be human. Much of the role of the author may be subsumed by programmers and programs, by digital "plot managers," rhetorical "expressivators," 'bots or agents who learn by going, but a good story will always require storytellers who are human, who address us directly, friend to friend, in all our bafflement and knowledge, in all our certainties and confusion. Our most powerful stories will always spring from a human voice, from human experience, from a sense of the beginning, middle, and end of a series of human events that resonate. The human voice of the storyteller is the counterpart to Benjamin's thumbprint on a pot, evidence of an originating presence that is alive and singular; evidence of a faith, perhaps naive, in the rhetorical capacity of an individual person to talk about how she or he has lived, even as the computer hums around that telling. The human storyteller is the fox standing on the road in the face of traffic. The storyteller's voice is recognizable as a way of speaking and knowing that springs ultimately from the lived experiences of ones wiser than ourselves.

Appendix: Timeline

1839   Charles Babbage (with the help of Ada Lovelace) develops the first self-powered mechanical "difference engine," a machine for solving mathematical problems and the prototype for the computer.

1942–1946 Army supports development of ENIAC (Electronic Numerical Integrator and Computer) at the University of Pennsylvania, developed originally to calculate firing tables for artillery weapons; formally dedicated on February 14, 1946.

1945   Publication of Vannevar Bush's "As We May Think" in the *Atlantic Monthly*, an article that establishes the concept of a "Memex," an early version of a comprehensive database and search engine.

1957   October 4: Launch of the Soviet *Sputnik*.

1958   January 7: President Eisenhower requests startup funds from Congress for the Advanced Research Projects Agency (ARPA).

1959   Publication of Vannevar Bush's *Memex II*.

1960   November 24: Oulipo (*Ouvroir de Littérature Potentielle*, or *Workshop of Potential Literature*), founded by several writers who were interested in "combinatorics" in fiction, or *combinatory literature*, in France.

1960   Hasbro starts selling the Think-A-Tron, an "electronic Q&A computer," a battery-operated toy in which the player manually feeds small punch cards to get a digital readout of "yes" or "no."

1961 Undergraduate members of MIT's Tech Model Railroad Club write *Space War*, a computer game that begins to be passed around as sets of punched cards to other computer enthusiasts.

1965 ARPA sponsors study of "cooperative network of time-sharing computers."

1968 ARPAnet officially commissioned by U.S. Department of Defense for Research into Networking.

1968–1969 Andries Van Dam and others develop a Hypertext Editing System (HES) and File Retrieval Editing System (1968), which become the basis for Brown University's Intermedia.

1969 ARPA installs the first nodes of a computer network at UCLA, UC-Santa Barbara, the University of Utah, and the Stanford Research Institute (now SRI).

1970 Alan Kay joins Xerox Corporation's Palo Alto Research Center (PARC), and in the early 1970s leads a group that develops modern workstations, the forerunners of the Macintosh, Smalltalk, Ethernet, laser printing, and network client-servers; Kay also conceives of the first laptop computer, the Dynabook.

1972 Marvin Minsky designs "The Muse," a random melody music synthesizer and player, manufactured by Triadex.

1974 Publication of Theodore Nelson's *Computer Lib: You Can and You Must Understand Computers Now.*

1976 At Yale University, James Meehan develops a story-generating program that he names "Tale-Spin," a program that tells stories for children in the style of Aesop's fables and folktales.

Will Crowther releases *Adventure*, "a text adventure."

Queen Elizabeth II sends out her first e-mail in February from RSRE (Malvern).

1976–1977 Donald Woods reworks *Adventure*, repairing bugs, adding new obstacles and a pirate, doubling the program in size, and referring to it as *Advent*.

1977   Jim Guyton writes *Mazewar*, the first networked, multi-user game.

1978   Roy Trubshaw, a student at the University of Essex, in England, writes a computer game he calls a *Multi-user Dungeon*, or MUD.

1979   Infocom is founded by several graduate students at MIT's Computer Research Laboratory. The Cambridge, Massachusetts, company releases *Zork!*

1979   Alan Klietz uses BASIC to write *Empire*, a multi-user variant of *Advent*. Players work together or fight against one another in a variety of settings including the Wild West, science fiction, and detective stories. *Empire* becomes *The Scepter of Goth*.

1980   Tim Berners-Lee writes a notebook program, "Enquire-Within-Upon-Everything," which allows links to be made between arbitrary nodes.

1980–1987   Michael Lebowitz, a faculty member from 1980 to 1987 in the Department of Computer Science at Columbia University, develops a "simple, prototype story-telling program, UNIVERSE."

1981   BITNET, the "Because It's There NETwork," is established as a cooperative network at the City University of New York, with the first connection to Yale.

            July: ALAMO (*Atelier de Littérature Assistée par la Mathématique et les Ordinateurs*, or a workshop for literature assisted by mathematics and computers) is founded by Paul Braffort and Jacques Roubaud.

            Dehn's AUTHOR is developed.

1982   Publication of Theodore Nelson's *Literary Machines*.

1985   Mike Sharples designs FANTASY, a story generation system for children.

1986–1987   Michael Joyce writes *Afternoon*.

            Eastgate Systems is founded.

1986–1990   Brown University researchers write Intermedia, one of the first hypermedia systems.

1987   Apple Computer releases HyperCard.

              Alan Cox designs *AberMUD,* named for the town of Aberystwyth, Wales, where Cox lived.

1989   Jim Aspnes of Carnegie Mellon University develops TinyMUD for the UNIX operating system, an MUD that becomes the first "social MUD."

1989   Interface designer and interactive multimedia artist Abbe Don releases *We Make Memories,* an interactive family photo album to which viewers can add their own stories and pictures.

1990   October: Tim Berners-Lee starts work on a hypertext browser and editor for CERN. He discards the names "Information Mesh" and "Information Mine" and names the project instead "World Wide Web."

1990   Voyager Company releases the first in its line of *Expanded Books.*

1991   The Oz Project, under the leadership of Joseph Bates, begins Story Generation.

1993   National Center for Supercomputing releases Mosaic, the first major HTTP browser.

1993   The White House comes online.

1994   Broderbund publishes *MYST,* one of the most successful graphic hypertext adventures to date.

              May 25–27: First International WWW Conference, CERN, in Geneva. Known as "the Woodstock of the Web."

1994   Netscape Navigator World Wide Web browser released.

1995   Compuserve, America Online, and Prodigy begin to provide Internet access.

              July: Amazon.com goes online.

1998–1999   Dedicated e-Book devices go on sale, including Librius Millennium, Softbook, Everybook (with dual facing screens), Glassbook, and Rocket eBook; the latter is touted as holding "some 4,000 pages of words and images," or the equivalent of 10 novels (see Michael Gross [1998] article).

Notes

1. For example, the overview of Shanahan and Lomax (1986) is so embedded in litera-ture on text processing and the cognitive model of reading and writing that not one of "the three theoretical models of reading and writing" it discusses includes an explicit awareness of context.

2. The second screen of *Deadline*, if the reader-player types "Go south. Knock on door."

3. Responses appearing in the text of *Deadline* when the program is not recognizing the reader-player's input.

4. Opening screen of *Deadline*. (See note #2.)

5. See Graves (1957). Yes, I deliberately end on a comma, in a discursive act that echoes Robert Graves's wonderful poem, "Leaving the Rest Unsaid," the last three stanzas of which conclude:

> Must the book end, as you would end it,
> With testamentary appendices
> And graveyard indices?
>
> But no, I will not lay me down
> To let your tearful music mar
> The decent mystery of my progress.
>
> So now, my solemn ones, leaving the rest unsaid,
> Rising in air as on a gander's wing
> At a careless comma, (p. 153)

6. As I write these words, I think about a newspaper story I recently read. According to that story, *Dr. Quinn, Medicine Woman*, is getting married. Not only is she getting married, but five other weddings are taking place during this last week of the network sweeps, in a beautiful example of a story delivery system (the television) being informed by its socioe-conomic contexts—and, as a result, constraining narrative. In their efforts to garner high ratings at this important end-of-season moment, writers of a popular television show resort to creating a wedding, knowing that this familiar ritual is sure to pack in the viewers. I see this televised fictional wedding as an unhappy example of the convergence of delivery sys-tem, narrative, and larger cultural and economic context that is echoed in today's com-

puter stories, their contexts, and their delivery systems, and that likewise demands our investigation.

7. Part of Hugo Ball's abstract poem, "O Gadji Beri Bimba," delivered at a public reading in which Ball tried to take on "the age-old cadence of priestly lamentation." Described in Dawn Ades's *Dada and Surrealism* (1978), p. 14.

8. *The Castle of Crossed Destinies* (Calvino, 1977), translated by William Weaver, begins with the time-honored device of several travelers arriving independently at a castle (as in Boccaccio, Chaucer, and many a fairy tale). The travelers decide to tell their stories. However, the moment that they open their mouths to speak, they realize they have all been struck dumb. So, they decide to use a Tarot pack to tell their stories, using the cards to cobble together their narratives, to frame the salient moments rather like a comic strip.

9. See both Landow (1992a) and Bolter (1990) for a more thorough discussion of these particular connections.

10. See Brande (1934/1984) and Ghiselin (1952).

11. I am indebted to a number of sites on the WWW, especially *Colossal Cave Adventure Page*, as well as the books *When Wizards Stay Up Late* and *Hackers*, for this account.

12. "Zork: A Computerized Fantasy Simulation Game" (1979) includes this example of MDL language, which I include as a simple illustration of the kinds of texts that invisibly underlie the texts on the screen:

The definition of the "verb" READ

```
<ADD-ACTION "READ:"
"Read"
[(READBIT REACH AOBJS ROBJS TRY)
        "restrictions on characteristics and location of objects for defaulting—filling in an
unadorned 'READ' command. The object must be readable and accessible."
["READ" READER] DRIVER]
        "READER is the function, and the form 'READ object' is preferred (the 'driver')"
[(READBIT REACH AOBJS ROBJS TRY) "WITH" OBJ ["READ" READER)]
        "specification for 'READ obj1 WITH obj2" ["READ READER")]
        "specification for 'READ obj1 THROUGH obj2'">
```

13. Marc Blank, a graduate of MIT, was co-author of the original mainframe version of *Zork* in 1977. He is also co-author of the *Zork* trilogy and *Enchanter,* and is sole author of DEADLINE, "the first interactive mystery," according to *The Lost Treasures of Infocom Manual* (1988, p. 100).

14. Opening screen of *A Mind Forever Voyaging* (1985).

15. At that time I observed a series of drama experiments orchestrated by Margaret Kelso of the Carnegie Mellon University Drama Department and designed and participated in my own narrative experiment. Mark Kantrowitz, a Carnegie Mellon graduate student developing a natural language base for Oz, and I created a "free" interactive fiction wherein I took the role of the narrator and Kantrowitz the user-player. We wished to simulate the experience of interactive fiction when unconstrained by a reluctant parser or limited vocabulary.

16. These data gloves or cyber gloves have been described in articles in *Mondo 2000, The Media Lab,* and *The Journal of Computer Game Design,* and are currently advertised as available from VPL Industries and Autodesk. They are commercially available alternative interfaces for engaging with computer simulations.

[17.] The Believable Agents 1994 Spring Symposium was collaboratively planned by Joseph Bates, Barbara Hayes-Roth, Brenda Laurel, and Nils Nilsson. The Interactive Story Systems: Plot & Character Symposium in 1995 was cochaired by Joseph Bates, Barbara Hayes-Roth, and Pattie Maes. The Socially Intelligent Agents Symposium was organized by Michel Aube, Universite de Sherbrooke, Canada; Joseph Bates, Carnegie Mellon University, Pittsburgh, PA; Kerstin Dautenhahn (cochair), VUB AI Lab, Belgium, and University of Reading, UK; Philippe Gaussier, ENSEA, France; Judith Masthoff (cochair), Institute for Perception Research, The Netherlands; Chisato Numaoka (cochair), Sony Computer Science Lab, Paris, France; and Aaron Sloman, University of Birmingham, UK.

[18.] Bates acknowledges the work of Agre and Chapman at Massachusetts Institute of Technology and the work at Yale of Firby in the development of HAP. Bates links the development of Prodigy (a "planner/learner") to the work of Jaime Carbonell's machine-learning group at Carnegie Mellon University.

[19.] Kantrowitz's summary of Hovy, "Overview of Natural Language Text Generation," (class lecture given at Carnegie Mellon University, November 6 & 8, 1990), 12.

[20.] From the overview of Oz presented in *ArtCom*. While such a parser would help readers successfully avoid the frustrating experience of not being "understood," Bates's model of the reader's input here reveals a predisposition to see the reader as having a limited participation in these stories.

[21.] After the Woggles' debut at AAAI-92, they were exhibited at the Hewlett Gallery of Carnegie Mellon University in January 1993, and then made part of the permanent exhibition of the Boston Computer Museum in February 1993. It won an honorable mention at the SIGGRAPH 1993 Art Show, in Anaheim, California.

[22.] Picard's (1998) summary and synthesis of various cognitive models of emotion ranges from the obscure to the wildly entertaining, at least to some readers. Clark Elliot's (DePaul University) "Affective Reasoner" has increased the OCC model of 22 emotions to 26 emotions, all of which can be "elicited" through encounters with other agents. Dolores Cañamero of the Free University of Brussels "has built a system in which emotions trigger changes in synthetic hormones" (Picard, 1998, p. 213).

[23.] According to Johnson (1987), this metaphor derives originally from René Descartes's *Discourse on Methods* and construes a dualism between rationalism and matter (and helped lay the groundwork for the building of calculating clocks, the precursor of computers). It connects, too, to Acquinas's *Treatise on Man* (1981).

[24.] Doug Lenat of MCC's Cyc, for example, at AAAI-90, gave a short presentation in which he asked, "Do you know the capital of [a distant country not often featured in U.S. news, whose precise name I cannot recall. Madagascar? Zimbabwe?]?" Audience members immediately shook their heads or politely demurred. Lenat explained that human beings know "instantly" when they do not know something, while computers must search through all their information and databases, before they can conclusively state they don't "know" something. Why this difference? How can human beings know so quickly when they lack some piece of knowledge?

[25.] According to Albertine Gaur, the Phaistos disc was found "in an outbuilding of the Minoan palace at Hagia Triada. The disc, 160 millimeters in diameter, and dated not later than 1700 BC ... is inscribed on both sides.... [It is] a text, arranged in bands spiraling towards the center, [that] has been impressed with forty-five different wooden or metal punches in the originally soft clay" (1984, p. 144). It remains to be successfully interpreted.

26. The Edinburgh literati proposed a new literary criticism and chose literary examples to underscore their claims, which themselves were knowledge very much situated and shared, and which probably evolved from their common Edinburgh High School training, common study in the principles of the sublime and of rhetoric, and rich conversations, exchanges of writing-in-progress, shared memories, and intermarriages among this exclusive, homosocial community.

27. "We Make Memories" (abbedon.com/Project/wemake.html) is a groundbreaking, important work of art made by Abbe Don in 1990 and exhibited in numerous locations. "We Make Memories" is an interactive family album to which viewers add their own stories and pictures. Don's more recent "Bubbe's Back Porch" (bubbe.com) is another nonfiction narrative, in which women from around the world participated in a "digital story bee," in which they shared stories and pictures of their family, and pioneered the idea of websites as sites for cross-cultural sharing of memories. In Don's work, the memories are ancestral as well as contemporary, and the sponsors Don notes on her website includes the *Jewish Heritage Online Magazine*. She also thanks the Bay Area Council for Jewish Rescue and Renewal "for making the collaboration with Kiev, Moscow, St. Petersburg, and the Bay Area Russian emigre community possible."

28. Guyer was interviewed in an e-mail communication dated May 3, 1996.

29. Moulthrop was interviewed in an e-mail communication dated April 22, 1996.

30. A word attributed by Alison Adam to Lorraine Code: "Malestream," a wonderful term conjuring up both maleness and mainstream at the same time appears to have originated in Code (1993).

31. Which does, of course, make one wonder where, in fact, the center lies. If all these people are disenfranchised from dominant narratives, as we all sometimes feel, then who writes the stories that the majority can relate to, identify with, and read with pleasure?

32. Graves (1988) reminds readers that in Celtic myth the labyrinth came to mean "royal tomb" and that the early Greeks probably used the word *labyrinth* to refer to mountain caves or subterranean caves. Graves points us toward Pliny's *Natural History* for the tale of Lars Porsena the Etruscan, who made a labyrinth leading to his own tomb. And Graves notes, finally, that there were labyrinths in the pre-Hellenic caves near Nauplia and on Samos and Lemnos. Graves ends with the matter-of-fact statement that "[t]o escape from the labyrinth, therefore, is to be reincarnate" (p. 318).

33. A list of current MUDs is available through the Web at the following URL: http://www.cm.ac.uk/User/Andrew.Wilson/MUDlist/dorans.html

34. According to an article published in the February 1999 *MIT Technology Review*, diabetic children playing Packy & Marlon, a story in which two elephants try to survive an outing while remembering to check their blood glucose and administer insulin to themselves, needed "77 percent fewer urgent-care visits to a doctor or emergency room than the kids who played the placebo game" (p. 24). One loves, of course, the notion of "a placebo game."

35. Of course, debates about the connections between visual and verbal arts are endless, erupting in arguments about aesthetics in the 18th century and critical theory in the 20th century (see, for example, Berger, 1991; Gombrich, 1961; Mitchell, 1986).

36. Scholes (1998) also discusses the need to transform English departments back into communities built on the shared enterprise of rhetorical analysis of language. He acknowledges the development of literary study from 18th-century Scottish rhetoric, citing Kames's *The Elements of Criticism* as an early textual example, but claims that the study of literature as a discipline was really consolidated by German Romantics like Schiller,

Schelling, and Hegel. Scholes says that the current minimal attention given to rhetoric in English departments shows signs of changing, owing in part to the pressures of contemporary students. At my own campus, we wait and watch and see.

References

Aarseth, Espen. (1993). Nonlinearity and literary theory. In G. Landow (Ed.), *Hypertext and literary theory* (pp. 51–86). Baltimore, MD: John Hopkins University Press.

Aarseth, Espen. (1997). *Cybertext: Perspectives on ergodic literature*. Baltimore, MD: Johns Hopkins University Press.

Abrams, M. H. (1953). *The mirror and the lamp*. New York: Oxford University Press.

Adam, Alison. (1998). *Artificial knowing: Gender and the thinking machine*. London: Routledge.

Addams, Shay. (1985, March). Interactive fiction. *Popular Computing*, 97–99, 180–182.

Ades, Dawn. (1978). *Dada and surrealism*. New York: Barron's Educational Series.

Alfau, Felipe. (1936). *Locos: A comedy of gestures*. New York: Farrar & Rinehart.

Ammons, A. R. (1993). *Garbage*. New York: Norton.

Anderson, John R., Corbett, Albert T., & Reiser, Brian J. (1987). *Essential LISP*. Reading, MA: Addison-Wesley.

Acquinas, Thomas. (1981). *Treatise on man*. Westport, CT: Greenwood.

Atlantis [Hypertext document]. (1995–1999). Available: http://atlantis.midsouth.net

Auster, Paul. (1990). *The New York trilogy*. New York: Penguin Books.

Ayckbourn, Alan. (1981). *Sisterly feelings*. London: Chatto & Windus.

Bacon, Francis. (1944). *Advancement of learning, and Novum organum*. New York: Wiley. (Original work published 1620)

Bakhtin, M. M. (1981). *The dialogic imagination* (Michael Holquist, Ed. & Trans.; Caryl Emerson, Trans.). Austin, TX: University of Texas Press.

Bakhtin, M. M. (1993). The spatial form of character. In Alla Efimova & Lev Manovich (Ed. & Trans.), *Tekstura: Russian essays on visual culture* (pp. 37–44). Chicago: University of Chicago Press.

Banks, Michael A. (1985). An introduction to interactive fiction. In *The 1985 writers yearbook* (pp. 64–73).

Barthes, Roland. (1974). *S/Z* (Richard Miller, Trans.). London: Farrar, Strauss, Giroux.

Barthes, Roland. (1977). The death of the author. In S. Head (Ed. & Trans.), *Image-music-text* (pp. 142–148). New York: Hill & Wang.

Barthes, Roland. (1992a). *The responsibility of forms: Critical essays on music, art, and representation* (Richard Howard, Trans.). Berkeley, CA: University of California Press.

Barthes, Roland. (1992b). The structuralist activity. In H. Adams (Ed.), *Critical theory since Plato* (Rev. ed.; pp. 1127–1133). Fort Worth, TX: Harcourt Brace Jovanovich.

Bartholomae, David. (1993). *Ways of reading: An anthology for writers.* Boston: Bedford Books of St. Martin's Press.

Baruchello, Gianfranco, & Martin, Henry. (1984). *How to imagine: A narrative on art and agriculture.* New Paltz, NY: Documentext/McPherson & Company.

Bates, J. (1990). *Computational drama in Oz.* In *Working notes of the AAAI-90 Workshop on Interactive Fiction and Synthetic Realities.* Boston, MA. Unpublished manuscript.

Bates, J. (1992). Virtual reality, art, and entertainment. *PRESENCE: Teleoperators and Virtual Environments, 1*(1), 133–138.

Bates, J., Loyall, A. B., & Reilly, W. S. (1991, August). Broad agents. *SIGART Bulletin, 2*(4), 38–40.

Bates, Joseph, & Smith, Sean. (1989). *Towards a theory of narrative for interactive fiction* (Technical Report No. CMU-CS-89-121). Pittsburgh, PA: Carnegie Mellon University.

Baudrillard, Jean. (1983). *Simulations* (Paul Foss, Paul Patton, & Philip Beitchman, Trans.). New York: Semiotext(e).

Baudrillard, Jean. (1988). For a critique of the political economy of the sign. In M. Poster (Ed.), *Jean Baudrillard: Selected writings* (pp. 57–97). Stanford, CA: Stanford University Press.

Baudrillard, Jean. (1989). *America* (Chris Turner, Trans.). London, Verso.

Baudrillard, Jean. (1990). The dual, the polar, and the digital. In *Seduction* (pp. 154–156; Brian Singer, Trans.). New York: St. Martin's Press.

Benedikt, Michael. (1987). *For an architecture of reality.* New York: Lumen Books.

Benjamin, Walter. (1988). *Illuminations: Essays and reflections.* New York: Harcourt, Brace, and World. (Original work published 1955)

Bereiter, Carl, & Scardamalia, Marlene. (1984). Learning about writing from reading. *Written Communication, 1,* 163–188.

Bereiter, Carl, & Scardamalia, Marlene. (1987). *The psychology of written composition.* Hillsdale, NJ: Lawrence Erlbaum.

Bereiter, Carl, & Scardamalia, Marlene. (1993). *Surpassing ourselves: An inquiry into the nature and implications of expertise.* Chicago: Open Court.

Berger, John. (1991). *About looking.* New York: Vintage International.

Berlin, James A. (1996). *Rhetoric, poetics, and cultures: Refiguring college English studies.* Urbana, IL: National Council of Teachers of English.

Betz, David. (1987, May). An adventure authoring system. *Byte,* 125–135.

Birkerts, Sven. (1995). *The Gutenberg elegies: The fate of reading in an electronic age.* New York: Fawcett Columbine.

Birkerts, Sven. (1999a, February). American nostalgias. *Writer's Chronicle, 31*(4), 27, 28, 36.

Birkerts, Sven. (1999b). *Readings.* St. Paul, MN: Graywolf Press.

Bishop, Wendy. (1992). *Working words: The process of creative writing.* London: Mayfield.

Blair, David. (1991). *Wax or the discovery of television among the bees* [Videotape]. Available: http://jefferson.village.virginia.edu/wax/

Bolter, J. David. (1991a). *Writing space: The computer, hypertext, and the history of writing* [Computer software]. Hillsdale, NJ: Lawrence Erlbaum.

Bolter, J. David. (1991b). *Writing space: The computer, hypertext, and the history of writing.* Hillsdale, NJ: Lawrence Erlbaum.

Bolter, J. David. (1996). Ekphrasis, virtual reality, and the future of writing. In Geoffrey Nunberg (Ed.), *The future of the book* (pp. 253–272). Berkeley, CA: University of California Press.

Bolter, J. David, Joyce, Michael, Smith, John B., & Bernstein, Mark. (1992). *Getting started with Storyspace*. Cambridge, MA: Eastgate Systems.

Booth, Wayne. (1983). *The rhetoric of fiction* (2nd ed.). Chicago: University of Chicago Press.

Borges, Jorge Luis. (1972). The garden of forking paths. In Donald A. Yates (Ed. & Trans.) & James E. Inby (Ed.), *Labyrinths: Selected stories and other writings* (pp. 19–29). New York: Penguin Books.

Borges, Jorge Luis. (1999). *Collected fictions* (Andrew Hurley, Trans.). New York: Penguin.

Bracewell, Robert J., Frederiksen, Carl H., & Frederiksen, Janet Donin. (1982). Cognitive processes in composing and comprehending discourse. *Educational Psychologist, 17*(3), 146.

Brande, Dorothea. (1984). *Becoming a writer*. Los Angeles: Jeremy P. Tarcher. (Original work published 1934)

Brandt, Deborah. (1990). *Literacy as involvement: The acts of writers, readers, and texts*. Carbondale, IL: Southern Illinois University Press.

Brandt, Deborah. (1992). The cognitive as the social: An ethnomethodological approach to writing process research. *Written Communication, 9*, 315–355.

Breton, Andre. (1972). *Manifestoes of surrealism* (Richard Seaver & Helen R. Lane, Trans.). Ann Arbor, MI: University of Michigan Press.

Brummett, Barry. (1990). Relativism and rhetoric. In Richard A. Cherwitz (Ed.), *Rhetoric and philosophy* (pp. 79–103). Hillsdale, NJ: Lawrence Erlbaum.

Buckles, Mary Ann. (1985). *Interactive fiction: The computer storygame "Adventure."* Unpublished dissertation, University of California, San Diego.

Buckles, Mary Ann. (1987, May). Interactive fiction as literature. *Byte*, 135–142.

Burgess, Anthony. (1986). *Little Wilson and big God*. New York: Weidenfeld & Nicolson.

Burka, Lauren P. (1995). *Untitled* [Hypertext document]. Available: http://www.apocalypse.org/pub/u/lpb/muddex/mudline.html

Burke, Kenneth. (1957). *The philosophy of literary form: Studies in symbolic action*. New York: Vintage Books.

Burke, Kenneth. (1966). *Language as symbolic action: Essays on life, literature, and method*. Berkeley, CA: University of California Press.

Burke, Kenneth. (1969). *A grammar of motives*. Berkeley, CA: University of California Press.

Busey, Andrew. (1995). *Secrets of the MUD wizards*. Indianapolis, IN: Sams.net.

Bush, Vannevar. (1945). As we may think. *Atlantic Monthly, 176*, 101–108.

Calvino, Esther. (1995). Introduction. In Italo Calvino, *Numbers in the dark* (pp. 1–3). New York: Pantheon Books.

Calvino, Italo. (1977). *The castle of crossed destinies* (William Weaver, Trans.). New York: Harcourt Brace Jovanovich.

Calvino, Italo. (1981). *If on a winter's night a traveler* (William Weaver, Trans.). New York: Harcourt Brace Jovanovich.

Calvino, Italo. (1983). *Comment j'ai ecrit un de mes livres*. Paris: Bibliotheque Oulipienne.

Calvino, Italo. (1986). *The uses of literature: Essays*. San Diego, CA: Harcourt Brace Jovanovich.

Calvino, Italo. (1995). *Numbers in the dark: And other stories* (Tim Parks, Trans.). New York: Pantheon Books.

Carpenter, Michael. (1981). *Corporate authorship: its role in library cataloging.* Westport, CT: Greenwood.

Caudill, Maureen. (1992). *In our own image.* New York: Oxford University Press.

Cervantes, Miguel de. (1950). *The adventures of Don Quixote.* Baltimore, MD: Penguin Books.

Chartier, Roger. (1997). *On the edge of the cliff: History, language, and practices* (Lydia G. Cochrane, Trans.). Baltimore, MD: Johns Hopkins University Press.

Chartier, Roger. (1994). *The order of books: Readers, authors, and libraries in Europe between the fourteenth and fifteenth centuries* (Lydia G. Cochrane, Trans.). Stanford, CA: Stanford University Press.

Chatman, Seymour. (1978). *Story and discourse: Narrative structure in fiction and film.* Ithaca, NY: Cornell University Press.

Cheuse, Alan. (1998, November 23). Alan Cheuse: Writer and raconteur. *Publishers Weekly,* 26.

Cixous, Hélène. (1990). The laugh of the Medusa. In Patricia Bizzell & Bruce Herzberg (Eds.), *The rhetorical tradition: Readings from classical times to the present* (pp. 1232–1245). Boston: Bedford Books of St. Martin's Press.

Code, Lorraine. (1993). Taking subjectivity into account. In Linda Alcoff & Elizabeth Potter (Eds.), *Feminist epistemologies* (pp. 15–48). New York: Routledge.

Collins, Wilkie. (1874). *The moonstone.* New York and London: Harper.

Compact edition of the Oxford English dictionary. (1971). New York: Oxford University Press.

Comstock, Anna Botsford. (1941). *Handbook of nature-study.* Ithaca, NY: Comstock.

Cooper, Marilyn. (1986). The ecology of writing. *College English, 48*(4), 364–375.

Coover, Robert. (1969). *Pricksongs & descants; fictions.* New York: .Dutton.

Coover, Robert. (1992, June 21). The end of books. *The New York Times Book Review,* pp. 1, 23–25.

Coover, Robert. (1993, August 29). Hyperfiction: Novels for the computer. *The New York Times Book Review,* pp. 1, 8–12.

Cortázar, Julio. (1975). *Hopscotch* (Gregory Rabassa, Trans.). New York: Avon.

Costanzo, William V. (1986, June). Reading interactive fiction: Implications of a new literary genre. *Educational Technology,* 31–35.

Costello, Matt. (1987). *Robert Silverberg's Majipoor: A Crossroads adventure.* New York: TOR Books.

Coverley, M. D. (1998). Remarks made during a "hypermedia performance" sponsored by the Committee on Computers and Emerging Technologies in Teaching and Research at the 1998 MLA, San Francisco.

Crawford, Chris. (1984). *The art of computer game design.* Berkeley, CA: Osborne/McGraw-Hill.

Daglow, Don L. (1987). Through hope-colored glasses: A publisher's perspective on game development. *The Journal of Computer Game Design, 1*(4), 3–5.

Damar, Bruce. (1998). *Avatars! Exploring and building virtual worlds on the Internet.* Berkeley, CA: Peachpit Press.

Deadline [Hypertext document]. (1991). In *The lost treasures of Infocom.* Los Angeles: Activision.

de Beaugrand, Robert. (1982). The story of grammars and the grammar of stories. *Journal of Pragmatics, 6,* 383–422.

de Certeau, Michel. (1984). *The practice of everyday life* (S. Randall, Trans.). Berkeley, CA: University of California Press.

Deely, John. (1990). *Basics of semiotics.* Bloomington, IN: Indiana University Press.

Dehn, Natalie. (1981). Memory in story invention. In *Proceeding of the Third Annual Conference of the Cognitive Science Society* (pp. 213–215). Berkeley, CA.

Dehn, Natalie. (1989). *Computer story-writing: The role of deconstructive and dynamic memory* (Document No. TR792). New Haven, CT: Yale University.

Delany, Samuel R. (1996). *Dhalgren.* Hanover, NH: University Press of New England.

De Landa, Manuel. (1992). *War in the age of intelligent machines.* Cambridge, MA: MIT Press.

De Lauretis, Teresa. (1984). *Alice doesn't: Feminism, semiotics, cinema.* Bloomington, IN: Indiana University Press.

Deleuze, Gilles, & Guattari, Félix. (1987). *A thousand plateaus: Capitalism and schizophrenia* (Brian Massumi, Trans.). Minneapolis, MN: University of Minnesota Press.

Derrida, Jacques. (1976). *Of grammatology* (Gayatri Chakravorty Spivak, Trans.). Baltimore, MD: Johns Hopkins University Press.

Derrida, Jacques. (1990). Signature event context. In Samuel Weber & Jeffrey Mehlman (Trans.), *The rhetorical tradition: Readings from classical times to the present* (pp. 1168–1184). Boston: Bedford Books of St. Martin's Press.

Derrida, Jacques. (1992). Structure, sign and play in the discourse of the human sciences. In Hazard Adams (Ed.), *Critical theory since Plato* (Rev. ed.; pp. 1116–1126). Fort Worth, TX: Harcourt Brace Jovanovich.

Descartes, Rene. (1987). *Discourse on method and the meditations.* New York: Viking.

Don, Abbe. (1985–1999). *We make memories* [Hypertext document]. Available: http://www.abbedon.com/Project/wemake.html

Doniger, Wendy. (1998). *The implied spider: Politics & theology in myth.* New York: Columbia University Press.

Douglas, Jane Yellowlees. (1993). I have said nothing [Hypertext document]. *The Eastgate Quarterly Review of Hypertext, 1*(2).

Douglas, Jane Yellowlees. (1994). "How do I stop this thing?": Closure and indeterminancy in interactive narratives. In George P. Landow (Ed.), *Hypertext theory* (pp. 159–188). Baltimore, MD: Johns Hopkins University Press.

Dreyfus, Herbert L. (1993). *What computers still can't do: A critique of artificial reason.* Cambridge, MA: MIT Press.

DuPlessis, Rachel Blau. (1985). *Writing beyond the ending: Narrative strategies of twentieth-century women writers.* Bloomington, IN: Indiana University Press.

Dyer, M. G. (1982). *In-depth understanding: A computer model of integrated processing for narrative comprehension* (Technical Report No. 219). New Haven, CT: Yale University, Department of Computer Science.

Eagleton, Mary. (Ed.). (1996). *Feminist literary theory: A reader* (2nd ed.). Oxford, England: Blackwell.

Eagleton, Terry. (1983). *Literary theory: An introduction.* Minneapolis, MN: University of Minnesota Press.

Eagleton, Terry. (1996). *Literary theory: An introduction* (2nd ed.). Minneapolis, MN: University of Minnesota Press.

Eco, Umberto. (1986). *Travels in hyperreality* (William Weaver, Trans.). San Diego, CA: Harcourt, Brace, Jovanovich.

Eco, Umberto. (1990). *The limits of interpretation.* Bloomington, IN: Indiana University Press.

Ede, Lisa, & Lunsford, Andrea. (1990). *Singular texts, plural authors: Perspectives on collaborative writing.* Carbondale, IL: Southern Illinois University Press.

Elbow, Peter. (1981). *Writing with power: Techniques for mastering the writing process.* New York: Oxford University Press.

Elbow, Peter. (1973). *Writing without teachers.* New York: Oxford University Press.

Eliot, Thomas Stearns. (1935). *Murder in the cathedral.* New York: Harcourt, Brace and Company.

Ellis, Estelle, Seebohm, Caroline, & Sykes, Christopher Simon. (1995). *At home with books: How booklovers live with and care for their libraries.* New York: Carol Southern Books.

Ellison, Ralph. (1972). *Invisible man.* New York: Vintage Books.

Eternal Struggle [Hypertext document]. (1998–2000). Available: http://eternal.oxonet.com

Falco, Edward. (1997). *A dream with demons* [Hypertext document]. Cambridge, MA: Eastgate Systems.

Fish, Stanley. (1989). *Doing what comes naturally.* Durham, NC: Duke University Press.

Flower, Linda. (1985). *Problem-solving strategies in writing* (2nd ed.). New York: Harcourt Brace Jovanovich.

Flower, Linda. (1989). Cognition, context, and theory building. *College Composition and Communication, 40,* 282–311.

Flower, Linda. (1994). *The construction of negotiated meaning: A social cognitive theory of writing.* Carbondale, IL: Southern Illinois University Press.

Flower, Linda, & Hayes, John R. (1980). The cognition of discovery: Defining a rhetorical problem. *College Composition and Communication, 31,* 21–32.

Flower, Linda, & Hayes, John R. (1981a). A cognitive process theory of writing. *College Composition and Communication, 32,* 365–387.

Flower, Linda, & Hayes, John R. (1981b). Plans that guide the composing process. In C. H. Frederickson & J. F. Dominic (Eds.), *Writing: The nature, development, and teaching of written communication* (pp. 39–58). Hillsdale, NJ: Lawrence Erlbaum.

Flower, Linda, & Hayes, John R. (1984). Images, plans, and prose: The representation of meaning in writing. *Written Communication, 1,* 120–160.

Forster, E. M. (1927). *Aspects of the novel.* London: Edward Arnold.

Foucault, Michel. (1977). What is an author? In Donald F. Bouchard (Ed.), *Language, counter-memory, practice: Selected essays and interviews* (Donald F. Bouchard & Sherry Simon, Trans.; pp. 113–138). Ithaca, NY: Cornell University Press.

Fowles, John. (1969). *The French Lieutenant's woman.* London: Cape.

Galloway, Janice. (1995). *Foreign parts.* Normal, IL: Dalkey Archive Press.

Gardner, John. (1983). *The art of fiction: Notes on craft for young writers.* New York: Alfred Knopf.

Gaur, Albertine. (1984). *A history of writing.* London: The British Library.

Getting started [Hypertext document]. (1994). *The Eastgate Quarterly Review of Hypertext, 1*(3), 4–5.

Ghiselin, Brewster. (1952). *The creative process.* Berkeley, CA: New American Library.

Gibson, William. (1984). *Neuromancer.* New York: Ace Books.

Gibson, William. (1988). *Mona Lisa overdrive.* Toronto and New York: Bantam Books.

Gilbert, Sandra, & Gubar, Susan. (1979). *The madwoman in the attic: The woman writer and the nineteenth-century literary imagination.* New Haven, CT: Yale University Press.

Gilbert, Sandra and Susan Gubar. (1994). *No man's land: The place of the woman writer in the twentieth century.* New Haven, CT: Yale University Press.

Glass, James. (1993). *Shattered selves: Multiple personality in a postmodern world.* Ithaca, NY: Cornell University Press.

Goldberg, Natalie. (1986). *Writing down the bones: Freeing the writer within.* Boston: Shambhala.

Goldberg, Natalie. (1990). *Wild mind: Living the writer's life.* New York: Bantam Books.

Goldman, Susan R. (1996). Reading, writing, and learning in hypermedia environments. In Herre van Oostendorp & Sjaak de Mul (Eds.), *Cognitive aspects of electronic text processing* (pp. 7–42). Norwood, NJ: Ablex.

Gombrich, Ernst Hans. (1961). *Art and illusion: A study in the psychology of pictorial representation.* New York: Bollingen Foundation.

Goody, Jack, Ed. (1968). *Literacy in traditional societies* (pp. 304–345). Cambridge, England: Cambridge University Press.

Goody, Jack. (1977). *The domestication of the savage mind.* New York: Cambridge University Press.

Goody, Jack, & Watt, Ian. (1968). The consequences of literacy. In Jack Goody (Ed.), *Literacy in traditional societies.* Cambridge, England: Cambridge University Press.

Graves, Robert. (1957). *Poems.* London: Penguin Books.

Graves, Robert. (1988). *The Greek myths.* Mt. Kisco, NY: Moyer Bell.

Graves, Robert. (1966). *The white goddess: A historical grammar of poetic myth.* New York: Farrar, Straus, and Giroux.

Gross, Michael Joseph. (1999, January 7). Rare, delicate books you can maul to your heart's content. *New York Times,* p. G6.

Guyer, Carolyn. (1992, December). *Buzz-daze and the quotidian stream.* Paper presented at the Annual Conference of the Modern Language Association, New York.

Guyer, Carolyn. (1993, November 15). Artist's statement. *Leonardo Electronic News 2*(11).

Guyer, Carolyn. (1993). *Quibbling* [Hypertext document]. Cambridge, MA: Eastgate Systems.

Guyer, Carolyn. (1994, April–May). Experimental women. *American Book Review,* 13.

Guyer, Carolyn, & Petry, Martha. (1991). Notes for *IZME PASS* exposé. *Writing on the Edge,* 2(2), 82–89.

Haas, C., & Hayes, John. (1986). What did I just say? Reading problems in writing with the machine. *Research in the Teaching of English, 20*(1), 22–35.

Haas, Christina. (1996). *Writing technology: Studies on the materiality of literacy.* Hillsdale, NJ: Lawrence Erlbaum.

Hackforth, Reginald. (Ed. & Trans.). (1952). *Introduction to Phaedrus by Plato.* Indianapolis, IN: Bobb-Merrill.

Hafner, Katie, & Lyon, Matthew. (1998). *Where wizards stay up late: The origins of the Internet.* New York: Simon & Schuster.

Haraway, Donna. (1985). A manifesto for cyborgs: Science, technology, and socialist feminism in the 1980s. *Socialist Review, 80,* 65–108.

Haraway, Donna. (1997). *Modest_witness@second_millennium.FemaleMan-Meets-OncoMouse: Feminism and technoscience.* New York: Routledge.

Haraway, Donna. (1991). *Simians, cyborgs, and women: The reinvention of nature.* New York: Routledge.

Haugeland, John. (1985). *Artificial intelligence: The very idea.* Cambridge, MA: MIT Press.

Havelock, Eric A. (1986). *The muse learns to write: Reflections on orality and literacy from antiquity to the present.* New Haven, CT: Yale University Press.

Hawisher, Gail, & Selfe, Cynthia. (Eds.). (1991). *Evolving perspectives on computers and composition studies.* Urbana, IL: The National Council of Teachers of English; Houghton, MI: Computers and Composition Press.

Hayes, John R., & Flower, Linda S. (1980). Identifying the organization of writing processes. In Lee W. Gregg & Erwin R. Steinberg (Eds.), *Cognitive processes in writing* (pp. 3–30). Hillsdale, NJ: Lawrence Erlbaum.

Heath, Shirley Brice. (1983). *Ways with words: Language, life, and work in communities and classrooms.* Cambridge and New York: Cambridge University Press.

Heim, Michael. (1987). *Electric language: A philosophical study of word processing.* New Haven, CT: Yale University Press.

Heim, Michael. (1993). *The metaphysics of virtual reality.* New York: Oxford University Press.

Herbert, Frank. (1984). *Dune.* New York: Berkley Books.

Hesse, Mary B. (1970). *Forces and fields.* Westport, CT: Greenwood Press.

Hikins, James W. (1990). Realism and its implications for rhetorical theory. In Richard A. Cherwitz (Ed.), *Rhetoric and philosophy* (pp. 21–78). Hillsdale, NJ: Lawrence Erlbaum.

Hirsch, E. D. (1987). *Cultural literacy: What every American needs to know.* Boston: Houghton Mifflin.

Hogan, James P. (1995). *Realtime interrupt.* New York: Bantam Books.

Horace. (1992). Art of poetry. In Hazard Adams (Ed.), *Critical theory since Plato* (pp. 68–75). Fort Worth, TX: Harcourt Brace Jovanovich.

Howard, Rebecca Moore. (1999). *Standing in the shadow of giants.* Stamford, CT: Ablex.

HyperCard Version 1.25 [Computer software]. (1987). Cupertino, CA: Apple Computer.

HyperCard basics. (1990). Cupertino, CA: Apple Computer.

Hunter, Lynette. (1999). Feminist thoughts on rhetoric. In Christine Mason Sutherland & Rebecca Sutcliffe (Eds.), *The changing tradition: Women in the history of rhetoric* (pp. 237–248). Calgary: University of Calgary Press.

Irigaray, Luce. (1985). *This sex which is not one* (Catherine Porter & Carolyn Burke, Trans.). Ithaca, NY: Cornell University Press. (Original work published 1977)

Iser, Wolfgang. (1978). *The implied reader: Patterns of communication in prose fiction from Bunyan to Beckett.* Baltimore, MD: Johns Hopkins University Press.

Iser, Wolfgang. (1991). Institutions of interpretation. *New Literary History, 22*(1), 231–239.

Jaggar, Alison. (1989). Love and knowledge: Emotion in feminist epistemology. In Alison Jaggar & Susan Bordo (Eds.), *Gender/body/knowledge: Feminist deconstructions of being and knowing.* New Brunswick, NJ: Rutgers University Press.

James, Henry. (1960). *The ambassadors.* New York: New American Library.

James, P. D. (1993). *The children of men.* New York: Knopf.

Jameson, Fredric. (1991). *Postmodernism: Or, the cultural logic of late capitalism.* Durham, NC: Duke University Press.

Janangelo, Joseph. (1991). Technopower and technoppression. *Computers and Composition, 9*(2), 95–129.

Johnson, George. (1986). *Machinery of the mind: Inside the new science of artificial intelligence.* New York: Random House.

Johnson, Mark. (1987). *The body in the mind.* Chicago: University of Chicago Press.

Johnson, Mark, & Lakoff, George. (1999). *Philosophy in the flesh.* Chicago: University of Chicago Press.

Johnson-Eilola, Johndan. (1997). *Nostalgic angels: Rearticulating hypertext writing.* Norwood, NJ: Ablex.

Joyce, James. (1958). *Finnegan's wake.* New York: Viking Press.

Joyce, Michael. (1987). *Afternoon, A Story* [Hypertext document]. Cambridge, MA: Eastgate Software.

Joyce, Michael. (1988, November). Siren shapes: Exploratory and constructive hypertexts. *Academic Computing, 10–14*, 37–42.

Joyce, Michael. (1995). *Of two minds: Hypertext, pedagogy, and poetics.* Ann Arbor, MI: University of Michigan Press.

Kahlo, Frida. (1995). *The diary of Frida Kahlo: An intimate self-portrait.* New York: H.N. Abrams.

Kalmbach, James. (1997). *The computer and the page: Publishing, technology, and the classroom.* Norwood, NJ: Ablex.

Kantrowitz, M. (1990). *Natural language text generation in the Oz interactive fiction project* (Technical Report No. CMU-CS-90-158). Pittsburgh, PA: School of Computer Science, Carnegie Mellon University.

Kantrowitz, M., & Bates, J. (1992, April). Natural language text generation in the Oz interactive fiction project. In R. Dale, E. Hovy, D. Rosner, & O. Stock (Eds.), *Aspects of automated natural language generation, Volume 587 of Lecture Notes in Artificial Intelligence* (pp. 13–28). London: Springer-Verlag.

Kantrowitz, Mark. (1990, November). *Summary of Hovy,* Overview of Natural Language Text Generation. Class lecture given at Carnegie Mellon University, Pittsburgh, PA.

Kay, Alan, & Goldberg, Adele. (1976, March). *Personal dynamic media* (Xerox PARC Technical Report No. SSL-76-1).

Kelso, Margaret, Weyhrauch, Peter, & Bates, Joseph (1992). *Dramatic presence* (Technical Report No. CMU-CS-92-195). Pittsburgh, PA: Carnegie Mellon University, School of Computer Science.

Kimbrell, Andrew. (1993). *The human body shop.* New York: HarperCollins.

Kinneavy, James. (1971). *A theory of discourse.* Englewood Cliffs, NJ: Prentice-Hall.

Kirby, Vicki. (1991). Corporeal habits: Addressing essentialism differently. *Hypatia, 6,* 4–24.

Kirby, Vicki. (1997). *Telling flesh: The substance of the corporeal.* New York: Routledge.

Kirsch, Gesa, & Roen, Duane H. (Eds.). (1990). *A sense of audience in written communication.* Beverly Hills, CA: Sage.

Kristeva, Julia. (1992). From one identity to another. In H. Adams (Ed.), In *Critical theory since Plato* (Rev. ed.; pp. 1162–1173). Fort Worth, TX: Harcourt Brace Jovanovich.

Krueger, Myron W. (1991). *Artificial reality II.* Reading, MA: Addison-Wesley.

Kucer, Stephen L. (1985). The making of meaning: Reading and writing as parallel processes. *Written Communication 2*(3), 318.

Kurzweil, Raymond. (1990). *The age of the intelligent machine.* Cambridge, MA: Institute of Technology Press.

Lake, Carlton. (1990). *Confessions of a literary archaeologist.* New York: New Directions.

Lakoff, George, & Johnson, Mark. (1980). *Metaphors we live by.* Chicago: University of Chicago Press.

Lammers, Susan. (1986). *Programmers at work: Interviews with 19 programmers who shaped the computer industry.* Redmond, WA: Microsoft Press.

Landow, George P. (1987, November). *Relationally encoded links and the rhetoric of hypertext.* Paper presented at Hypertext '87, Chapel Hill, NC.

Landow, George P. (1992a). *Hypertext: The convergence of contemporary critical theory and technology.* Baltimore, MD: John Hopkins University Press.

Landow, George. (1992b). Hypertext, metatext, and the electric canon. In Myron Tuman (Ed.), *Literacy online: The promise (and peril) of reading and writing with computers* (pp. 67–94). Pittsburgh, PA: University of Pittsburgh Press.

Landow, George P. (Ed.). (1994). *Hypertext theory.* Baltimore, MD: John Hopkins University Press.

Lanham, Richard. (1993). *The electronic word: Democracy, technology, and the arts.* Chicago: University of Chicago Press.

Lanham, Richard. (1990). Unpublished lecture given at Ohio State University.

Lanier, Jaron. (1986). *Programmers at work: Interviews with 19 programmers who shaped the computer industry.* Redmond, WA: Microsoft Press.

Larkin, Patti. (1997). The book i'm not reading [Song]. In *Perishable fruit.* New York: High Street Records.

Larsen, Deena. (1993). *Marble springs* [Hypertext document]. Cambridge, MA: Eastgate Systems.

Larsen, Deena. (1997–1998). *Samplers: Nine vicious little hypertexts* [Hypertext document]. Cambridge, MA: Eastgate Systems.

Lashley, K. S. (1951). The problem of serial order in behavior. In L.A. Jeffress (Ed.), *Cerebral mechanisms in behavior* (pp. 112–136). New York: Wiley.

Laurel, B. (1986). *Toward the design of a computer-based interactive fantasy system.* Unpublished doctoral thesis, Ohio State University, Columbus.

Laurel, B. (1991). *Computers as theater.* Reading, MA: Addison-Wesley.

Leather goddesses of Phobos [Computer software]. (1991). In *The lost treasures of Infocom.* Los Angeles: Activision.

Lebling, D. (1980, December). Zork: A computerized fantasy simulation game. *Byte,* 172–182.

Lebowitz, Michael. (1984). Creating characters in a story-telling universe. *Poetics, 13,* 171–194.

Lebowitz, Michael. (1992). All work and no play makes Hal a dull program. In Raymond Kurzweil (Ed.), *The age of intelligent machines* (pp. 390–393). Cambridge, MA: MIT Press.

Lederer, Katherine. (1998). A dream of mimesis. *The American Poetry Review, 27,* 6.

Levy, Steven. (1992). *Artificial life.* New York: Vintage Books.

Liebold, Jay. (1987). *Beyond the Great Wall.* New York: Bantam Books.

Liebold, Jay. (1990). *Fight for freedom.* New York: Bantam Books.

Loader, Jane. (1989). *Wild America.* New York: Grove Press.

Lotman, Yury. (1993). Movement-immobility. In Alla Efimova & Lev Manovich (Eds. & Trans.), *Tekstura: Russian essays on visual culture* (pp. 56–69). Chicago: University of Chicago Press.

Lunsford, Andrea Abernethy. (1999). Rhetoric, feminism, and textual ownership. *College English, 61*(5), 529–544.

Lunsford, Andrea, & Ede, Lisa. 1990. *Singular texts/plural authors: Perspectives on collaborative writing.* Carbondale, IL: Southern Illinois University Press.

Lyotard, Jean-Francois. (1984). *The postmodern condition: A report on knowledge* (Geoff Bennington & Brian Massumi, Trans.). Minneapolis, MN: University of Minnesota Press.

Mac, Kathy. (1994, Summer). Unnatural habitats [Compter software]. *The Eastgate Quarterly Review of Hypertext,* 1(3).

Malloy, Judy, & Marshall, Cathy. (1998). *Forward anywhere* [Hypertext document]. Cambridge, MA: Eastgate Systems.

Malmgren, Carl D. (1986) Romancing the reader: Calvino's *If on a winter's night a traveler. The Review of Contemporary Fiction, 6*(2), 106–116.

Marks, Elaine, & de Courtivron, Isabel. (Eds). (1981). *New French feminisms: An anthology.* Sussex, England: New Harvester Press.

Marriott, Michael. (1998, October 29). I don't know who you are, but (click) you're toast. *New York Times*, pp. D1, D6.

Martin, Henri-Jean. (1994). *The history and power of writing* (Lydia G. Cochrane, Trans.). Chicago: University of Chicago Press.

Martin, Wallace. (1986). *Recent theories of narrative*. Ithaca, NY: Cornell University Press.

Mathews, Harry, & Brotchie, Alastair. (Eds.). (1998). *Oulipo compendium*. London: Atlas Press.

Matsuhashi, A. (1981). Pausing and planning: The tempo of written discourse production. *Research in the Teaching of English 15*(2), 113–134.

McAdam, E. L., Jr., & Milne, George. (1963). *Johnson's dictionary: A modern selection*. New York: Pantheon Books.

McLuhan, Marshall. (1964). *Understanding media: The extensions of man* (2nd ed.). New York: Signet.

Mead, Margaret. (1949). *Coming of age in Samoa*. New York: New American Library.

Meehan, J. R. (1976). The metanovel: Writing stories by computer (Technical Report 74). New Haven, CT: Yale University, Department of Computer Science.

Merwin, W. S. (1998, Fall). *The folding cliffs. Doubletake*, 117.

A mind forever voyaging [Computer software]. (1991). In *The lost treasures of Infocom*. Los Angeles: Activision.

Miller, J. Hillis. (1987). *The ethics of reading*. New York: Columbia University Press.

Minsky, Marvin. (1986). *The society of mind*. New York: Simon and Shuster.

Mitchell, W. J. T. (1986). *Iconology: Image, text, ideology*. Chicago: University of Chicago Press.

Moffett, James. (1983). *Teaching the universe of discourse*. Boston: Houghton Mifflin.

Montgomery, Raymond A. (1977). *Journey under the sea*. New York: Bantam Books.

Moriarty, Brian. (1998). *Interview* [Online]. Available: http://www.xyzzynews.com/xyzzy.16f.html

Morrison, Toni. (1987). *Beloved: A novel*. New York: Knopf.

Motte, Warren. (1986). *Oulipo: A primer of potential literature*. Lincoln, NE: University of Nebraska Press.

Moulthrop, Stuart. (1991a). The politics of hypertext. In Gail Hawisher & Cynthia Selfe (Eds.), *Evolving perspectives on computers and composition studies: Questions for the 1990's* (pp. 253–271). Urbana, IL: National Council of Teachers of English.

Moulthrop, Stuart. (1991b). *Victory garden* [Hypertext document]. Cambridge, MA: Eastgate Systems.

Moulthrop, Stuart. (1995). *Hegirascope* [Hypertext document]. Available: http://raven.ubalt.edu/staff/moulthrop/hypertexts/hgs/hegirascope.html

Moulthrop, Stuart. (1997). *Hegirascope 2.0* [Hypertext document]. Available: http://raven.ubalt.edu/staff/moulthrop/hypertexts/hgs/hegirascope.html

Murray, Donald. (1985). *A writer teaches writing*. Boston: Houghton Mifflin Co.

Murray, Janet. (1997). *Hamlet on the holodeck*. New York: The Free Press.

Nelson, Theodor H. (1987a). *Computer lib/dream machines* (2nd ed.). Redmond, WA: Microsoft Press. (Original work published in 1974).

Nelson, Theodor H. (1987b). *Literary machines*. Palo Alto, CA: Project Xanadu.

Neumann, Erich. (1954). *The origins and history of consciousness* (R. F. C. Hull, Trans.). New York: Pantheon Books.

Newell, Allen, & Simon, Herbert A. (1972). *Human problem solving*. Englewood Cliffs, NJ: Prentice-Hall.

Newkirk, Thomas. (1986). *Only connect: Uniting reading and writing*. Upper Montclair, NJ: Boynton/Cook.

Niesz, Anthony, & Holland, Norman. (1984). Interactive fiction. *Critical Inquiry, 11*, 110–129.

Nietzsche, Friedrich Wilhelm. (1993). *The birth of tragedy out of the spirit of music* (Michael Tanner, Ed., & Shaun Whiteside, Trans.). New York: Penguin Books.

Nord and Bert [Computer software]. (1991). In *The lost treasures of Infocom*. Los Angeles: Activision.

Nunberg, Geoffrey. (Ed.). (1996). *The future of the book*. Berkeley, CA: University of California Press.

Nyce, J. M., & Kahn, P. (Eds.). (1991). *From memex to hypertext: Vannevar Bush and the mind machine*. Boston: Academic Press.

Obermeier, Klaus. (1989). *Natural language processing technologies in artificial intelligence*. New York: John Wiley.

O'Brien, Flann. (1976). *At swim two-birds*. New York: New American Library.

Oliphant, Mike. (1996). *Gumshoe* [Computer software]. Available: http://www.cogsci.ucsd/~oliphant

Ong, Walter. (1982). *Orality and literacy: The technologizing of the word*. New York: Routledge Press.

van Oostendorp, Herre, & de Mul, Sjaak. (Eds.). (1996). *Cognitive aspects of electronic text processing*. Norwood, NJ: Ablex.

Ortony, A., Clore, G., & Collins, A. (1988). *The cognitive structure of emotions*. Cambridge, England: Cambridge University Press.

Park, D. B. (1982). The meanings of "audience." *College English, 44*, 247–257.

Pavic, Milorad. (1991). *Landscape painted with tea*. New York: Knopf.

Peterson, Steve. The design process????

Pfeil, Fred. (1990). *Another tale to tell: Politics and narrative in postmodern culture*. London and New York: Verso.

Phelan, James. (1989). *Reading people, reading plots*. Chicago: University of Chicago Press.

Phelan, Peggy. (1993). *Unmarked: The politics of performance*. London and New York: Routledge.

Picabia, Francis. (1979). Cerebral undulations. In *Surrealists on art* (pp. 184–186). Englewood Cliffs, NJ: Prentice-Hall.

Picard, Rosalind W. (1997). *Affective computing*. Cambridge, MA: MIT Press.

Piercy, Marge. (1991). *He, she, and it*. New York: Knopf.

Pirandello, Luigi. (1998). *Six characters in search of an author* (Eric Bently, Trans.). New York: Penguin Books.

Plato. (1942). *Five great dialogues* (Louise Ropes Loomis, Ed.). New York: Random House.

Plato. (1952). *Phaedrus*. In Reginald Hackforth (Ed. & Trans.), *Introduction to Phaedrus by Plato*. Indianapolis, IN: Bobb-Merrill.

Plato. (1998). *Cratylus* (C. D. C. Reeve, Ed. & Trans.). Indianapolis, IN: Hackett.

Plundered hearts [Computer software]. (1991). In *The lost treasures of Infocom*. Los Angeles: Activision.

Poe, Edgar Allan. (1841). *Forty-two tales: Including the fall of the house of Usher; the murders in the Rue Morgue; the pit and the pendulum*. London: Octopus Books.

Poe, Edgar Allan. (1986). *The raven, with the philosophy of composition*. Boston: Northeastern University Press.

Poster, Mark. (1990). *The mode of information: Post-structuralism and social context*. Chicago: University of Chicago Press.

Postman, Neil. (1992). *Technopoly: The surrender of culture to technology*. New York: Knopf.

Powers, Richard. (1995). *Galatea 2.2*. New York: Farrar, Strauss, Giroux.

Putnam, Hilary. (1983). *Reason, truth, and history.* Cambridge, England: Cambridge University Press.

Pylyshyn, Zenon W. (1984). *Computation and cognition: Toward a foundation for cognitive science.* Cambridge, MA: MIT Press.

Pylyshyn, Zenon W. (Ed.). (1998). *Constraining cognitive theories: Issues and options.* Stamford, CT: Ablex.

RACTER. (1984). *The policeman's beard is half constructed: Computer prose and poetry by RACTER.* New York: Warner Books.

Radway, J. A. (1984). *Reading the romance: Women, patriarchy, and popular literature.* Chapel Hill, NC: University of North Carolina Press.

Randall, Neil. (1988). Determining literariness in interactive fiction. *Computers and the Humanities, 22* , 83–191.

Reid, Elizabeth. (1994, January). *Cultural formations in text-based virtual realities.* Masters thesis, University of Melbourne, Australia.

Reilly, W. S., & Bates, J. (1992). Building emotional agents (Technical Report CMU-CS-92-143). Pittsburgh, PA: School of Computer Science, Carnegie Mellon University.

Reilly, Scott Neal. (1996). *Believable social and emotional agents.* Unpublished doctoral thesis, School of Computer Science, Carnegie Mellon University, Pittsburgh, PA.

Richards, I. A. (1936). *The philosophy of rhetoric.* New York and London: Oxford University Press.

Rico, Gabrielle. (1983). *Writing the natural way: Using right-brain techniques to release your expressive powers.* Los Angeles: J.P. Tarcher.

Riven (1997). [Computer software]. Novato, CA: Red Orb Entertainment.

Rosenblatt, Louise. (1995). *Literature as exploration.* New York: Modern Language Association.

Roubaud, Jacques. (1998). Introduction. In Harry Mathews & Alastair Brotchie (Eds.), *Oulipo compendium* (pp. 37–44). London: Atlas Press.

Rummelhart, David E. (1977). *Introduction to human information processing.* New York: Wiley.

Rummelhart, David E, & Norman, Donald A. (1981). Introduction. In Geoffrey E. Hinton & James A. Anderson (Eds.), *Parallel models of associative memory* (pp. 15–21). Hillsdale, NJ: Lawrence Erlbaum.

Salvaggio, Ruth. (1999). *The sounds of feminist theory.* Albany, NY: State University of New York Press.

Scardamalia, M., Bereiter, C., Brett, C., Burtis, P. J., Calhoun, C., & Smith Lea, N. (1992). Educational applications of a networked communal database. *Interactive Learning Environments, 2,* 45–71.

Scardamalia, Marlene, Bereiter, Carl, & Fillion, Bryant. (1981). *Writing for results: A sourcebook of consequential composing activities.* Toronto: OISE Press; La Salle, IL: Open Court.

Schank, Roger. (1990). *Tell ne a story.* New York: Charles Scribner's Sons.

Schank, Roger, & Abelson, R. P. (1977). *Scripts, plans, goals, and understanding: An inquiry into human knowledge structures.* Hillsdale, NJ: Lawrence Erlbaum.

Scholes, Robert E. (1998). *The rise and fall of English: Reconstructing English as a discipline.* New Haven, CT: Yale University Press.

Searle, John. (1983). *Intentionality.* Cambridge, England: Cambridge University Press.

Selfe, Cynthia. (1989). Redefining literacy: The multilayered grammars of computers. In Gail Hawisher & Cynthia L. Selfe (Eds.), *Critical perspectives on computers and composition instruction* (pp. 3–15). New York: Teacher's College Press.

Selfe, Cynthia L., & Selfe, Richard J. (1994). The politics of the interface: Power and its exercise in electronic contact zones. *College Composition and Communication, 45*, 480–504.

Sengers, Phoebe. (1998, August). *Anti-boxology: Agent design in cultural context* (Technical Report No. CMU-CS-98-151). Unpublished doctoral thesis, Department of Computer Science and Program in Literary and Cultural Theory, Carnegie Mellon University, Pittsburgh, PA.

Shah, Rawn, & Romine, James. (1995). *Playing MUDs on the Internet.* New York: John Wiley.

Shakespeare, William. (1989). *A midsummer night's dream* (Dominic Hyland, Ed.). Harlow, Essex, England: Longman.

Shanahan, Timothy. (1987). The shared knowledge of reading and writing. *Reading Psychology: An International Quarterly, 8*(2), 93–102.

Shanahan, Timothy, & Lomax, Richard G. (1986). An analysis and comparison of theoretical models of the reading–writing relationship. *Journal of Educational Psychology, 78*(2), 116–123.

Sharples, Michael. (1985). *Cognition, computers, and creative writing.* New York: Halsted Press.

Sharples, Michael. (1999). *How we write: Writing as creative design.* New York and London: Routledge.

Shirk, Henrietta Nickels. (1991). Hypertext and composition studies. In Gail Hawisher & Cynthia Selfe (Eds.), *Evolving perspectives on computers and composition studies: Questions for the 1990's* (pp. 177–202). Urbana, IL: National Council of Teachers of English.

Slatin, John M. (1990). Reading hypertext: order and coherence in a new medium. *College English, 52*, 870–883.

Sloane, Sarah. (1991). *Interactive fiction, virtual realities, and the reading–writing relationship.* Unpublished doctoral dissertation, Ohio State University, Columbus.

Sloane, Sarah. (1994). Close encounters with virtual worlds. *Educators' Tech Exchange, 2*(1), 23–29.

Sloane, Sarah. (1999a). The haunting story of J: Genealogy as a critical category in understanding how a writer composes. In Gail E. Hawisher & Cynthia L. Selfe (Eds.), *Passions, pedagogies, and 21st century technologies* (pp. 49–65). Logan, UT: Utah State University Press; Urbana, IL: National Council of Teachers of English.

Sloane, Sarah. (1999b). Interpreting computer-based fictional characters, a reader's manifesto: Or, remarks in favour of the accommodating text. In Ray Paton & Irene Neilson (Eds.), *Visual representations and interpretations* (pp. 186–195). London: Springer-Verlag.

Sloane, Sarah. (1999c). Postmodernist looks at the body electric: E-mail, female, and hijra. In Kris Blair & Pamela Takayoshi (Eds.), *Feminist cyberscapes: Mapping gendered academic spaces* (pp. 41–61). Stamford, CT: Ablex.

Smith, Barbara. (1996). Towards a black feminist criticism. In M. Eagleton (Ed.), *Feminist literary theory: A reader* (pp. 121–126). Cambridge, MA: Blackwell.

Smith, Catherine F. (1991). Reconceiving hypertext. In Gail Hawisher & Cynthia Selfe (Eds.), *Evolving perspectives on computers and composition studies: Questions for the 1990's* (pp. 224–252). Urbana, IL: National Council of Teachers of English.

Smith, S., & Bates, J. (1989). *Toward a theory of narrative for interactive fiction* (Technical Report No. CMU-CS-89-121). Pittsburgh, PA: School of Computer Science, Carnegie Mellon University.

Sorrentino, Gilbert. (1979). *Mulligan stew: A novel.* New York: Grove Press.

Souhami, Diana. (1992). *Gertrude and Alice.* San Francisco: Pandora.

Spender, Stephen. (1952). The making of a poem. In Brewster Ghiselin (Ed.), *The creative process* (pp. 112–124). Berkeley, CA: University of California Press.

Stephenson, Neal. (1992). *Snow crash.* New York: Bantam Books.

Sternglass, Marilyn. (1997). *Time to know them.* Hillsdale, NJ: Lawrence Erlbaum.

STORYSPACE for the Macintosh, Version 1.12 [Computer software]. (1991). Cambridge, MA: Eastgate Systems.

Stotsky, Sandra. (1983, May). Research on reading/writing relationships: A synthesis and suggested directions. *Language Arts, 60*(5), 627–642.

Street, Brian. (1995). *Social literacies: Critical approaches to literacy development, ethnography, and education.* Reading, MA: Addison-Wesley.

Sullivan, P. A. (1995). Review: Social constructionism and literacy studies. *College English, 57*(8), 950–959.

Susser, Bernard. (1998). The mysterious disappearance of word processing. *Computers and Composition Journal, 15*(3), 347–371.

Swift, Jonathan. (1960). *Gulliver's travels.* Cambridge, MA: The Riverside Press.

Tey, Josephine. (1983). *The singing sands.* New York: Garland.

Tierney, Robert J., & Pearson, David P. (1988). Toward a composing model of reading. In Eugene R. Kintgen, Marry M. Kroll, & Mike Rose (Eds.), *Perspectives on literacy* (p. 272). Carbondale, IL: Southern Illinois University Press.

Todorov, Tzvetan. (1990). *Genres in discourse* (Catherine Porter, Trans.). Cambridge and New York: Cambridge University Press.

Tolkien, J. R. R. (1984). *The hobbit, or, there and back again.* Boston: Houghton Mifflin.

Tolstoy, Count Leo. (1965). *Anna Karenina* (Leonard J. Kent & Nina Berberova, Trans.). New York: The Modern Library.

Tompkins, Jane. (1988). A short course on post-structuralism. *College English, 50,* 733–747.

Tompkins, Jane. (1990). Pedagogy of the distressed. *College English, 52,* 653–660.

Tompkins, Jane (Ed.). (1992). *Reader-response criticism: From formalism to post-structuralism.* Baltimore, MD: Johns Hopkins University Press.

Tompkins, Jane. (1992). *West of everything.* New York: Oxford University Press.

Troyka, Lynn Quitman. (1995). *Structured reading.* Englewood Cliffs, NJ: Prentice Hall.

Tuman, Myron C. (Ed.). (1992a). *Literacy online: The promise (and peril) of reading and writing with computers.* Pittsburgh, PA: University of Pittsburgh Press.

Tuman, Myron C. (1992b). *Word perfect: Literacy in the computer age.* Pittsburgh, PA: University of Pittsburgh Press.

Turkle, Sherry. (1984). *The second self: Computers and the human spirit.* New York: Simon and Schuster.

Turkle, Sherry. (1997). *Life on the screen: Identity in the age of the Internet.* New York: Simon and Schuster.

Ueland, Brenda. (1987). *If you want to write.* St. Paul, MN: Gray Wolf Press.

Ulmer, Gregory L. (1989). *Teletheory: Grammatology in the age of video.* New York: Routledge.

Ulmer, Gregory L. (1994). *Heuretics: The logic of invention.* Baltimore, MD: John Hopkins University Press.

Valéry, Paul. (1952). The course in poetics: First lessons. In Brewster Ghiselin (Ed.), *The creative process* (pp. 92–106). Berkeley, CA: University of California Press.

van Dijk, T. (1987). Episodic models of discourse processing. In R. Horowitz & S. J. Samuels (Eds.), *Comprehending oral and written language* (pp. 161–196). San Diego, CA: Academic Press.

Vipond, Douglas. (1993). *Writing and psychology: Understanding writing and its teaching from the perspective of composition studies.* Westport, CT: Praeger.

Vipond, Douglas, & Hunt, Russel A. (1984). Point-driven understanding: Pragmatic and cognitive dimensions of literary reading. *Poetics, 13,* 261–277.

Vitanza, Victor (Ed.). (1996). *CyberReader.* Boston: Allyn and Bacon.

Watson, Craig. (1985, Fall). The project of language. *Credences, III,* 160.

Weizenbaum, Joseph. (1976). *Computer power and human reason: From judgment to calculation.* San Francisco: W.H. Freeman.

Welch, Kathleen. (1999). *Electric rhetoric: Classical rhetoric, oralism, and a new literacy (digital communication).* Cambridge, MA: MIT Press.

West, David M., & Travis, Larry E. (1991). The computational metaphor and artificial intelligence: A reflective examination of a theoretical falsework. *AI Magazine, 12*(1), 73.

Whitford, Margaret (Ed.). (1991). *The Irigaray reader.* Oxford, England: Basil Blackwell.

Wiener, Norbert. (1964). *God and Golem, Inc.* Cambridge, MA: MIT Press.

Williams, Raymond. (1983). *Culture & society: 1780–1950.* New York: Columbia University Press.

Wilson, Johnny. (1991, November). A history of computer games. *Computer Gaming World,* 16–26.

Winterson, Jeannette. (1994). *Written on the body.* New York: Vintage Books.

Wittig, Monique. (1992). The straight mind. In *The straight mind and other essays* (pp. 21–32). Boston: Beacon Press.

Wright, Patricia. (1991). Cognitive overheads and prostheses: Some issues in evaluating hypertexts. *Proceedings of Hypertext '91,* ACM, San Antonio, TX.

Yankelovich, Nicole, Haan, Bernard J., Meyrowitz, Norman K., & Drucker, Steven M. (1988). INTERMEDIA: The concept and construction of a seamless information environment. *Computer, 21*(1), 81–96.

Yates, Francis. (1966). *The art of memory.* Chicago: University of Chicago Press.

Yazdani, Masoud, & Lawler, Robert W. (1987). *Artificial intelligence and education.* Norwood, NJ: Ablex.

Yeats, W. B. (1951). *Collected poems.* New York: Macmillan.

Zavarzadeh, Mas'ud, & Morton, Donald. (Eds.). (1991). *Theory/pedagogy/politics: Texts for change* (pp. 1–32). Urbana, IL: University of Illinois Press.

Ziegfeld, Richard. (1989). A new literary genre? *New Literary History: A Journal of Theory and Interpretation, 20*(2), 341–372.

Zinik, Zinovy. (1993). Sots-art. In Alla Efimova & Lev Manovich (Eds. & Trans.), *Tekstura: Russian essays on visual culture* (pp. 70–88). Chicago: University of Chicago Press.

Zork, a computerized fantasy simulation game. (1979, April). *Computer,* 51–59.

Zuboff, Shoshana. (1988). *In the age of the smart machine: The future of work and power.* New York: Basic Books.

Author Index

Subject Index

About the Author

Sarah Sloane is an associate professor in the Department of English and the Women Studies Program at the University of Puget Sound. A junior sabbatical grant from the University of Puget Sound aided in parts of this research. Correspondence concerning this book may be addressed to sarah_sloane@hotmail.com.